A DICTIONARY OF WOMEN IN CHURCH HISTORY

A DICTIONARY OF WOMEN IN CHURCH HISTORY

by

Mary L. Hammack

MOODY PRESS
Chicago

Library of Congress Cataloging in Publication Data

Hammack, Mary L. 1922-
A dictionary of women in church history.

Bibliography : p.
1. Christian biography. 2. Women—Biography.
I. Title.
BR1713.H33 1984 270'.092'2[B] 84-14710
ISBN 0-8024-0332-8

1 2 3 4 5 6 7 Printing/EB/Year 87 86 85 84

Printed in the United States of America

To the many "unknown" Christian women whose prayers, sacrifices, dedication, and faithful stewardship have greatly influenced church history, yet written accounts of them are lacking. Great is their reward in heaven!

Acknowledgments

A personal word of appreciation for the prayers, encouragement, and assistance from friends, unseen church and missionary personnel, archivists, unnamed librarians, secretaries, and others. A special thanks to my friend, church librarian, and music educator Miss Frances D. Sibley, who is largely responsible for the research on hymnists.

Preface

Women played a decisive role in the ministry of Christ and have continued to influence Christianity throughout history. Special mention was given the women in the upper room after the ascension (Acts 1:14), to the believers in Acts 13:50; 17:4, 12, and elsewhere in Scripture. Although Paul clearly excluded women from leadership ministry in the church, he expressed the importance of women in service within the church body. He extended greetings to various women in the church at Rome (Romans 16). Phoebe, a deaconess, signifies the service ministry of women to which Paul referred. The distinctive role of women in church history since Bible days has been tremendous and far-reaching.

Such an inclusive title as "dictionary" implies that women are included who have influenced the church both negatively and positively. Remember that education for women has not always been expected, and during some periods of history the monasteries were the only "universities" that existed. Yet, the influence of women behind the ruling classes, the evangelists, missions, and spread of Christianity has been beyond measure. It was necessary to comb church history books page by page during parts of the research. In addition to the many books researched, questionnaries and letters for suggestions on entries were sent out to some fifty denominations, thirty-seven non-denominational missionary societies, and various other independent groups such as the Salvation Army, the Women's Christian Temperance Union (WCTU), the Young Women's Christian Association (YWCA), the American Hymn Society, selected colleges, universities, Bible schools, seminaries, publishers, and individuals. The Evangelical Library in London has provided valuable bibliographies, and sources of research such as the Billy Graham Archives at Wheaton College, other archives, librarians, and interested individuals have contributed.

Basic prerequisites for inclusion were: (1) the impact of influence the woman had on church history, negatively or positively; (2) the availability of reliable, sufficient information about the person; and (3) the person must be deceased. The scope of this work is worldwide and the time span is all of the A.D. era designation. John Foxe's *Book of Martyrs* and James and Marti Hefley's book *By Their Blood* provide names of dedicated women who died in their service for the Lord, but many could not be included in this work because of the lack of information.

The compilation of a biographical dictionary of this nature is an awesome task. But the Lord can do the impossible, and so it is that He has directed this author through many months of intensive research, while prayer has consistently gone up on behalf of the project. May He be glorified!

KEY TO PRONUNCIATION

â as in âir
ā as in māte
ă as in căt
ä as in äre

ē as in tēe
ĕ as in mĕt
ẽ as in hẽr
ê as in thêre

ī as in mīte
ĭ as in ĭt

ō as in nōte
ŏ as in hŏt
ô as in nôr
ȯ as in sȯft
ö as in Böhm (Boehm)

ū as in mūle
ŭ as in ŭp
û as in bûrn
ü as in Müller (Mueller)

o͝o as in bo͝ok
o͞o as in to͞ot

Introduction to Indexes

The role of most women in church history involved several capacities. For example, a number of missionaries combined the talents of teaching, translating, and writing. Also, most hymnists were poets, but not all poets were hymnists. Some women have been included primarily because of their influence on the church as helpmates to their husbands; their power as royalty; or their leadership of a country or organization. Therefore, an attempt to categorize the entries by role was abandoned. Rather, they are presented chronologically.

It is hoped that the following index provides sufficient help for the reader to visualize the relationship that each entry had with church history.

Chronological Index According to Periods in Church History

Entries are placed alphabetically within various time periods. Placement of entries into these periods has been determined by death dates. The following periods of church history are used:

Ancient Church History (A.D. 33—590)
Medieval Church History (590—1500)
Reformation (1500—1650)
Expansion, Denominationalism (1650—1800)
Revivals, Missions, Further Expansion (1800—Present)

ANCIENT CHURCH HISTORY (A.D. 33—590)

Agape	c. 272-304
Agatha	c. 225-251
Agnes	c. 340
Anastasia	c. 25-c. 70
Anastasia	c. 230-c. 259
Anastasia	c. 279-c. 304
Anastasia	c. 553-c. 580
Anthusa	c. 331-c. 374
Barbara	c. 259-c. 306
Beatrix	c. 249-303
Blandina	d. 177
Blesilla	c. 350
Candace	c. 25-c. 41
Cecilia	c. 141-177
Clotilda	c. 475-545
Domitilla, Flavia	c. 60
Dorothea	c. 313
Eudocia	c. 401-460
Eudoxia	375-404
Eustochium, Julia	c. 370-418
Fabiola	c. 143-199
Felicitas	c. 107-164
Felicitas	d. 203
Genevieve (Genoveta)	c. 422-c. 500
Helena	c. 250-c. 330
Hypatia	c. 375-415
Macrina	327-379
Marcella	325-410
Marcellina	c. 330-c. 398
Margaret of Antioch	c. 350
Mary of Egypt	c. 344-c. 421
Monica	c. 331-387
Nonna	c. 329-374
Olympias	368-408
Paula	347-404
Pelagia	c. 296-311
Perpetua, Vibia	181-203
Priscilla	First Century
Pulcheria, Augusta	399-453
Radegonde	518-587
Sambine	c. 99-125
Scholastica	480-543
Seraphia	d. c. 125
Thecla	First Century
Theodora	508-548
Ursula	Fourth Century
Zoe	c. 255-286

Medieval Church History (590-1500)

Adela of Blos	1062-1137
Adeloga, Martel	c. 775
Aelfled	c. 630
Aethelthryth	630-679
Agnes	1274-1317
Agnes of Assisi	1207-c. 1232
Agnes of Bohemia	1200-c. 1227
Aldegonde	630-680
Amboise, Francise d'	1427-1485
Angela of Foligno	c. 1248-1309
Anne of Bohemia	1366-1394
Audry, Etheldreda	c. 632-679
Austrebertha	633-704
Austrudis	c. 635-c. 700
Bathilda	c. 651-680
Bertha	c. 570-612
Bertha	646-725
Bridget of Sweden	c. 1303-1373
Bryennius, Anna Comnena	c. 1038-c. 1150
Catherine of Alexandria	c. 950
Catherine of Bologna	1413-1463
Catherine of Siena	1347-1380
Catherine of Sweden	1331-1381
Clare of Assisi	1194-1253
Elizabeth of Hungary	1207-1231
Elizabeth of Portugal	1271-1336
Elizabeth of Thuringia	1207-1235
Ethelberga	c. 601-c. 673
Falconieri, Juliana	1270-1341
Gertrude the Great	1256-1302
Hedwig	c. 1174-1243
Heloise	c. 1098-1164
Hilda	614-680
Hildegard	1098-1179
Hroswitha	935-1002
Irene	752-803
Joan of Arc	1412-1431
Joan of Kent	c. 1306-1385
Juliana of Norwich	c. 1342-c. 1413
Kempe, Margery	c. 1373-1433
Lioba	c. 710-779
Margaret of Scotland	c. 1045-c. 1093
Mathilda	c. 1046-c. 1115
Matilda	c. 895-968
Mechthild of Magdeburg	1210-1280
Odilia	c. 690-720
Olga	c. 902-969
Rose of Viterbo	1235-1252
Theodelinda	568-628
Thrutgeba, Leoba	c. 703-779

Reformation (1500-1650)

Acarie, Mme. Barbe	1566-1618
Albright, Anne	c. 1504-1556
Allin, Catherine	c. 1517-1557
Angela, Merici	1474-1540
Appleby, Petronil	c. 1507-1557
Askew, Anne	1521-1546
Astoo, Margery	c. 1511-1557
Audebert, Ann	c. 1502-1549
Barton, Elizabeth	c. 1506-1534
Beaufort, Margaret	1443-1509
Benden, Alice	c. 1531-1557
Boleyn, Anne	c. 1507-1536
Bonzaga, Guilia	c. 1512-1566
Bresegna, Isabella	1510-1567
Bullinger, Anna	c. 1504-1564
Calvin, Idelette de Bures Stordeur	c. 1499-1549
Catherine of Aragon	1485-1536
Catherine de Medici	1519-1589
Catherine of Genoa	1447-1510
Ciro, Caterino	1501-1557
Colonna, Victtoria	1490-1549
Cunningham, Ann	c. 1591-1647
d'Albret, Jeanne	1528-1572
de Bourbon, Catherine	1559-1604
de Bourbon, Charlotte	c. 1546-1582
de Chantal, Jane Frances Fremyot	1572-1641
de Cologyn, Louise	1553-1620
de Roye, Eleonore	1535-1564
de Souboise, Madame	c. 1475
de Xainctonge, Anne	1567-1621
Elizabeth I	1533-1603
Elizabeth of Brandenburg	1485-1545
Elizabeth of Brunswick-Calenberg	1510-c. 1548
Grey, Lady Jane	1537-1555
Harley, Brilliana Conway	1600-c. 1644
Hutchinson, Anne Marbury	1591-1643
Hyde, Margaret	c. 1495-1557
Isabella of Castile	1451-1504
Knox, Margaret Stuart	c. 1547-1612
Knox, Marjory Bowes	1538-1560
Lomelino, Vicentina	c. 1553-1605
Luther, Katherine von Bora	1499-1552
Marguerite of Valois (or Navarre)	1492-1549
Maring, Margaret	c. 1516-1557
Mary Stuart (Queen)	1542-1587
Mary Tudor (Mary I)	1516-1558

Melanchthon, Katherine Krapp — c. 1500-1557
M'Naught, Marion — 1585-1643
Morata, Olympia — 1526-1555
Nelli, Suora Platella — 1523-1588
Parr, Catherine — 1512-1548
Pocahontas — 1595-1617
Poniatowa, Christine — 1610-1644
Potkins, Alice — c. 1501-1556
Ranfaing, Marie Elizabeth — 1592-1649
Renee of France — 1510-1575
Rose of Lima — 1586-1617
Rutherford, Eupham Hamilton — c. 1567-1630
Sidney, Mary — c. 1530-1601
Stanley, Agnes — c. 1501-1557
Teresa of Avila — 1515-1582
Ursula of Musterberg — c. 1491-5; d. after 1534
Ward, Mary — 1585-1642
Waste, Joan — c. 1500-1556
Welsh, Elizabeth Knox — 1568-1625
Wilbrandis Rosenblatt — 1504-1564
Willoughby, Catherine — 1514-1580
Winthrop, Margaret Tindal — 1590-1647
Zell, Katherine — c. 1497-1562
Zwingli, Anna Reinhard — c. 1487-c. 1538

Expansion and Denominationalism (1650-1800)

Agnesie, Maria Gaetana — 1718-1799
Alacoque, Marguerite Marie — 1647-1690
Anne — 1665-1714
Anne, Lady — 1630-1716
Armyne, Lady — c. 1594-c. 1675
Arnauld, Jacqueline-Marie-Angelique — 1591-1661
Baxter, Margaret Charlton — 1639-1681
Beaumont, Agnes — 1662-1730
Bendish, Bridget Ireton — 1649-1729
Belasyse, Mary Cromwell — 1636-1712
Bell, Ann Mary — 1706-1775
Bendish, Bridget Ireton — 1649-1729
Biscott, Jeanne — 1601-1664
Blackhouse, Sarah — c. 1626-1706
Bourgeoys, Marguerite — 1620-1700
Bourignon, Antionette — 1616-1680
Bradstreet, Anne Dudley — 1612-1672
Buchan, Elspeth Simpson — 1738-1791
Bunyan, Elizabeth — c. 1630-1692
Bunyan, Mary — c. 1625-1656
Buttlar, Eva von — 1670-1717
Cornaro, Helena — 1646-1684
Cromwell, Elizabeth Bouchier — c. 1598-1672
Cromwell, Elizabeth Stewart — c. 1562-c. 1654
Cunningham, Barbara — c. 1630
de l'Incarnation, Marie Guyard — 1599-1672
de Marillac, Louise — 1591-1660
d'Matel, Jeanne Chezard — 1596-1670
Douglas, Lady Margaret — 1592-1678
Dutton, Annie — 1698-1765
Dyer, Mary — c. 1604-1660
d'Youville, Marie Marguerite — 1710-1771
Eleanor — 1655-1720
Eliot, Ann — c. 1611-c. 1675
Elizabeth, Albertine — 1618-1680
Fisher, Mary — c. 1623-c. 1698
Fleetwood, Bridget Cromwell — 1624-c. 1701
Fox, Margaret Fell — 1614-1702
Gaunt, Elizabeth — c. 1649-1685
Glenorchy, Wilhelmina Maxwell — 1741-1786
Godolphin, Margaret Blagge — 1652-1678
Govona, Rosa — 1716-1776
Guyard, Marie — 1599-1672
Guyon, Jeanne Marie Bouvier de la Motte — 1648-1717
Hayn, Henrietta Luise von — 1724-1782
Henry, Katharine — 1629-1707
Hobart, Lady — 1603-1664
Hooten, Elizabeth — 1598-1672
Hume, Lady Grisell — 1665-1746
Huntingdon, Selina Hastings — 1707-1791
Hutchinson, Lucy Apsley — c. 1620
Lecsinska, Mary — 1703-1768
Lee, Ann — 1736-1784
l'Huillier, Marie de Villeneuve — c. 1610
Lindsey, Anne — c. 1645-c. 1730
Ludamilia, Elizabeth — 1640-1672

Mackenzie, Anne Alexander	c. 1619-1706
Marguerite Bourgeyos	1620-1700
Maria Theresa	1717-1780
Miramion, Marie Bonneau	1629-1696
Nagle, Nano	1728-c. 1790
Nitschmann, Anna	1715-1760
Pembroke, Anne	1589-1674
Penn, Gulielma	1644-1694
Polallion, Marie de Lumague	1599-1657
Quatremere, Ann Bourjet	1732-1790
Ranelagh, Lady Katherine B.	1614-1691
Reuss, Benigna Von	1695-1751
Rogers, Hester Ann Roe	1756-1794
Roldan, Luisa	1654-1704
Rowe, Elizabeth Singer	1674-1737
Russell, Frances Cromwell	1638-1720
Rutherford, Jean McMath	c. 1618
Schurmann, von Anna Maria	1607-1678
Steele, Annie	1716-1778
Tekakwitha, Catherine	c. 1657-1680
Vere, Mary Tracey	1581-1671
Wesley, Susanna Annesley	1669-1742
West, Elizabeth	1672-1735
Whitefield, Elizabeth Burnell	c. 1705-c. 1757

REVIVALS, MISSIONS, AND FURTHER EXPANSION (1800-PRESENT)

Adams, Abigail Smith	1744-1818
Adams, Hannah	1756-1831
Adams, Sarah Flower	1805-1848
Addams, Jane	1860-1935
Agnew, Eliza	1807-1883
Aguilar, Grace	1816-1847
Aguillard, Verna	1902-1981
Ahlstrand, Ruth von Malborg	1878-1962
Aldrich, Doris Coffin	1906-1958
Alexandar, Ann	1767-1849
Alexander, Cecil Frances Humphreys	1823-1895
Allen, Elizabeth	1787-1871
Allen, Frances Grace	1864-1957
Allen, Phoebe	1769-1856
Amandon, Martha D. Byington	1834-1937
Anderson, Minnie Susan	1892-1967
Andre, Hattie	1865-1952
Anthony, Mary O'Connell	1815-1897
Anthony, Susan Brownell	1820-1906
Araki, Iyo	c. 1875-c. 1938
Armstrong, Annie	1850-1938
Armstrong, Laura Dell Malotte	1886-1945
Ashby, Mary	1773-1835
Asher, Virginia	1869-1937
Auber, Harriet	1773-1862
Augusta, Caroline	c. 1799-c. 1850
Aylward, Gladys	1902-1970
Baerg, Anna	1897-1972
Baldwin, Mary Briscoe	1811-1877
Bannister, Catherine	1855-1910
Barat, Madeline Sophie	1779-1865
Barbauld, Anna Letitia Aikin	1743-1825
Bargen, Elizabeth Regehr	1897-1976
Barker, Lillie Easterby	1865-1925
Barlow, Ann	1787-1867
Barton, Clara Harlowe	1821-1912
Bates, Katherine Lee	1859-1929
Bauman, Mary Melissa Wagoner	1876-1909
Baxter, Lydia	1809-1874
Becker, Magdalena Herbert	1878-1938
Bell, Martha E. McIntosh	1848-1922
Bell, Virginia Myers Left	1892-1974
Bender, Bertha Berkholder	1896-1978
Bennett, Belle Harris	1852-1922
Bernadette of Lourdes Soubirous	1844-1879
Bert, Sarah	1860-1948
Besant, Annie	1847-1933
Bethune, Joanna Graham	1770-1860
Bethune, Mary McLeod	1875-1955
Bevan, Emma Frances	1827-1909
Billart, Marie Rosa Julia	1751-1816
Binns, Mary	1775-1851
Bishop, Isabella Bird	1831-1902
Blackwell, Antoinette Louise Brown	1825-1921

Blackwell, Elizabeth	1821-1910
Blake, Louise	1888-1975
Blavatsky, Elena Petrovna	1831-1891
Bookwalter, Lulu G.	1883-1958
Booth, Catherine Mumford	1829-1890
Booth, Elizabeth Charlesworth	1865-1948
Booth, Evangeline Cory	1865-1950
Booth, Florence Eleanor Soper	1862-1957
Booth-Clibborn, Catherine	1858-1955
Booth-Tucker, Emma Moss	1860-1903
Borthwick, Jane Laurle	1813-1897
Bose, Kheroda	c. 1887-1948
Bose, Mona	c. 1860
Boss, Martha	1913-1973
Bothwell, Marie Hankey	1914-1979
Bown, Emma Jane	1858-1924
Boyd, Maud Sisley	1851-1937
Boynton, Grace M.	1890-1970
Bragg, Margaret Wilson	1775-1840
Bragg, Mary Furnas	1762-1849
Brand, Evelyne Constance Harris	1880-1975
Breck, Carrie E.	1855-1934
Brewster, Ann Shewell	1762-1835
Bridgman, Clara Davis	1872-1956
Bridgman, Eliza Jane Gillett	c. 1803-1871
Broomhall, Amelia Hudson Taylor	1835-1918
Brown, Antionette L.	1825-1921
Brown, Cecil	1906-1958
Brown, Phoebe Hinsdale	1783-1861
Browning, Elizabeth Barrett	1806-1861
Brunk, Ada Zimmerman	1908-1954
Brunner, Marie Anna	1800-1836
Brunonia, Mary	c. 1830
Buck, Theresa R.	1912-1964
Buell, Harriett Eugenia Peck	1834-1910
Buhlmaier, Marie	1859-1938
Bulmer, Agnes Collinson	1775-1837
Burgess, Georgia Anna Burrus	1866-1948
Burrus, Noni	c. 1918-1958
Busby, Beryl Elizabeth	1903-1983
Butler, Fanny J.	c. 1837-1899
Butler, Josephine Elizabeth	1828-1907
Buyse, Mabel Easton	1882-1977
Byers, Emma D. Lefevre	1875-1946
Cable, Mildred	1877-1952
Cabrini, Frances Xavier	1850-1917
Camp, Mabel Johnston	1871-1937
Campbell, Jane Corneigle	1763-1835
Campbell, Louise	1883-1968
Carey, Charlotte Emilia Rumohr	1761-1821
Carey, Dorothy Plackett	1755-1807
Carey, Grace Hughes	1778-c. 1840
Carmichael, Amy Wilson	1867-1951
Cary, Alice	1820-1871
Cary, Maude	1878-1967
Cary, Phoebe	1824-1871
Case, Adelaide T.	1887-1948
Cassidy, Bertha E.	c. 1881-1963
Caviness, Agnes Elvira Lewis	1889-1973
Cayley, Lady	1748-1828
Charles, Elizabeth Rundle	1828-1896
Chestnut, Eleanor	1868-1905
Choi, Pilley Kim	1884-c. 1939
Christiansen, Avis Burgeson	1895-1966
Claassen, Katharine Reimer	1827-1869
Clark, Grace Agnes	1898-1955
Clark, Mary Elizabeth Brown	c. 1838-c. 1913
Clarke, Mary Lane	1872-1970
Clarke, Sarah Dunn	1835-1917
Clement, Lora E.	1890-1958
Clephane, Elizabeth Cecilia	1830-1869
Coghill, Annie Louise Walker	1836-1907
Coillard, Christina Mackintosh	1829-1891
Cole, Hannah Hunter	1919-1951
Coleman, Alice Blanchard Merriam	1858-c. 1918
Collins, Elizabeth	1755-1831
Connelly, Cornelia Peacock	1809-1879
Cook, Jennie Siemens	1902-1975
Cook, Sylvia Soetenga	1930-1960

Copenhaver, Laura Scherer	1868-c. 1939
Cordell, Bessie	1894-1981
Cousins, Anne Ross	1824-1906
Covette, Aurelia	c. 1825
Cowman, Lettie B.	1870-1960
Cox, Blanche B.	1864-1940
Cox, Ethelene Boone	1890-1965
Cox, Frances Elizabeth	1812-1897
Cox, Vercia P.	c. 1891-1946
Crewdson, Jane Fox	1809-1863
Croll, Martha B.	c. 1847-1906
Crosby, Frances Jane	1820-1915
Crowell, Grace Noll	c. 1898-c. 1963
Culbertson, Belle Caldwell	1857-c. 1938
Cu, Lu Bi	c. 1850
Cure, Apollonie Pelissier	1809-1869
Cushman, Emma Darling	1865-1930
Cushman, Mary Floyd	1870-1965
Danforth, Clarissa	1792-c. 1851
Davidson, Hannah Frances	1860-1935
Day, Emma V.	1853-1894
de Bonnault, Marie Madelene de Bengy	1781-1858
Dederer, Anna	1902-1976
De Forest, Charlotte	1879-1973
de Lamoignon, Louise Elizabeth	1763-1825
de Meester, Marie Louise	1856-1928
Depew, Mary Kinney	1836-1892
de Prayer, Eva	1866-1928
Dickson, Lillian LeVesconte	1901-1983
Diehl, Nona M.	1894-1981
Dillon, Margaret Neely	1865-1913
Dix, Dorothea Lynde	1802-1887
Dixon, Helen Cadbury Alexander	1877-1969
Doane, Margaret Treat	1868-1954
Doremus, Sarah Platt Haines	1802-1877
Doyle, Mary	1763-1834
Drexel, Katherine	1858-1955
Druillard, Nellie Helen Rankin	1844-1937
Dryer, Emma	c. 1833-1925
Duff, Ann Scott Drysdale	c. 1805-c. 1889
Duff, Mildred	1860-1932
Duncan, Mary Ludlie	1814-1839
Dunn, Catherine Hannah	1815-1863
Dunn, Geneva Mildred Oldham	1911-1969
Durocher, Marie Rose	c. 1804-c. 1873
Ebersole, Melinda	1860-1933
Eddy, Mary Morse Baker, Glover, Patterson	1821-1910
Edwards, Mary Kelley	1829-1927
Eitzen, Sara Block	1840-1917
Elliot, Clara Elizabeth Luginbuhl	1895-1981
Elliott, Charlotte	1789-1871
Elliott, Emily Steele	1836-1897
Eng, Hu King	1865-c. 1949
Enss, Amy Evelyn Greaves Sudermann	1878-1975
Eo-ing, Mary	c. 1807
Eva of Friedenshort	1865-1921
Evald, Emmy Carlsson	1857-1946
Falck, Elizabeth	1894-1980
Farrell, Monica	1898-1982
Fay, Lydia Mary	c. 1802-1878
Fedororna, Mary	c. 1759-1828
Feller, Henrietta	1800-1865
Ferguson, Manie Payne	1850-c. 1927
Field, Adele	1839-1916
Findlater, Sarah Borthwick	1823-1907
Fiske, Fidelia	1816-1864
Fleming, Lulu Cecilia	1862-1899
Flower, Eliza	c. 1801-1846
Flowerdew, Alice	1759-1830
Fox, Margaret	1833-1893
Frey, Amanda	1890-1975
Fromman, Erma Valentine	1904-1976
Fry, Elizabeth Gurney	1780-1845
Frykenberg, Doris Skoglund	1909-1981
Fuller, Grace L. Payton	1886-1966
Garnett, Christine Margaret	1886-1972
Garrett, Elizabeth Clark	1805-1855
George, Eliza Davis	1879-1979
Gilbert, Ann Taylor	1782-1866
Goforth, Florence Rosalind Bell-Smith	1864-1942
Good, Mary	1890-1982
Gordon, Anna	1835-c. 1926
Gorle, Ruth Thomas	1899-1971
Graffam, Mary Louise	1871-1922
Graham, Isabella	1742-1814
Graham, Mary Jane	1803-1830

Graham, Morrow Coffey	1892-1981
Grammer, Katharine Arnett	1902-1980
Green, Harriet Maria	c. 1839-1905
Greene, Olive	1883-1966
Gregg, Alice H.	1893-1978
Gregg, Jessie	1875-1942
Griffiths, Ann Thomas	1776-1805
Grijalva, Dorothy Clinkenbeard	1920-1970
Grimke, Emily	1805-1879
Grimke, Sarah Moore Angelina	1792-1873
Gruen, Olive	1883-1963
Guérin, Anne Therese	1798-1856
Guérin, Eugénie de	1805-1848
Guilding, Clara Wight	1886-1974
Gurney, Dorothy Frances	1858-1932
Gwinn, Alice E.	1896-1969
Habershon, Ada	1861-1918
Hale, Mary Whitwell	1810-1862
Hale, Sarah Josepha Buell	1795-1879
Hamer, Lilian	1912-1959
Hanaford, Phoebe Ann Coffin	1829-1921
Hanke, Sarah Emma Catherine Harer	1897-1959
Hankey, Katherine	1834-1911
Harkness, Georgia Elma	1891-1974
Harper, Frances Ellen Watkins	1825-1911
Harrison, Alda B. Haworth	1877-1959
Hartzler, Sadie	1896-1972
Havergal, Frances Ridley	1836-1879
Haviland, Laura Smith	1808-1898
Hawks, Annie Sherwood	1835-1918
Hayashi, Utako	c. 1850-c. 1937
Hayes, Lucy Webb	1831-1889
Haygood, Laura Askew	1845-1900
Heatwole, Lydia	1887-1932
Heck, Barbara Ruckle	1734-1804
Heck, Fannie Exile Scudder	1862-1915
Hedrick, Laura Gossnickle	1858-1934
Hedwig, Eleanora Von Haartman	1860-1902
Hershey, Mae Elizabeth Hertzler	1877-1974
Heusser, Meta Schweizer	1797-1876
Hewitt, Eliza Edmunds	1851-1920
Hiebert, Mary J. Regier	1884-1970
Hill, Grace Livingston	1865-1947
Hinderer, Anna Martin	1827-1870
Hinz, Hansina Christina Fogdal	c. 1803-1896
Holecek, Ruth Stevens	1921-1968
Hopkins, Emma Curtis	1853-1925
Hoppe, Anna Bernardine	c. 1882-1941
Horton, Rose	1883-1972
Hourani, Almaz	c. 1860-c. 1925
Howe, Julia Ward	1817-1910
Hsieh, Wan Ying	c. 1830
Hull, Eleanor Henrietta	1860-1935
Hunt, Helen	1890-1975
Huntley, Amelia Elmore	1844-c. 1920
Hussey, Jennie Evelyne	d. c. 1850
Huston, Ruth	1899-1982
Ingalls, Marilla Baker	1830-1895
Inouye, Tomo	d. c. 1900
Irene	1832-1896
Isherwood, Cecile	1862-1905
Iwamato, Kashi Shimada	1863-1896
Iwasa, Rin	1891-1949
Jackson, Alice	1876-1906
James, Minnie Lou Kennedy	1874-1963
Jameson, Anna	1797-1860
Jersey, Margaret Elizabeth Villiers	1849-c. 1930
Johnston, Dorothy Grunbock	1915-1977
Johnston, Julia Harriette	1849-1919
Johnston, Ruby	1909-1983
Judson, Ann Hasseltine	1789-1826
Judson, Emily Chubbuck	1817-1854
Judson, Sarah Hall Boardman	1803-1845
Jugan, Jeanne (Marie de la Croix)	1792-c. 1861
Kahn, Ida	1872-1932
Kalopothakis, Mary	d. c. 1910
Kanagy, Minnie	1891-1976
Karmarker, Dr. Bububa	d. c. 1920
Kasper, Catherine	c. 1820
Kauffman, Emily Strunk	1873-1960
Kauffmann, Christmas Carol	1901-1969

Mott, Lucretia Coffin	1793-1880
Muller, Gary Groves	1797-1870
Muller, Susannah Grace Sangar	1817-1895
Musselman, Rose Lambert	1878-1974
Nation, Cary Amelia Moore	1846-1911
Nelson, Effie Victoria	1901-1977
Newell, Harriett Atwood	1793-1812
Newman, Angela F.	1837-c. 1905
Nightingale, Florence	1820-1910
Noel, Carolina Maria	1817-1877
Okken, Nellie	1915-1983
Ouchterlony, Hanna	1838-1924
Pak, Esther Kim	c. 1857-1910
Palmer, Phoebe Worral	1807-1884
Parmelee, Ruth Azniv	1885-1973
Parsons, Edith F.	1878-1959
Paru, Dr. P.	c. 1900
Patrick, Mary Mills	1850-1940
Pattison, Dorothy Wyndlow	1832-1878
Paul, Elizabeth Riemann	1894-1966
Pavlova, Rada Evanova	c. 1800
Paxson, Ruth	c. 1889-1949
Peabody, Lucy McGill	1861-1949
Peck, Sara Elizabeth	1868-1968
Pelletier, Mary	1796-1868
Penn-Lewis, Jessie Jones	1861-1927
Perkins, Eva	1858-1942
Petrie, Irene Eleanora Verita	1809-1896
Petter, Bertha Kisinger	1872-1967
Philip, Sarah	c. 1800
Piccard, Jeannette Ridlon	1895-1981
Playfair, Joyce Nethercott	1886-1978
Plummer, Hilda	1899-1980
Plummer, Lorena Florence Fait	1862-1945
Pounds, Jessie Brown	1861-1921
Prentiss, Elizabeth Payson	1819-1878
Preston, Ann	1810-1906
Procter, Adelaide Ann	1825-1864
Rader, Alma	1885-1966
Rainer, Caroline Elizabeth Farabee	1927-1983
Ramabai Pandita Sarasvati	1858-1922
Randall, Sally Parsons	1775-c. 1850
Reed, Mary	1854-1943
Rehwinkel, Angela	1882-1973
Ressler, Lina Zook	1869-1948
Rhodes, Mary	c. 1760
Ridley, Mrs. W.	c. 1810-1896
Roberts, Ellen Lois Stowe	1825-1908
Robinson, Jane Marie Bancroft	1847-1932
Ross, Dorothy Blatter	1901-1977
Rossetti, Christina Georgina	1830-1894
Rowell, Mable G.	1889-1969
Royer, Christina Newhouser	1875-1967
Rupp, Grace Kennedy	1883-1967
Sa, Ma Saw	c. 1860
Sales, Jane Magorian	1931-1974
Sandell, Lina	1832-1903
Sather, Myrtle	1905-1971
Sayer, Mary Geneva	1895-1980
Sayers, Dorothy Leigh	1893-1957
Schellenberg, Katharina	1870-1945
Schroll, Eleanor Allen	c. 1880
Schultz, Elizabeth Unruh	1866-1943
Scott, Clara H.	1841-1897
Scott, Helen May	1882-1963
Scudder, Catherine Hastings	1825-1849
Scudder, Ida Sophia	1870-1960
Sears, Minnie Sandberg	1894-1968
Selzer, Gertrude	1892-1979
Seton, Elizabeth Ann Bayley	1774-1821
Sexton, Lydia Casad	1799-1873
Shank, Clara Brubaker	1869-1958
Shank, Crissie Yoder	1888-1929
Shank, Emma Hershey	1881-1939
Shattuck, Corinna	1848-1910
Shaw, Anna Howard	1847-1919
Shaw, Frances Jervis	c. 1857-1903
Shenk, Alta Barge	1912-1969
Shepherd, Anne Houlditch	1809-1957
Sherwood, Mary Martha	1775-1848
Shuck, Henrietta Hall	1817-1844
Sibley, Georgiana H.	1887-1980
Siedliska, Frances	1842-1902
Sieveking, Amalia	1794-1859
Singh, Lilavati	c. 1860
Slessor, Mary	1848-1915
Smet, Eugenie Marie	1825-1871
Smith, Amanda	1837-1915
Smith, Elizabeth Lee	1817-c. 1888
Smith, Hannah Whitall	1832-1911

A

ACARIE, BARBE (Madame) (1566-1618), a person of considerable spiritual influence. From an aristocratic family in Paris; daughter of Nicolas Avrillot. In 1583 she married Pierre Acarie, who was wealthy at one time but had misused his money. She was able to restore the funds and use them to help many needy people. She knew both Francis de Sales and Vincent de Paul and opened her home to many in need of spiritual counsel. Her dedicated life is believed to have had much influence on the writings of de Sales in particular. It was likely because of her influence on King Henry IV that the reformed Carmelites originated in France in 1604. Although frail in health, she was an active Christian witness. She spent her final years at the Carmelite convent in Amiens, where her three daughters later followed.

ADAMS, ABIGAIL SMITH (1744-1818), Christian first lady of America and daughter of William Smith, a minister in Weymouth, Massachusetts. Common with many women of that time, she had little formal education. She was taught at home, read widely, and became one of the best-informed women of her time. In 1764 she married John Adams, America's second president. Her personal life was one of sincere Christian dedication. She loved her family, taught the Scriptures at home, and counseled her children in spiritual matters. Their oldest son, John Quincy Adams, became America's sixth president. Their oldest child (also named Abigail) married Colonel William Stephens Smith. The quiet Christian influence of Abigail Adams was a significant contribution to the church. As the first hostess of the White House, she took advantage of unique opportunities to serve her Lord in a prominent role.

ADAMS, HANNAH (1744-1831), one of the first women to become a historical and religious writer in America. A student of both Latin and Greek, she lived near Boston and is remembered for her *Dictionary of Religion, History of the Jews,* and *History of New England.* Details of her childhood are obscure.

ADAMS, SARAH FLOWER (1805-1848), hymnist and poet born in England; the daughter of Benjamin Flower, editor of a Cambridge weekly paper. She was married to William B. Adams, a writer and engineer. She wrote one of her most familiar hymns in 1840, "Nearer, My God, to Thee." This hymn is said to have been the author's response to the Genesis story of Jacob's vision at Bethel, and also is reported to have been the dying prayer of President William McKinley. In addition to her poetry, she had prose published in the magazine *The Repository.* Her pastor, William Johnson Fox, published *Hymns and Anthems* in 1841, including thirteen of her hymns for use in his church. Some of her writings were published in 1845 in a catechism with hymns called *The Flock at the Fountain,* although some critics consider her major literary work to be a religious drama, *Vivia Perpetua.*

ADDAMS, JANE (1860-1935), author and social worker, especially known as the founder of Hull House, one of the first social settlements in America. Born in Cedarville, Illinois, of Quaker parents, she had great compassion for the poor, the immigrants, and displaced people. A graduate of Rockford College, she traveled in Europe and exerted much influence for support of reforms, including improved working conditions for women and children. In 1889 she and her friend Ellen Gates Starr founded Hull House in Chicago. It was located in a poor neighborhood and set up to help those in special need, especially immigrants, and was similar to Toynbee Hall in London. In 1909 she was elected the first woman president of the National Conference of Charities and Correction, and in 1915 became president of the International Peace Congress in The Hague. She shared the Nobel peace prize with Nicholas Murray Butler in 1931. Among her writings, the most familiar to Americans is *Twenty Years at Hull House*.

ADELA OF BLOS (1062-1137), a devout Christian woman of France who had significant influence during the First Crusade. Her father was William the Conqueror and her husband was Stephen Henry, Count of Blos. When attempts were made to unite Christians to gain full control of the Holy Land from the Moslems, she urged her husband to join in the Crusade efforts and was appointed regent in his absence. He was killed during a battle at Ramula in 1101, leaving her a widow with several children. She carried on the business of the country until her son, Theobald, became of age and succeeded her. Theobald's daughter, Adela, later became the wife of Louis VII. Another son of Adela of Blos, Stephen, became king of England, reigning for nineteen years. Two other sons, Philip and Henry, held influential positions in the church. Adela was considered a serious scholar of Latin and Greek. The bishops of LeMans and Hildebert, among others, corresponded with her concerning ecclesiastical matters.

ADELOGA, MARTEL (Eighth Century), daughter of Charles Martel by Kunehilda. She was influential in building convents or Catholic communities for women, and became an abbess of a convent. She was sainted by the Roman Catholic church.

AELFLED, daughter of Edwin, king of Northumbia, and his wife, Ethelberga, who was the granddaughter of Bertha. Aelfled established the first Christian church at Canterbury, England. She was educated by Hilda and later succeeded her as abbess in 680.

AETHELTHRYTH (630-679), a princess in ancient England who founded a convent at Ely. An East Anglican was betrothed to her, but she persuaded him to refuse to consummate the marriage so that she could become a nun. She became quite well known as the abbess of the convent she founded, having been referred to as St. Audrey. June 23 became a feast day known as St. Audrey's.

AGAPE (c. 272-304), one of three sisters martyred for her Christian stand. All three sisters lived in Thessalonica. They were instructed in the Christian faith and doctrines but were warned to remain unknown and to live in seclusion and prayer. Agape, along with her sisters, were discovered and examined before the governor, Dulcatius. During the questioning her Christian testimony was firm, indicating that she could not comply with laws that enforced the worship of idols and devils. This angered the governor, and he condemned her to death. She was martyred on March 25, 304.

AGATHA (c. 225-251), a Christian woman of Sicily with unusual beauty. Quintain, the pagan governor of Sicily, was greatly attracted to her and attempted to seduce her. She tried to relocate so as not to be seen by him, but she was discovered and brought to Catana. Realizing her circumstances, she prayed for death. In a further attempt to gratify his desires, the governor assigned Agatha to a licentious woman, Aphrodica, who tried to persuade Agatha to give in to prostitution. All such efforts were wasted, and Agatha's Christian testimony remained firm. This caused Quintain great resentment, especially when Agatha spoke so clearly of her Christian faith. The governor was determined to have his revenge and had Agatha scourged, burned with red-hot irons, torn with sharp hooks, and finally laid naked on live coals intermingled with glass. She died as a result of that torture on February 5, 251.

AGNES (Fourth Century), considered a Christian martyr of Rome; especially recognized for her defense of chastity. The daughter of the Emperor Constantine is said to have built a basilica over her grave near Via Nomentana. Exact dates and details of her life are uncertain.

AGNES (St.) (1274-1317), born in area of Monte Pulciano in Tuscany. When she was nine years old she entered a convent of the order of St. Francis, called Sacchine or Sackins, because their habit was of coarse linen. She became cellarist of the house at age fourteen, and later abbess of another house at Proceno. She established a monastery at Mounte Pulciano with the St. Benedict rule of St. Dominic and was a leader highly respected for her faith and leadership abilities.

AGNES OF ASSISI (1207-c. 1232), sister of Clare who, with St. Francis of Assisi, founded the Franciscan Order of Poor Clares. She and Clare were installed by St. Francis of Assisi as the first two nuns of the Second Order of Franciscans. Later their mother joined them. She was influential because of her Christian service in this order.

AGNES OF BOHEMIA (1200-c. 1227), daughter of King OttokarI of Bohemia and a niece of the king of Hungary. Agnes entered the convent established by Clare and St. Francis of Assisi, the Franciscan Order of Poor Clares. Like a number of other women of nobility, she preferred to dedicate her life to this means of Christian service.

AGNESIE, MARIA GAETANA (1718-1799), a Christian intellectual of noble parents who used her wealth and knowledge to help others. Born in Milan, Maria was a Latin student. At the age of nine she composed a Latin essay; at eleven years of age she knew Greek and Hebrew as well as several other languages; and at age thirteen translated Latin into Italian, French, German, and Greek. She translated *The Spiritual Combat*, a work by Lorenzo Scupoli, from Italian into Greek. She turned to mathematics and at age fourteen studied the *Elements of Euclid*. In 1738 she published 191 theses, which were accepted by distinguished scholars of Milan. Later she published *Analytical Institutions*, which drew considerable attention from mathematicians and scientists. Not only was she highly recognized for her other scholarly work, but she was well read in religion, and some theologians sought her opinions about religious issues. She sought to serve the Lord with her material means, dedicating her income and life to the Lord as she worked in hospitals and helped where the needs were evident. In 1771 Prince Trevulzi founded a hospital and asked her to govern the women's section.

AGNEW, ELIZA (1807-1883), believed to have been the first single woman missionary to Ceylon, where she served forty years. Born in New York City, she dedicated her life to missions when only eight years old. After her parents died, she applied to the American Board of Missions, and in 1840 began her work as administrator of the Central Boarding School for Girls, founded in 1824 in the area of Uduville, in the Jaffna province, Ceylon. She continued in that position for the next forty years and did not return to the United States. Her influence was outstanding in the furtherance of Christian training and witness.

AGUILAR, GRACE (1816-1847), a Jewess writer, born near London. Her family was one of many Hebrew merchants in Spain who had to flee because of religious persecutions. She died in Frankfort, Germany, in 1847, and is especially remembered for her book *Women of Israel*. Details of her short life are obscure.

AGUILLARD, VERNA (1902-1981), American home missionary, native of southern Louisiana. She became a Christian as a young adult and felt the burden of the French-speaking people in that area. She attended college and prepared to serve in home mission work. She is believed to have been the first home missionary to the French-speaking people of the southern United States. So successful were her efforts in that vicinity that she was sent elsewhere in the southern United States to organize Sunday schools and establish churches under the sponsorship of the Southern Baptist Convention. She was much sought as a speaker, not only to testify of her own conversion but to present the needs of the work in which she was involved. She served for many years as a field representative of the Southern Baptists, stimulating interest in home missions.

AHLSTRAND, RUTH von MALBORG (1878-1962), Swedish author and missionary to China for more than forty-six years under The Evangelical Alliance Mission. Born in Sweden, she grew up in a family with the unusual combination of nobility, wealth, and Christian dedication. She married Gustav Ahlstrand, a missionary in China seven years previously. They arrived in Shensi, China, in 1900 as the Boxer Rebellion was beginning. She assisted her husband, taught, and maintained a home for missionary activity. It was said that her kitchen offered "seminary" training, and a number of their household workers became evangelists and pastors. Ruth wrote historical articles in Swedish, was proficient in English and Chinese, and could speak German and French as well. Her husband and two children preceded her in death. One child, Natalie, died in infancy. Their son, George, was martyred at age ten when, during the Revolution of 1911, an attack on the missionary children's school at Sian killed five other missionary children and two teachers. Faithful witnessing in the home, church, jails, and outstations increased the Christian community remarkably. Returning to Sweden to retire, they left their church of nearly 900 fully self-supported, with strong leaders in eight or nine missionary outstations. Several thousand Chinese gathered for the farewell services. Ruth retired to Sweden, where she remained until her death at Stockholm in 1962.

ALACOQUE, MARGUERITE MARIE (1647-1690), founder of a religious order in Lhautecour, France, called *The Devotion to the Sacred Heart of Jesus*. Her early education and training was at a convent of the Visitation Nuns in Burgundy, central France. The Visitation Nuns originated in 1610, organized by the widow of Baron de Chantal. Their work was largely visiting the sick. Marguerite Alacoque, also known as St. Margaret Mary, was canonized in 1920.

ALBRIGHT, ANNE (c. 1504-1556), an outspoken Christian and one of seven at Smithfield burned at the stake for their faith. Details of her life are uncertain.

ALDEGONDE (630-680), born in Hainaut, France, of aristocracy and wealth. She gave a fortune for the building of a monastery and took Catholic vows at the Abbey of Hautmount. Her name is mentioned in calendars during the time of Louis le Debonnaire. Her religious views and faith influenced nobility and the wealthy, yet she was seriously devoted to her Christian faith.

ALDRICH, DORIS COFFIN (1906-1958), author and popular speaker; born in Seattle, Washington, and attended the University of Washington, and Biola College. She married Willard M. Aldrich and worked with him in the growth and development of Multnomah School of the Bible in Portland, Oregon. Dr. Aldrich became president of that school, and she not only assumed a vital role as his wife, but she wrote a regular column for *The Multnomah Miniature* periodical and often spoke to women's groups. She was much loved by the students and faculty. They had nine children, six of whom entered full-time Christian service with one son, Joe, becoming president of Multnomah School of the Bible when his father retired. The column by Doris in *The Multnomah Miniature* was appropriately titled "Out of the Mixing Bowl" and was based on many personal experiences and contained Scriptural parallels and applications. After her death in an automobile accident in 1958, a collection of her writings were compiled in book form, *Mommie of the Mixing Bowl.*

ALEXANDAR, ANN (1767-1849), an English-born minister in the Society of Friends church. She was the daughter of William and Esther Tuke. She ministered first in Scotland in 1788, then in Ireland in 1791, effectively increasing a religious awakening. She came to America briefly but is especially remembered for having started the publication devoted to the interest of the Society of Friends called *Annual Monitor* in 1811.

ALEXANDER, CECIL FRANCES HUMPHREYS (1823-1895), an Irish hymnist. She was the daughter of Major John Humphreys. In 1850 she married William Alexander, who later became Bishop of Derry and primate of Ireland. Many of her nearly 400 hymns and poems were translated into several languages. Her more familiar hymns are

"Jesus Calls Us," "Once in David's Royal City," and "There Is a Green Hill Far Away." The latter one was written in 1847 and first published in her book *Hymns for Little Children.* The composer, Charles Gounod, considered it a near-perfect hymn in the English language with simplicity its greatest beauty. *Hymns for Little Children,* although small, was published in more than one hundred editions. Her best-known poem probably was "The Burial of Moses," which had wide circulation. Even Tennyson was complimentary of it.

ALLEN, ELIZABETH (1787-1871), an influential minister in the Society of Friends church. Born in England, she began preaching in 1828 and actively ministered in many areas until a serious fall in 1863 caused her to be disabled for the rest of her life.

ALLEN, FRANCES GRACE (1864-1957), a missionary educator, school founder, and administrator who served for fifty-two years in Africa under the General Mission Board of the Free Methodist church. Born in Michigan, she grew up in a Methodist family and attended teacher training school after graduating from high school in Lawrence, Kansas. In 1888 she went to Mozambique with the second party of missionaries to be sent out by the Free Methodist board. In 1891 she was transferred to Natal and later founded a school for girls at Fairview and served as its principal. In 1926 she took charge of a mission in Pondoland serving two main and seven branch stations with schools.

ALLEN, PHOEBE (1769-1856), born in England and served as a minister for the Society of Friends. She held important positions in the society and served many years along with her husband. Details of her early life are obscure.

ALLIN, CATHERINE (c. 1517-1557), wife of Edmund of Frytenden. They were burned at Maidstone along with five others on June 18, 1557, because of their steadfast testimony for the Lord.

ALSTYNE, FRANCES JANE VAN. *See* **CROSBY, FRANCES (FANNY)**

AMANDON, MARTHA D. BYINGTON (1834-1937), oldest daughter of the John Byington family, pioneer workers in the Seventh Day Adventist movement. She was the first teacher in the first school for Adventist children organized in this country by her father in 1853 at Buck's Ridge, New York. In 1860 she married George W. Amandon and served as the first president of the Dorcas Society of that denomination.

AMBOISE, FRANCISE d' (1427-1485), daughter of Louis Amboise; was married to PeterII, Duke of Brittany; founded the first monastery in Brittany of the order of Carmelites.

ANASTASIA (c. 25-c. 70), believed to have become a Christian after hearing one of Christ's disciples preach. She was martyred for her faith, probably about 70 A.D., during Emperor Nero's persecution. Although details of her life are obscure, her name has come down in history as a martyr because of her testimony and witness.

ANASTASIA (c. 230-c. 259), believed to have been the daughter of Constantius Chlorus. Her Christian influence in the home was accredited as a major contribution to Constantine. Details of her life are obscure.

ANASTASIA (c. 279-c. 304), born into a Roman family and under the teaching of Chrysogonus. Her father opposed her acceptance of Christianity, and her husband, Publius, betrayed her faith to authorities. She was martyred by the request of Florus, an official in Illyricum, because of her Christian faith.

ANASTASIA (c. 553-c. 580), a Greek woman who lived at Constantinople. It is reported that she fled to Alexandria, Egypt, after she was threatened with being forced into Emperor Justinian's harem, and that she lived for twenty-eight years in Egypt disguised as a monk.

ANDERSON, MINNIE SUSAN

(1892-1967), author, teacher, and pioneer missionary, a native of Haversham County, Georgia. Converted as a teenager, she graduated from the Women's Training School in Louisville, Kentucky, in 1915. She served as assistant to the pastor of the First Baptist Church in Charlotte, North Carolina for two and a half years, and in 1918 was appointed a missionary to Nigeria by the Foreign Mission Board of the Southern Baptist Convention. In Nigeria she taught at the Baptist Girls School in Abeokuta throughout her forty-three-year missionary career. Thus, her life influenced many for the Lord. She taught English and Bible and counseled many Nigerian girls, helping them to realize their potential in God's service. In her first book, *So This Is Africa,* published in 1943, she related many of her experiences in Africa, serious and humorous. Her second book, *May Perry of Africa,* was a biography of her closest associate in Nigeria, the principal of the girls school. Although retired and living in Kansas at the time of her death, she had begun working on yet another book.

ANDRE HATTIE (1865-1952), a missionary teacher and school administrator. She graduated from Battle Creek College in 1892 and served under the Seventh Day Adventist Church in the Pitcairn Islands, where she organized and conducted schools. Later she served as a teacher in Australia and for eleven years as dean of women at Pacific Union College. Her life influenced many young people for Christian service.

ANGELA, MERICI (1474-1540), born in Desenzano, a small town at the base of the Alps in Lombardy, Italy. In 1535 she founded the Ursuline Order in Italy. As a Catholic school for girls, it was well received with various branches established later in other European countries and much later in the United States. Education was the purpose of the Ursulines.

ANGELA OF FOLIGNO (c. 1248-1309), daughter of a wealthy family in Foligno. Although she married and had children, later, as a widow, she devoted her life in lay work of the Franciscan order. Records indicate that she reported having a number of visions as she communicated with God. Details of her life are obscure, but her life influenced many.

ANNA COMNENA. *See* **BRYENNIUS**

ANNE (1665-1714), Protestant Christian queen of the British Isles and first queen of the joint kingdoms of Great Britain and Ireland. Born at Twickenham near London, she was the second daughter of King James II and Anne Hyde. At the request of her uncle, King Charles II, who ruled from 1660-1685, her education was under the Protestant influence of the Church of England. In 1689 Anne married a Lutheran, Prince George of Denmark. In 1689 Anne's immediate family went into exile because they were Catholics, but she remained in England and faithful to the Protestant church. She was the last Stuart ruler and had a great desire to uphold Christian principles in all affairs of state. She exercised her religious convictions by appointing Church of England people to high positions. Anne was much influenced by her close friend Sarah Jennings Churchill, who advised Anne to seek favor from the Protestant ruler, William III of Orange, when he overthrew James II in 1688. The very next year by the Bill of Rights, William and his wife, Mary, Anne's oldest sister, were made king and queen of England. This placed Anne in succession for the throne, which she took in 1702 when William died and had no heirs. Anne was unsuccessful in providing a successor for herself, although it is reported that between 1683 and 1700, Anne became pregnant eighteen times, gave birth to six children, none of whom survived her. Thus, it was by the Act of Settlement of 1701 that her successors were the Hanoverian descendants of King James I. Her Christian faith was strong even to her final days, and one of her last acts as queen was to secure the Protestant succession by placing the Lord Treasurer's staff in charge of Charles Talbot, who administered the succession.

ANNE, Lady (1630-1716), Christian monarch, Duchess of Hamilton, and daughter of James, third Marquis and first Duke of Hamilton and Lady Mary Fielding. She was nineteen when her father was executed. In 1656 she married Lord William Douglas, oldest son of William. When Cromwell was overthrown and Charles II succeeded the throne, all of Lady Anne's estates were returned to her, although Charles II opposed an ecclesiastical form of church government in Scotland. Lady Anne (the Duchess of Hamilton) was in full sympathy with the Christian ministers and supported her husband's efforts to insure religious toleration. She permitted her palace to become a refuge for Christians, the poor, and needy. Among Anne's many influences were financial aid to colleges, help for youth preparing for the ministry, and sponsorship in building churches.

ANNE OF BOHEMIA (1366-1394), Christian queen of Richard II and the daughter of Charles IV of Bohemia by his fourth wife, Elizabeth. Anne was born in Prague; details of her early years are obscure, but at the age of fifteen she married King Richard II, and it is recorded that he was deeply devoted to her. His mother, Joan of Kent, studied the Bible with Anne. Anne's personal spiritual life was especially commendable, for she was a diligent student of the Bible, reading it daily in three languages—Bohemian, Latin, and English. She corresponded with John Wycliffe and assisted in translating the gospels into English. Reportedly she made a practice of having the Scriptures read aloud to her household, including the servants, and that this practice was followed not only by members of her household but by many of the lords and ladies of the land. In fact, she introduced Wycliffe's tracts to her native land. The influence of her Christian testimony is said to have laid the scriptural foundation needed for the time in royal circles. It was by Anne's request that pardons were issued for unjustly imprisoned people. Her faith and courage brought hope to many oppressed and discouraged.

ANTHONY, MARY O'CONNELL (Sister) (1815-1897), a native of Ireland. She emigrated to the United States with her family, and at the age of twenty took Catholic vows in the Order of the Sisters of Charity. She served as a nurse during the Civil War and was recognized for her bravery and nursing care, receiving the "Angel of the Battlefield" award following the Pittsburg Landing Battle. She took many of the disabled soldiers by boat to the convent in Cincinnati, Ohio, for further care.

ANTHONY, SUSAN BROWNELL (1820-1906), born in Adams, Massachusetts, of a Quaker family. After graduating from a Friends school in West Philadelphia she taught for fourteen years. Encouraged by her father, who had a group of abolitionists meet regularly in their home, she became actively involved with several social reform movements. She was also an outspoken proponent of temperance, antislavery, and equal rights for women. In 1852 she helped organize the first state chapter of the Women's Christian Temperance Union in New York. During and after the Civil War she was especially concerned with suffrage movements—black and woman. In 1856 she assumed an active role in the American Anti-Slavery Society and in 1869 was president of the American Woman Suffrage Association, which she helped organize. Miss Anthony traveled extensively in Britain and the United States lecturing to promote the cause of reform and in 1888 organized the International Council of Women. Her last public appearance was as a delegate to the International Council of Women in London, England, in 1900.

ANTHUSA (c. 331-c. 374), remembered as the mother of John Chrysostom. She lived in Antioch and became the wife of Secundus, who was in the Imperial Army of Syria. She was left a widow with an infant son, John, when only about twenty years old. She did not remarry but centered her efforts on the education and training of John. She taught him to love the Word of God and influenced him to become an expositor of the Bible.

APPLEBY, PETRONIL (c. 1507-1557), a Christian martyr; wife of Walter from Maidstone where they were both burned because of their testimonies for the Lord.

Although recorded as a martyr for the cause of Christ, other details of her life are uncertain.

ARAKI, IYO (c. 1875-c. 1938), a Japanese missionary nurse, graduate of St. Margaret's School in Tokyo. She came to America with an American missionary, taking postgraduate work at Johns Hopkins University. She returned to Japan in 1902 and became head of the nurses training program in Tokyo started by Dr. Teusler. She served during two emergencies with the Red Cross—relief work in Vladivostok and after the great Tokyo earthquake and fire in 1923. It is said of her twenty-five years of service that she proved a Christian commitment of missions by her devotion by a ministry of service.

ARMSTRONG, ANNIE (1850-1938), pioneer home missionary and organizer reared in Baltimore, Maryland; served at the Eutaw Place Baptist Church. She was largely responsible for the organized promotion of home missions, including framing the constitution of Women's Missionary Union of the Southern Baptist Convention. "Miss Annie" spearheaded extended ministries to meet specific needs for the disabled, the mountain people, blacks and Indians, and promoted an annuity fund for retiring pastors. She wrote extensively, started a Scripture department for young people in the publication *Kind Words,* and wrote for two departments in *The Teacher* and two mission publications, *Foreign Mission Journal* and *Our Home Field.* She wrote hundreds of letters by hand for the work of missions. Memorials to Annie Armstrong reflect her influence and include gifts to a hospital in China, a home mission school, the Annie Walker Armstrong building in Burnsville, North Carolina, and others.

ARMSTRONG, LAURA DELL MALOTTE (1886-1945), a native of Missouri, daughter of James W. and Mary Malotte of distinguished Huguenot and pilgrim background. Both her father and grandfather were well-known Baptist ministers in the area. She graduated from Northwest Missouri State Teachers College, taught in the public schools, and in 1907 married Frank W. Armstrong, an attorney. Laura Armstrong is remembered for her long administrative leadership in various offices of the Missouri Baptist General Association and in national and worldwide positions. She served on the executive board of the Missouri Baptist General Association (1919-1936); as state president of the Women's Missionary Union (1923-1934); of the convention-wide organization (1933-1945), the executive committee of the Southern Baptist Convention (1927-1945); and a member-at-large of the Baptist World Alliance (1934-1945). She was influential in establishing the first mission study institute and first Baptist Student Union conference in Missouri. Part of her varied official responsibilities included the editorial staff for several publications of the Women's Missionary Union, chairman of the Board of Trustees of the Training School for Women's Missionary Union built adjacent to the Southern Baptist Theological Seminary in Louisville, Kentucky, and she was responsible for promoting funds for the National Baptist Negro Women's work. Reflecting her influence on missions, many memorials have been established honoring her such as: the Armstrong Terrace at Carver School, the maternity ward of the first Southern Baptist Hospital in South America, the Armstrong Memorial Training School in Rome, Italy, and the Baptist Seminary in Cuba.

ARMYNE, Lady (c. 1594-c. 1675), a wealthy English Christian woman who gave liberally for the conversion of Indians in New England. She aided the nonconforming ministers, who by the Act of Uniformity (passed in 1660) lost many of their personal and family possessions. She provided money by her will for the needs of many of those people for years. Details of her personal life are obscure, but she influenced many for the Lord.

ARNAULD, JACQUELINE-MARIE-ANGELIQUE (1591-1661), a promoter of Jansenism and an abbess. She was born in Paris; her father was a distinguished attorney. At the age of eight she entered the Cistercian abbey of Port-Royal-des-

Champs. When only eleven, she became the abbess and claimed a spiritual conversion experience in 1608. In 1630 and no longer an abbess, she influenced the circumstances that brought Saint Cyran into a leadership position there. He was a fellow-student and a close friend of Cornelius Jansen, who promoted plans for reforming Roman Catholicism. He was associated with the Arnauld family from 1623, using Port Royal as a center for Jansenism in France. Again she served as an abbess between 1642 and 1655, having a distinct influence for Jansenism, especially with the many refugees who came to this convent.

ASHBY, MARY (1773-1835), born in England, became a minister in the Society of Friends, serving for nearly twenty years. She had strong convictions and was especially interested in New Testament studies.

ASHER, VIRGINIA (1869-1937), evangelist and co-worker with Billy Sunday, known also for founding the National Federation of Business Women's Councils. Born in Chicago, she studied voice under Gottschalk and Frederick Root. She became a Christian at the age of eleven at Moody Memorial Church in Chicago, later attended Moody Bible Institute, and in 1887 married William Asher. They worked as an evangelistic team assisting J. Wilbur Chapman and Billy Sunday. Besides singing, she led meetings especially for businesswomen in various cities, organizing those groups into a federation to carry on regularly. Her work with Billy Sunday had to do with arranging meetings for women. She and her husband also worked as evangelists in eighteen countries outside of the United States.

ASKEW, ANNE (1521-1546), a British Protestant martyr born in Stallingborough, Lincolnshire, England. She was converted through the study of the Bible and the preaching of a Reformer. When twenty-four she was arrested and tried for heresy, then released. She refused to accept the Roman Catholic views of the eucharist, did not attend confession, and in general opposed Catholic interpretation of the Scriptures. In 1546 she was arrested and tried again, but this time she was condemned to death as a heretic. Her husband, Thomas Kymn, a Catholic, renounced her because of her faith. She was imprisoned in the Tower of London but remained firm in her Christian commitment. In 1546 she was taken to Smithfield, chained to a stake and burned with several others. Her faithful witness for Christ drew the attention of the Duchess of Suffolk and other women of prominence.

ASTOO, MARGERY (c. 1511-1557), one of five Christian women burned at Islington for her faith and resistance to popish idolatrous practices.

AUBER, HARRIET (1773-1862), a British poet and hymnist remembered especially for her beautiful hymn "Our Blest Redeemer, Ere He Breathed." It is said that she first wrote this as a poem on a glass window of her home. Miss Auber was born in London. Her father, James Auber, was rector of the Anglican Church at Tring. Her great-grandfather, Pierre Auber, went to England from Normandy as a Huguenot refugee in 1685. She and another writer friend, a Miss Machenzie, made their home together in her later years. She is described as being a quiet, devout member of the Church of England. A book of her poems based on the Psalms was published in 1829, titled *The Spirit of the Psalms.*

AUDEBERT, ANN (c. 1502-1549), a martyr burned at Orleans for her faith and rejection of popish domination.

AUDRY, ETHELDREDA (c. 632-679), daughter of Anna and queen of Northumberland. She was married twice; her second husband consented to her desire to go into the Abbey of Caldingham. Later she had built a monastery on the Isle of Ely and became an abbess.

AUGUSTA, CAROLINE (c. 1799-c. 1850), daughter of FranzI, Emperor of Austria. She founded the Vincentian Religious Community of Sisters of Charity in 1835. It was located in Austria with the primary purpose of education.

AUSTREBERTHA (633-704), daughter of Badefroi, Count Palatine, and St. Frametilda. She was born in the area of Terouane. Little is known of her early years, but at age sixteen she was to be married against her wishes. To avoid such an arranged marriage, she chose to take Catholic vows. In 649 she received such vows from St. Omer, the Bishop of Terouane. She became the first abbess of Port in 672 and later the first abbess of Pavilly, a Catholic community founded by St. Philibertus. Her influence was effective in training other women and especially those who took the vows in circumstances comparative to hers. She was considered an example of humility and self-sacrifice.

AUSTRUDIS or **ANSTRUDIS** (c. 635-c. 700), born in the diocese of Toul, daughter of Blandinus Boson and his wife, Salabarna. Austrudis took Catholic vows at the age of twelve in a monastery at Laon where her mother was an abbess.

AYLWARD, GLADYS (1902-1970), devoted missionary to China. She was born in London of humble circumstance and converted at an early age. She felt a definite call to serve the Lord in China. As a young woman, she applied to a number of missionary societies, but they would not sponsor her, largely because of educational reasons. She worked as a maid, saving her meager wages for several years to finance her own way to China. She proved that those in God's will never lack His supply, and in 1932 she realized the initial part of her goal by making the long journey to China. Her trip in itself was a series of miracles as she traveled via Siberia and Japan into China. Unexpected problems resulting from the Russo-Chinese war complicated her plans, but she continued to exercise great faith. The Lord blessed her with a companion in Mrs. Jennie Lawson, and together they had an effective ministry in Yancheng. She learned the language and, with Mrs. Lawson, opened an inn for muleteers that served as a means for their Bible classes. At first they simply told Bible stories as they shared the plan of salvation. This was a pioneer ministry and an effective means of reaching the nationals. After the death of Jennie Lawson, Gladys continued with this work, finding help in the local mandarin. In 1940 the Japanese invaded that area, and Gladys miraculously led a group of 100 Chinese children over the mountains to safety. The experience and ordeal of that trek was so incredible that later a film was made based on it. Miss Aylward became seriously ill and returned to England in 1947 for a period of ten years. Then she went to Taiwan, established an orphanage, and worked there until the Lord called her Home.

B

BAERG, ANNA (1897-1972), Russian teacher and poet of considerable influence. Because of a physical disability she was confined to her home much of the time, but kept an extensive journal that has proved useful in Mennonite history. Her father was manager of a large Molotschna Mennonite colony in southern Russia. During the Russian Revolution her family suffered much, and when the Bolsheviks approached their colony, her family and others fled to a neighboring village of Wassilewka and later to Alexanderkrone. She taught a kindergarten class, and eventually the family sought emigration permission to America. After her father died, she and her mother moved to Winnipeg, Canada, later to Alberta, and she lived her final days with her sister in British Columbia. Much of her poetry has been included in Mennonite publications. Her work expresses deep faith in the Lord, trust, and comfort for many who have suffered as she did.

BALDWIN, MARY BRISCOE (1811-1877), American teacher-missionary for forty-two years in Greece. Born in Virginia, she received a private education. By the time she was twenty, she had lost both parents. She moved to Stanton, Pennsylvania, where she taught in a seminary for women. She answered a call to the mission field and went with friends, Dr. and Mrs. Hill, to Greece to teach in a school the Hills had established there under the Protestant Episcopal Society. She became an effective Christian educator among the women and girls of Greece. She was especially successful in helping Christians of Crete who in 1866 revolted against the Turkish government and fled to Athens as refugees. She opened schools and Sunday schools for them, even providing work and necessities.

BANNISTER, CATHERINE (1855-1910), British missionary, translator, leader, and pioneer of missions in India. Born in England to a refined family, she had an excellent education and was brought up in the Church of England. Converted at the age of sixteen, she cared for her invalid mother. She and her sister organized a mission in their village, invited lay preachers and served the ill, aged, and needy. Catherine heard Mrs. William Booth speak and in London attended meetings of the Salvation Army. Soon she dedicated her life to the Lord, later pioneering the work of the Salvation Army in India for thirteen years. She became known as Colonel Yudda Bai, her Indian name, serving as a Salvation Army Commander of both the Marathi and Punjab territories. She translated Marathi songs, encountered many difficult situations, but remained a fervent worker dedicated to spreading the good news of salvation. In spite of the advice of her physician, Catherine chose to remain in India until her death at age 55.

BARAT, MADELINE SOPHIE (1779-1865), born in Burgundy, a scholar, linguist, and founder of the Society of the Sacred Heart Catholic community in France in 1800. This order was established in the United States in 1818. She saw the need for missionary work in providing for the educational needs of poor children. She was the sister of Father Louis Barat.

BARBARA (c. 259-c. 306), became a Christian without her parents' knowledge. Her testimony became evident in her living habits, and she was criticized by her father. It is believed that he even turned against her for her faith and contributed to her martyrdom. She was killed for her faith in Christ likely at either of two locations: Heliopolis in Egypt or at Nicomedia. Details about her life are lacking.

BARBAULD, ANNA LETITIA AIKIN (1743-1825), a British author, hymnist, and teacher. She was born in Leicester, England, and was the daughter of John Aikin. She married a minister, Rochemont Barbauld, a descendant of a French Protestant family. They opened a school in Palgrave. In 1773 she published a volume of poems so popular that it went through four printings. Her other literary pursuits included the preparation of lesson materials for children in addition to many poems, some which were set to music as hymns. Collections of those hymns are complied in *Early Lessons for Children* and *Hymns in Prose for Children*. In 1775 her *Devotional Pieces* included work composed from the Psalms and Job. She wrote many other works, some of which were published in a six-volume work, *Evenings at Home*. Her best-known hymn was "Praise to God, Immortal Praise."

BARGEN, ELIZABETH REGEHR (1897-1976), author and amazing survivor of the persecutions of the Russian Revolution of 1917-1919. She was the daughter of the K. Regehrs, who lived in a Mennonite community in the Ukraine. Bandits ruthlessly mistreated her and her family; some members were killed and their homes burned. This was in the area of Molotschna, Russia. Much later the remaining family members migrated to Canada. Her account appeared in Mennonite literature and is but an example of what many women of the time endured. She helped many others, yet was often ill and in extreme circumstances.

BARKER, LILLIE EASTERBY (1865-1925), a native of Richmond, Virginia, and a graduate of the Chester Female Institute. She married John Alexander Barker in 1888. They went to Brazil as missionaries but had to return because of her health. She is remembered for her work and leadership in the Women's Missionary Union of the Southern Baptist Convention. During her leadership she established the Margaret Home Fund and the promotion of missionary education for youth.

BARLOW, ANN (1787-1867), a British missionary; at age eleven became a Wesleyan Methodist, and much later she committed her life to the Quaker doctrine and eventually became a minister in the Society of Friends. She had an effective ministry among women.

BARTON, CLARA HARLOWE (1821-1912), humanitarian, nurse, author, and founder of the American Red Cross. Born in Massachusetts, she graduated from the Liberal Institute in Clinton, New York. In the early part of the American Civil War she became greatly concerned with the need for better care of the wounded soldiers. In addition to takng supplies to them she helped care for them on the battlefield. Her devoted efforts brought wide attention to the needs she had discovered. In 1864 she was officially appointed superintendent of nurses for the Army. Later, President Lincoln appointed her to oversee the search for men missing in action and the marking of the thousands of graves at Andersonville, Georgia. She went to Switzerland in 1869, and during the Franco-Prussian War helped care for the wounded. There it was that she saw the great work of the International Committee of the Red Cross, and after returning to the United States sought support for a Red Cross in the United States. Her efforts prompted the formation of the American Red Cross in 1881. She served as its first president from 1881 to 1904. Before long, the Red Cross activities broadened to offer far more than caring for wounded soldiers by including emergency care in many situations. She represented the United States for the Red Cross Conference at the International Peace Convention in Geneva in 1884. Clara Barton was more than an organizer; she actually participated in carrying out the needed action. She did not hesitate to work at the scene of need and traveled wherever Red Cross help was sought: floods, earthquakes, explosions, and numerous other disaster locations. Her work called her to South Africa, Cuba, and Russia in addition to the United States. Her spiritual convictions tended toward universalism. Her several books include: *The Red Cross in Peace and War* (1898), *A Story of the Red Cross* (1904), and an autobiographical sketch, *The Story of My Childhood* published in 1907.

BARTON, ELIZABETH (c. 1506-1534), a martyr. Little is recorded about her, but she lived in Kent, England, and was known for her deep spiritual insight. She is reported to have prophesied a number of dramatic happenings but was criticized because of a physical handicap she had. She entered a convent at Canterbury and was later beheaded.

BATES, KATHERINE LEE (1859-1929), a native of Massachusetts whose father and grandfather were Congregational ministers. Miss Bates is included here for her hymn "O Beautiful for Spacious Skies." She graduated from Wellesley College in 1880, taught in high school and then returned to Wellesley as head of the English department. She wrote or edited more than twenty books, including a *History of American Literature* (1908) and her well-known hymn "America, the Beautiful" (1911). That hymn was result of a tour of the United States in 1893 that included the Columbia Exposition in Chicago, the summit on Pike's Peak in Colorado, and other places of beauty. She was inspired to write that tribute with each verse rounded by the idea of God's beauty and grace.

BATHILDA (c. 651-680), first Christian queen of France. She was born in England and was sold as a slave on the coast of France to Clovis II. About 640 she became his wife and thus queen. Bathilda and Clovis II had three sons. When her husband died she became regent and exercised her authority to reform many abuses that had come about in the church. Among the churches she founded was the monastery of Corbie at Picardy and restored houses of St. Vandrille and others in Paris.

BAUMAN, MARY MELISSA WAGONER (1876-1909), teacher, author, and minister. Born Mary Melissa Wagoner in Kansas, she graduated with honors from the Lawrence High School and taught in the public schools. In the spring of 1898 she married Louis S. Bauman, and became affiliated with the Brethren church. In December of 1899 she was ordained at Roann, Indiana. Mrs. Bauman wrote a number of articles for her denominational magazine and often served as speaker for a variety of groups in addition to her preaching. She may best be remembered for having organized the first Sisterhood of Mary and Martha, the girl's movement of the Brethren church, in Philadelphia in 1906. The meetings were held regularly at ten o'clock on Sunday mornings and before the weekly church services. Mrs. Bauman contracted typhoid fever in young womanhood and died at the age of thirty-three in Ashland, Ohio.

BAXTER, LYDIA (1809-1874), a native of New York and a poet of a Baptist background. In 1855 a volume of her poems was published under the title *Gems by the Wayside*. Although she wrote several gospel songs, the only one used commonly today is "Take the Name of Jesus with You."

BAXTER, MARGARET CHARLTON (1639-1681), devoted wife of Richard Baxter, born in Shropshire near Wellington, England. Her father died when she was quite young; her mother remarried. The influence of her Christian mother was evident, but Margaret was not very serious about her faith until she heard Richard Baxter preach. Margaret was convicted and converted, yet she seemed easily discouraged. Baxter counseled her and prayed for her. In 1659 she became quite ill and was thought to be dying. The church devoted a day of prayer for her recovery. Margaret gradually improved. Her mother invited those who had banded together to pray for Margaret's health to gather for a time of thanksgiving and praise in the spring of 1660. It was at this meeting that Margaret gave her testimony of gratitude. The friendship of Margaret and Richard Baxter grew into romance. They were married in 1662. Neither had been married before; she was twenty-three and he was forty-six. She was from a wealthy family, he was not, but their love deepened for each other and for the Lord. She stayed and comforted him when he was imprisoned for his evangelistic preaching. In 1674, while he was preaching in London, part of the church building caved in, and it was Margaret who sought to calm the hysterical crowd and help all to safety. The influence of her prayers and quiet ministry cannot be measured.

BEATRIX (c. 249-303), little is known about this woman, but her concern and resulting actions indicate something of her Christian principles. She is said to have been the sister of Faustinus and Simplecius and that she was condemned for her attempts to rescue their bodies from the Tiber River in order to give them a proper burial. She was put in prison and later beheaded.

BEAUFORT, MARGARET (1443-1509), born at Bletsoe, England, and the daughter of the Duke of Somerset. It is said that she was largely responsible for arranging the marriage of Henry VII so that he would be assured the throne. She was Countess of Richmond and Derby but is remembered especially for founding the Lady Margaret professorships of divinity at Oxford and Cambridge (1503), in addition to a preachership at Christ's and St. John's Colleges, Cambridge.

BEAUMONT, AGNES (1662-1730), a faithful friend of John Bunyan and converted through his preaching. Because of her faith, her father was unusually hostile. He would not accept her back into his home and would not allow her to attend church services, so she made her home with a sister. Her firm testimony and prayer for her father penetrated the situation, and he became a Christian. She was an influential, devout Christian, although her general circumstances have probably been experienced by untold numbers.

BECKER, MAGDALENA HERBERT (1878-1938), a pioneer missionary to the Comanche Indians of Oklahoma. She served thirty-seven years on this mission field. She and her husband, Abraham J. Becker, established a mission in what is now Oklahoma, but she was also officially appointed a field matron by the United States Government. The Comanche Indians looked to her for many things, thus helping her to encourage them in spiritual matters as well. Records show that she participated in more than 600 funerals or burials and was used effectively in consoling the bereaved. Her unusual combination of being a missionary and field matron for the government afforded a successful service for the Lord.

BELASYSE, MARY CROMWELL (1636-1712), daughter of Oliver Cromwell and wife of Thomas Belasyse, Earl of Fauconberg. Her letters reflect a devout Christian attitude and special sympathy for the cause of Christ and her own family.

BELL, ANN MARY (1706-1775), British teacher and minister in the Society of Friends. She taught at a Friends school in London; then traveled about England preaching and teaching the Bible. In 1753 she returned to London and faithfully preached in the streets.

BELL, MARTHA E. McINTOSH (1848-1922), the first president of the Women's Missionary Union of the Southern Baptist Convention. She was born in South Carolina, converted at an early age, and attended St. David's Academy and a private school in Charleston. Before her leadership on a national level, she was active in missionary leadership in her local church. In 1892 she married T. P. Bell, also a church leader and editor of *The Christian Index*.

BELL, VIRGINIA MYERS LEFT (1892-1974), nurse, missionary, wife of Dr. Nelson Bell and mother of Ruth Graham. She grew up in Waynesboro, Virginia, and attended nurses training school at St. Luke's Hospital in Richmond, Virginia. She and her husband served as Presbyterian missionaries in China between 1916 and 1941, while he was chief surgeon at Tsiangkiangpo General Hospital. Between 1941 and 1956 he practiced medicine in Ashville, North Carolina. Because of her background in nursing, she was able to help as needed. She survived her husband only a few months.

BENDEN, ALICE (c. 1531-1557), an English martyr. Little is recorded about her life apart from her Christian testimony and the consequences of her mistreatment and martyrdom. In Kent, England, she was interrogated concerning her faith. Her replies were firm, reflecting a deep Christian commitment, and left no doubt concerning her belief. When asked why she did not attend church, she answered that it was because of the idolatry there against the glory of God. After she realized that even her husband was about to give her over to the enemy, she went of her own accord. She was imprisoned, put in stocks, lay for nine weeks with only bread and water, and was then burned on June 19, 1557.

BENDER, BERTHA BERKHOLDER (1896-1978), a Mennonite educator of some influence. She graduated from Hesston College in 1925, then went to Goshen College in Indiana, where she earned an M.A. degree and became an instructor of French. She taught at Goshen College and later served there as dean of women.

BENDISH, BRIDGET IRETON (1649-1729), devout wife of Thomas Bendish and granddaughter of Oliver Cromwell, who supervised her education. Her testimony of faith under the leadership of Charles II and James II was one of nonconformity. She had great respect and admiration for her grandfather, Oliver Cromwell, and upheld Calvinistic doctrine. She was an active member of Dr. John Owen's congregation in London. Her husband died in 1707, and she never remarried. The poem of Isaac Watts "Against Tears" was addressed to her in 1699.

BENNETT, BELLE HARRIS (1852-1922), a Southern Methodist educator and lay leader born near Richmond, Virginia. She was active in Sunday school work, and after attending a meeting at Chautauqua, New York, she saw the need for a training school for women missionaries. She established the Scaritt Bible and Training School, which later moved to Nashville under the name of Scaritt College for Christian Workers. In 1896 she became president of the Home Mission Society and worked for the establishment of an industrial department for girls at Paine Institute for Negroes in Augusta, Georgia. She also headed a successful fund drive for mission work abroad. A woman's college was named after her in Rio de Janeiro, and she was was influential in establishing a Woman's Christian Medical College in Shanghai.

BERNADETTE OF LOURDES SOUBIROUS (1844-1879) Although born to the humble French family of Francois and Louise Soubirous, Bernadette gained considerable attention for her reported visions of the virgin Mary. At least eighteen times Bernadette claimed Mary appeared to her in a grotto at Lourdes near the Pyrenees Mountains, telling her to make known the healing quality of the waters in the Gave River there. Bernadette reported these visions when she was about fourteen. At one time she tended sheep, which explains why some artists have depicted her as a shepherd girl. She took vows at age twenty and entered the Convent of the Sisters of Charity at Nevers. A chapel was built on the spot where Bernadette had the visions, for in the final one she said the virgin Mary informed her that a chapel should be built there. A chapel was constructed in 1876 with millions of dollars contributed by Roman Catholics throughout the world. In more recent years, a huge underground basilica has been built in the shape of a fish, a familiar Christian symbol. It was dedicated in 1958, the one-hundredth anniversary of Bernadette's visions. This spot, including the grotto, chapel, and basilica has become one of the most-visited shrines of Christendom, and even to this day people claim to experience healing powers from the waters of Lourdes. The experiences of Bernadette have been reflected in several pieces of literature, particularly *The Song of Bernadette* by Franz Werfel, which was made into a film, and the story by Michel de Saint-pierre, *Bernadette and Lourdes*.

BERT, SARAH (1860-1948), pioneer mission founder and leader in the Brethren in Christ church. Born near Chambersburg, Pennsylvania, of French Huguenot parents who had immigrated from Germany in 1830. After schooling in Pennsylvania, she pioneered mission work in Chicago in 1894, founding the first mission of its kind for the Brethren in Christ church. She served as the mission's superintendent, organizing sewing classes for women, carrying on relief work both in and out of the mission itself. Sarah Bert is credited with introducing to her denomination such worship aids as the organ and choir. She also served as a transportation officer, arranging clergy fares and train schedules. She also served as hostess at the mission to many church persons passing through Chicago each year. She was one of the few women gaining recognition in her denomination before the 1970s. She died in Chicago at the age of eighty-eight.

BERTHA (c. 570-612), England's first Christian queen, she is credited with establishing the first church in England among the Anglo-Saxons. She was the daughter of Charibert, king of the Franks, and granddaughter of Clovis and Clotilda. When she agreed to become the wife of Aethelbert, king of East Anglia in ancient England, she requested that she be free to openly practice her religion, for she was a devout Christian. Her husband honored her wishes and became a Christian himself. He gave his testimony at a public baptism ceremony. This opened the way for many, including Augustine, to preach the gospel of Christ, thereby allowing Christianity to spread through England. Many Anglican churches were dedicated to this king. He and Bertha worshiped in a Roman edifice outside the walls of Canterbury and later gave Augustine their home, the present site of Canterbury Cathedral. Bertha's daughter was Ethelberga.

BERTHA (646-725), born in Artois, the daughter of Count Rigobertus and Ursana. At the age of twenty she married a man by the name of Sigefroi, although little is known about him. Twenty years later he died, and she retired to a monastery that she had built at Blany, the diocese of Terouanne. She became an abbess, had three churches built within the monastery, and was influential in promoting Christianity. Although she lived there until her death, she resigned her responsibilities as abbess, turning them over to her daughter, Deotila. The monastery she established was burned by the Normans in 895 and restored by the Benedictines in 1032.

BESANT (bèzánt) ANNIE (nee WOOD) (1847-1933), as an author, British-born theosophist, and political figure in India, exercised considerable influence in the late nineteenth century. A native of London, she received her education at London University and through tutors. Annie Besant's father was a minister as was her husband. In 1867 she married Frank Besant in Lincolnshire, the Vicar of Sibsey. Their marriage lasted only six years when she requested a divorce. She expressed considerable mental and spiritual confusion, unrest, and despondency as she left not only her husband but also the Church of England and Christianity in general. She became a kind of "free" thinker, a socialist, a follower of Madame Blavatsky, joined the Theosophical Society and became its president and continued in that office until her death. She founded the Central Hindu College of Benares, India, in 1898 (later the Central Hindu Girls School), the University of India, the Indian Home Rule League and became its president, and the Indian National Congress in 1917. In 1923 she became general secretary of the National Convention of India. She traveled widely with Jidder Krishnamurti, an Indian mystic she adopted, and even declared him the reincarnated Messiah, a claim he repudiated. She wrote a number of books: *The Religious Problems of India, The Wisdom of the Upanishads, The Basis of Morality, A World Religion, Theosophy and the New Psychology,* and others.

BETHUNE, JOANNA GRAHAM (1770-1860), pioneer in the American Sunday school movement. She was born in New York state and converted in 1794. She worked with her widowed mother, Isabella Graham, in organizing the first group to promote Sunday schools in the United States. In 1795 she married Divie Bethune, a businessman from Scotland. They went to England and Scotland on a business trip and to observe the work of Robert Raikes and his Sunday classes. Although their classes were to teach reading and writing in addition to the Bible, there was some opposition because of plans to hold them on Sunday. Only two years after her mother's death, Joanna Bethune, a Presbyterian, and women from several other denominations organized the Female Union for the Promotion of Sabbath Schools, the first such group in this country. This idea spread rapidly and included men. In 1817 Joanna and her husband were instrumental in organizing a more inclusive organization that came to be known as the American Sunday School Union. She wrote several books on the teaching of young children, and taught until she was past the age of eighty.

BETHUNE, MARY McLEOD (1875-1955), the daughter of former slaves, Mary Bethune became a leader and college president. Born in South Carolina, she accepted Christ quite young and was encouraged by a Presbyterian missionary to attend school. After her initial schooling she went to Moody Bible Institute to prepare for service in Africa but did not find a sponsoring mission board. She concluded that this was an indication that she was to minister to Africans in the United States. She believed education to be her primary means of Christian witness and social service to her own people. She taught and in 1904 began her own school. Initially, only five students came to her home, but the number soon grew. She named it the Daytona Normal and Industrial School for Girls and taught the Bible along with basic subjects, in addition to teaching a Sunday school. So successful were her efforts that others became interested and gave much-needed funds. In 1928 the school merged with the Cookman Institute, and she became its president. The school became an outstanding coeducational college. During the presidency of Herbert Hoover, she served on the National Commission for Child Welfare; during the Franklin D. Roosevelt administration she became a special advisor on minority affairs; and in President Truman's administration she was chosen to visit William Tubman, Christian president of Liberia. She founded the National Council of Negro Women and traveled throughout the United States on behalf of blacks.

BEVAN, EMMA FRANCES (1827-1909), British hymnist, daughter of the anti-Tractarian bishop of Chichester, P. N. Shuttleworth. Thus, she was considered a High Churchwoman. In 1856 she married R. C. L. Bevan, an Evangelical Anglican, who was a banker of Quaker background. In 1858 and later she anonymously published several hymn collections, largely paraphrased from German. Her best-known translation was "Sinners Jesus Will Receive."

BILLART, MARIE ROSA JULIA (1751-1816), founder of the Catholic community Sisters of Notre Dame in France in 1803. She devoted her life largely to the education of orphans. This order was introduced in the United States in 1840.

BINNS, MARY (1775-1851), an influential minister in the Society of Friends. She did evangelistic work in England. Although little is recorded about her, she was an invalid for a time.

BISCOTT, JEANNE (1601-1664), a French noblewoman, youngest daughter of Arras, and called "heroine of charity." She dedicated her life to God in a ministry of caring for the needy. During wartime she literally turned her home into an orphanage, providing food, and clothing, and shelter. When a plague hit, she assumed leadership in providing care. In 1645 she founded a sisterhood of St. Agnes and also cared for wounded soldiers during the war in 1654.

BISHOP, ISABELLA BIRD (1831-1902), a native of Edinburgh, Scotland. In 1881 she married Dr. Bishop, an eminent surgeon of Edinburgh. Together they planned to help missionaries and establish hospitals, but he died in 1886. She carried out his desire to erect a hospital in Nazareth and traveled extensively, visiting missions. She returned to Britain to speak out about the needs of missionaries. Her work was effective, and she was received by Queen Victoria in 1893. She also did some writing and was a Christian influence among educated Christians of Great Britain especially.

BLACKHOUSE, SARAH (c. 1626-1702), a British minister ordained by the Society of Friends. She was converted at the age of twenty-seven under the preaching of George Fox. Although not prominent, she had an effective ministry.

BLACKWELL, ANTOINETTE LOUISE BROWN (1825-1921), one of the first American women to be ordained, she graduated from Oberlin College in 1847. After graduate studies in theology she became pastor of the Congregational Church of South Butler, New York. Four years later she resigned because of theological differences and became a Unitarian. She was outspoken on women's rights and temperance.

BLACKWELL, ELIZABETH (1821-1910), pioneer woman physician, born near Bristol, England. She came to the United States with her family in 1832. Her parents were Samuel and Hannah (Lane) Blackwell. Although her father was in business, he was also a lay minister, and his home life reflected Christian principles and devotion. Much of her early education was with tutors. She became a teacher, but after teaching no longer became a challenge, she explored the possibilities of medicine. She tried to enter such medical schools as Harvard, Yale, Bowdoin, and schools in Philadelphia and New York, but was refused largely because she was a woman. At last she was accepted by Geneva College in New York state, where she graduated in 1849. She was one of the first women in the United States to become a physician.

BLAKE, LOUISE (1888-1975), home missionary and community leader. Mrs. Blake was born in Montana, attended the University of Wyoming, and served as a rural missionary from 1926 to 1956. After having services for some time in an old store building, she donated property and was instrumental in the building of All Soul's Church in Edgerton, Wyoming. She was an active community leader as well. Her husband was the justice of the peace in Edgerton.

BLANDINA (d. 177), a slave girl of Lyons martyred for her Christian faith and testimony. Little is known about her except that she was greatly tortured for publicly proclaiming her faith and then martyred.

BLAVATSKY, ELENA PETROVNA (nee HAHN) (1831-1891), a native of Russia, born in Ekaterinoslav of a noble family. At the age of seventeen she married N. V. Blavatsky, who was much older than she. They soon separated, and she traveled widely to study spiritualism and Eastern religions. In 1858 she declared herself a spiritualist and began to recruit followers in Russia and in America. Along with Henry Steel Olcott and others she founded the Theosophical Society and established its magazine.

BLESILLA (Fourth Century), a Christian woman of which little is recorded. Jerome spoke highly of her learning, and it was at her request that Jerome began his translation of Ecclesiastes. Blesilla died quite young. She is believed to have been the daughter of Paula and sister of Eustochium.

BOLEYN, ANNE (c. 1507-1536), the second wife of Henry VIII. She was a victim of difficult circumstances, yet a student of the Scriptures, and she exerted much influence in spite of her enemies. She protected believers, received a copy of the New Testament from William Tyndale. Through her influence an edict was issued to allow the Bible to be read openly. She made the necessary arrangements in London for publishing Tyndale's translation of the New Testament. Her enemies sought to destroy her character. Only three years after she went to the throne, she went to a scaffold to be martyred. Her final request from Henry was granted, that she be decapitated with a sword instead of an axe.

BONZAGA, GUILIA (c. 1512-1566), an Italian princess who promoted the Reformation. She was married to Prince Vespasiano Colonna at the age of fourteen. He was much older, a widower with a daughter named Isabella. When he died his estate went to Guilia until she remarried, then it went to Isabella. Again Guilia was married and widowed. Her home, located between Rome and Naples, became a center of learning, for many in the church came there to study the Scriptures, Calvin's *Institutes*, and tracts. She encouraged Bernardino Ochino who had become head of the Capuchins; whereas this displeased the pope, learning was a challenging activity in her home. Ochino denounced the sins of Venice and Rome and became "too popular" in the eyes of the pope. Guilia eventually lived within a convent, although she never took vows. She sent a copy of the commentary on the book of Romans to Vittoria Colonna and unreservedly accepted the doctrines preached by Valdes on justification by faith. Although she felt she should observe Paul's admonition for women to keep quiet, she could encourage those of influence in the study of the Bible and interpretation of its message without the domination of the pope. He accused her of haboring heretics and helping others flee.

BOOKWALTER, LULU G. (1883-1958), pioneer educator and missionary. She was born in the state of Tennessee, and received a B.A. degree from Smith College in 1908. She went on in graduate studies received an M.A. degree in 1919 from the State University of Kansas, and did further work in London. She became administrator for the Girls English School in Uduvil, Ceylon, now Sri Lanka. She served there from 1911 to 1941. Then she administered the William Mather Memorial Women's Center from 1943 to 1952. This was an interdenominational school, orphanage, and industrial center. Also she was manager of Jaffna College Schools and was sponsored by the Women's Board of Missions and later the American Board of Commissioners for Foreign Missions of the Presbyterian Church.

BOOTH, CATHERINE MUMFORD (1829-1890), author, evangelist, often referred to as the "mother" of the Salvation Army organization, as she was the wife of William Booth, its founder. A native of England, she was born in Derbyshire of a strict Christian family. Her father was an itinerant minister; her education was at home. After moving to London with her parents in 1844, she became affiliated with the Wesleyan church at Brixton. There she met William Booth; they were married in 1855, and eight children were born to them. The Booths and others in that church felt a need for greater emphasis on evangelism, and Catherine was especially concerned to share in the preaching of the gospel. The result of strife within the church about these matters caused them to break away and form another fellowship of believers. Later this group was divided again as the foundation of the Salvation Army organization was being formed. For a variety of reasons, this group, the Booths in particular, saw the value of organizing along militaristic lines including ranks and uniforms. Catherine conducted a series of successful evangelistic meetings in Britain in 1886 and the following year. A short time later she became ill with cancer, and her health began to decline. Her important writings include: *The Salvation Army in Relation to the Church and State, Godliness, Practical Religion, Aggressive Christianity,* and *Popular Christianity.*

BOOTH, ELIZABETH CHARLESWORTH (1865-1948), evangelist, leader, pioneer in prison reform, and wife of the second son of Catherine and William Booth. She was born in England but ministered in the United States for sixty-six years, fourteen with the Salvation Army. She began to work with prisoners while in the Salvation Army (1881-1896); then from 1896 until her death in 1948 she continued the work with the newly formed organization Volunteers of America, of which she and her husband were co-founders. Mrs. Booth was responsible for founding the Auxiliary League program of the Salvation Army. Under the Volunteers of America she founded and directed the Volunteer Prison League and the Hope Hall program of halfway houses. She served as General of the Volunteers from 1940 to 1948. A precedent involving her early life with the Salvation

Army was set in 1892 when she was the first Salvation Army woman officer to be licensed to perform the marriage ceremony in the United States. Following her precedent, all women officers in the Salvation Army were so licensed.

BOOTH, EVANGELINE CORY (1865-1950), author, hymnist, evangelist, gifted administrator, and the first general of the International Salvation Army. She was the fourth daughter and seventh child of Catherine and William Booth, founders of the Salvation Army. Born in England the same year the Salvation Army was formed, she served it well throughout her life. She worked in the slums of London, served as principal of the Salvation Army International Training College, led as Territorial Commander in Canada and Newfoundland (1896-1904), led within the United States (1904-1934), and then exerted worldwide influence as general (1934-1939). Her evangelistic work was demonstrated in the practical application of her faith to relieve suffering and need around the world. She was alert to the tragic situations of emergencies: earthquakes, famines, fire, war, and other such needs, whereon she acted quickly by sending food, materials, and relief help. Honors presented to her included the Distinguished Service Medal bestowed on her by President Woodrow Wilson, honorary degrees from Columbia University and Tufts College, the Fairfax Gold Medal for "eminent patriotic services," and the Vasa Gold Medal from the king of Sweden, among other distinctions. As a musician she was a harpist, wrote hymns, and composed the music for a number of Salvation Army hymns. These are included in her book *Songs of the Evangel,* published in 1927. Her other books include: *Love Is All, Toward a Better World,* and *Women.*

BOOTH, FLORENCE ELEANOR SOPER (1862-1957), author, administrator, commissioner in the Salvation Army, and daughter of a prominent physician in Plymouth, England. She was well-educated and in her youth attended a preaching service by Catherine Booth in London. After her conversion, she joined the Salvation Army and was assigned to France. In 1882, then a lieutenant, she married the oldest son of William and Catherine Booth, Bramwell, who succeeded his father as leader of the Salvation Army. She organized and directed the Women's Social Service work of the Salvation Army from 1882 to 1912 and inaugurated the Home League, which introduced women of the slums to simple but efficient methods of homemaking and child care. She served as a justice of the peace for the London district and as one of the visiting justices for prisons for the County of London in addition to serving on various committees, such as Britain's Central Control Board of the Liquor Traffic and other important positions of social service. She lived to see the fiftieth anniversary of the International Home League, which she had inaugurated in 1907. Many of her articles appeared in Salvation Army periodicals, and two of her books are *Mothers and the Empires* and *Friendship with Jesus.*

BOOTH-CLIBBORN, CATHERINE (1858-1955), was born in England. She was a pioneer evangelist in France, a field marshall in the Salvation Army, and the first daughter of Catherine and William Booth. She was married to Arthur Sidney Clibborn in 1887, at which time he changed his surname to Booth-Clibborn. They served in France, but after twenty-one years in the Salvation Army they broke away over several disagreements with William Booth, who had seemed to become more autocratic in his advancing years. She was a pioneer in opening France to the Salvation Army and responsible for establishing their work there. She was much loved and her preaching reached many lives for Christ.

BOOTH-TUCKER, EMMA MOSS (1860-1903), leader, writer, hymnist, and second daughter and fourth child of Catherine and William Booth, founders of the Salvation Army. She was born at Gateshead-on-Tyne, England, and by the age of twenty had become much involved with the work of the Salvation Army. When she married Fredrick St. George de Lautour Tucker, he changed his surname to Booth-Tucker. She became director of the first Salvation Army Training College for Women and held influential positions in the United States and India and served as counsel at the International Headquarters of the Salvation Army as well. Her husband held a commander post in India, where they worked together. Twice she was a guest at the White House and was a friend of some of the most prominent statesmen and women leaders of the world. As a mother of several children, it was at times difficult for her to meet travel requirements for her work. When their oldest child was just thirteen, Mrs. Booth-Tucker was killed in a train derailment in Dean Lake, Missouri.

BORA, KATHERINE von (1499-1552). *See* **LUTHER**

BORTHWICK, JANE LAURIE (1813-1897), was a native of Edinburgh, Scotland and is remembered for her work in the translation of German hymns. She and her sister, Sarah (Mrs. Eric Findlater), worked together. Perhaps their best-known work was compiled in *Hymns from the Land of Luther* published in four series in 1854, 1855, 1858, and 1862. She translated sixty-one of the hymns, many of which have appeared in *The Family Treasury*. "Be Still, My Soul" is one of her best-known translations.

BORTHWICK, SARAH (1823-1907). *See* **FINDLATER**

BOSE, KHERODA (c. 1887-1948), a national of India, she was a physician in charge of a large missionary work at Asrapur. Her work was commended by the government of India. Details of her personal life are not available in English.

BOSE, MONA, notable Christian educator in the latter part of the nineteenth century. She was born near Calcutta. Her parents became Christians and sent her to a mission school and later to school in England. She returned to India becoming headmistress of the Victoria School for Girls in Lahore. She was active in the Naulakha Presbyterian Church there.

BOSS, MARTHA (1913-1973), an outstanding missionary nurse and teacher. She served in China under the Lutheran church of the Missouri Synod. Although born in Cleveland, Ohio, of German parentage, some of her early education was in Germany: three years at the Bredower Madohen Gemeinde Schule and four years at the Hindenburg Geminde Schule. She then returned to Cleveland for further education. In 1933 Martha became a registered nurse and served in the Cleveland Gospel Center and in an orphanage in Illinois before going to the Enshih Hospital in Chengtu, China, in 1946. Later she served in Hong Kong, working with Chinese pastors. As a memorial to her ministry, a beautiful community center there is named for her. While home on furlough in 1973 she was tragically killed in an automobile accident near Elgin, Illinois.

BOTHWELL, MARIE HANKEY (1914-1979), a pioneer missionary evangelist in the Congo (now Zaire), and among the first missionaries sponsored by the Conservative Baptist Foreign Mission Society to enter that part of Africa. She was born in Wisconsin and received her training at the Teachers College of Oshkosh, Wisconsin. She had a special ministry in the teaching African women. After Congo independence, she and her husband, Robert, pioneered the Conservative Baptist work in Senegal. There, too, she had a wide influence among women and youth.

BOURGEOYS, MARGUERITE (1620-1700), founder of the first uncloistered Roman Catholic missionary group for women in the New World at Montreal, Canada—the Church of Bonsecours in Ville Marie in 1658. Also part of her pioneer work was the Congregation of Notre Dame of Montreal and several missions, mainly for education purposes.

BOURIGNON, ANTIONETTE (1616-1680), born in the Spanish Netherlands of Roman Catholic background, she claimed to have special revelations or visions. Her views opposed established churches, teaching the "inner light" and direct communication with God. She attracted some followers, especially in Scotland. The sect gradually disappeared in the 1700s. Some of her writings were published in Amsterdam.

BOWN, EMMA JANE (1858-1924), faithful leader and pioneer social worker in the Salvation Army for thirty-eight years. She influenced thousands of lives. She did a remarkable job of organizing the various women's social service programs in the United States, which included settlement houses, slum work, day nurseries, maternity homes for unwed mothers, and hospitals. She had the honor of being the first woman appointed to the rank of major and the first appointed to the rank of brigadier and later became a lieutenant, the highest rank in the Salvation Army.

BOYD, MAUD SISLEY (1851-1937), Christian educator. She was born in England and came to the United States at age eleven. She became a pioneer Bible instructor and the first Seventh Day Adventist woman missionary to Europe. In 1877 she was sent to assist J. N. Andrews in publishing religious materials in Switzerland. She set the type for the first Seventh Day Adventist tract in the Italian language. She returned to America and later married Charles L. Boyd, and both served as missionaries to Africa. After the death of her husband in 1898, she went to Australia as an instructor at Avondale and later as a Bible teacher in New South Wales and Victoria. Again returning to the United States, she taught Bible at Loma Linda and Glendale Sanitariums in California.

BOYNTON, GRACE M. (1890-1970), author and professor, served in China and Japan under the American Board of Commissioners for Foreign Missions, a forerunner of the United Church Board for World Ministries. She received her B.A. degree from Wellesley College in 1912 and an M.A. degree from the University of Michigan in 1916. She also attended Radcliffe College. She was a professor of English language and literature from 1919 to 1950 at Yenching University in Peking, China. She also taught at Nanking University; Chengtu, Szechuan, and at Kobe College in Nishinomiya, Japan. She wrote *The River Garden of Pure Repose*, published in 1951.

BRADSTREET, ANNE DUDLEY (1612-1672), author whose volume of poems was the first original book of poems written in the North American colonies. Born in England, she was the daughter of Thomas Dudley and became the wife of Simon Bradstreet about 1628. She and her husband came to the Massachusetts Bay Colony in 1630. Her collection of verse was titled *The Tenth Muse Lately Spring Up in America*, and she also wrote an autobiographical prose volume called *Religious Experiences*. Her life and writings influenced and encouraged many colonists, especially women.

BRAGG, MARGARET WILSON (1775-1840), pioneer evangelist, born in Kendal, England, and daughter of Isaac Wilson. In 1790 she married Hadwen Bragg of Newcastle-upon-Tyne. At the age of thirty-four she began her life as a minister in the Society of Friends. She made an evangelistic tour of Ireland in 1825.

BRAGG, MARY FURNAS (1762-1849), a British minister in the Society of Friends, born at Liverpool. She was married to Henry Bragg in 1785, after which they worked together in Christian education. In 1817 they were appointed administrators of the provincial Friends school near Lisburn, Ireland. Later they worked in Belfast.

BRAND, EVELYNE CONSTANCE HARRIS (1880-1975), an outstanding missionary to southern India. She was the mother of Dr. Paul Brand, known for his pioneer surgery and treatment of leprosy or Hanson's disease. Evelyne Brand was born in the London area of a prosperous merchant and was the ninth of eleven children. She grew up in a strict Christian family of Baptist persuasion; was taught at home and showed much artistic talent. Missionaries were welcome to the Harris home, and Evelyne became especially aware of the needs of India as she served on a church committee whose purpose was to form a woman's auxiliary to sponsor missionaries to the zenanas of

India. She read of the work in southern India by Jesse Mann Brand, and when he was on furlough she heard him speak at the St. John's Wood Chapel. He visited their home, telling of his trip to India in 1907 after his studies at Livingstone College, where he took a brief medical course. He also studied at Madras University. Later, Evelyne went to India, and in 1913 she and Jesse were married at Sendamangalam near the Kolli Mountains. Jesse had already built their home. Trust and Triumph was their motto. Jesse helped Evelyne learn the language and together they served faithfully in telling the nationals of the gospel of salvation. Jesse was able to reach many with his limited medical knowledge and treated as many as 1,500 patients during one year. In addition to reaching the nationals with God's Word, she taught them how to build and perform many other useful skills. Both their son, Paul, and their daughter, Connie, were born at Ootacamond. Evelyne taught the children at home, but later they went to England for schooling. Evelyne was widowed in 1929 when Jesse did not recover from a fever. She returned to England for reappointment, although that was not common. She appealed and was permitted to return to India to complete the work they had so well established. She had remarkable stamina and commitment, serving until ninety-five years of age in rugged conditions. Her final years were shared by a nurse, Carolyn Weeber, an American from Pennsylvania, who had spent many years in nursing, eighteen of them among the Tamil-speaking people of South India. More than one biography has been written about Evelyne Brand, known to many as "Granny" Brand.

BRECK, CARRIE E. (1855-1934), after a childhood in Vermont, she moved to the West Coast of the United States, settling in Portland, Oregon, with her husband, Frank A. Breck. She was a Presbyterian, and although she wrote many poems, the only one that remains popular as a hymn is the beautiful "Face to Face with Christ, My Saviour."

BRESEGNA, ISABELLA (1510-1567), an influential Italian Christian refugee in a difficult time of history. Although she was born in Spain, she was reared in Naples, Italy. While in her teens she married Garcia Manriquez, a Spanish military man who later became the governor of Piacenza. She inherited wealth and was a capable businesswoman, having begun several industries near Naples. Later, with the intensity of the Inquisition, she became interested in theology and read much about it. She used her position and influence to help many who were opposed to the papal authority and resisted the misinformation given to them. She lived in the Italian-speaking part of Switzerland for a while and was described as a faithful Christian example.

BREWSTER, ANN SHEWELL (1762-1835), an English minister in the Society of Friends; born in London. Not until 1821, at the of age fifty-nine, was she recognized as a Friends minister. She married Thomas Brewster in 1784.

BRIDGET OF SWEDEN (c. 1303-1373), founder of the Brigittines about 1346 at Vadstema. Bridget was a widow with several children and devoted much of her time and efforts to church work. The Roman Catholic community she founded was unusual in that it included both nuns and priests. There were sixty nuns and thirteen priests (to represent the twelve apostles and Paul). Her daughter, Catherine, became the abbess of this monastery, which was later banished from Sweden.

BRIDGMAN, CLARA DAVIS (1872-1956), a missionary and pioneer worker among women in South Africa. She was born in Japan of missionary parents. She and her husband Frederick, a medical doctor, served more than forty years in Africa. She founded the Tabitha Home for Girls, worked in Imfumi, Durban, and Johannesburg. After the death of Dr. Bridgman in 1925, she raised funds for the founding of the Bridgman Memorial Hospital, the first hospital for Bantu women in Johannesburg. The Bridgmans were sponsored by the American Board of Commissioners for Foreign Missions, a forerunner of the United Church Board for World Ministries.

BRIDGMAN, ELIZA JANE GILLETT (c. 1803-1871), a missionary teacher, native of New York state. She married Elijah Coleman Bridgman in 1845. She and her husband are believed to have established the first American mission in China. They first went to Canton, where Eliza she taught Chinese girls and established a school. She served thirty-two years in China; her husband died in 1861. She returned to China, after furlough, working in the Peking area, and founded a school for girls. Her long service was one of dedication and humility.

BROOMHALL, AMELIA HUDSON TAYLOR (1835-1918), beloved sister of J. Hudson Taylor; a native of Barnsley, Yorkshire, England, was educated largely at home. She and her brother, J. Hudson Taylor, were very close. She was married in 1859 and became the mother of ten children. She and her husband worked at the home office of the China Inland Mission. After her brother's wife died, she took his children to raise with hers. She was a gracious hostess at the mission headquarters where the Broomhalls lived.

BROWN, ANTIONETTE L. (1825-1921), considered to be the first woman to be formally ordained in the United States. She was ordained in 1853 at the Congregational Church of South Butler in her home state of New York. She graduated from Oberlin College and did some graduate work in theology. Officials of Oberlin and even her own family were opposed to her ordination. Later she became a Unitarian. In 1855 she married Samuel Blackwell; they had six daughters. She wrote ten books including *Shadows of Our Social System.*

BROWN, CECIL (1906-1958), missionary in the Great Smoky Mountains of the United States. She established and developed the mountain mission work of the Salvation Army. Through her influence many isolated communities not only received the gospel but were supplied with electricity, the telephone, medicine, and other necessities. Twenty-eight years of her life were invested in this ministry. Born in North Carolina, she was well acquainted with the needs of those living in the mountains. Her Bible classes grew and many were converted.

BROWN, PHOEBE HINSDALE (1783-1861), considered to be America's first woman hymnist; born in New York state. She was orphaned very young and grew up in the home of a married sister. Her early life included many hardships and deprivations. She was not permitted to attend school and did not learn to read and write until she was an adult. When she was twenty-two, she married Timothy H. Brown, a house painter and fine man, although poor. They had several children. Because her days were full of domestic responsibilities, she found it difficult to enjoy even a few moments alone for quiet devotion and prayer. Thus, she made a habit of taking an evening walk to a beautiful garden at the edge of an estate. She found that brief recluse a time to "steal away" and be alone with God. She did not realize that she was being observed by the mistress of the estate, who openly criticized Mrs. Brown for her actions, thinking she had some deceptive motive. Mrs. Brown's diary reveals how crushed she felt about this and tearfully wrote, "My Apology for My Twilight Rambles," which was sent to the lady of the estate. Her hymn "The Hymn of a Wounded Spirit" referred to as her "twilight hymn," was included in *Village Hymns,* compiled by Dr. Nettleton seven years later. She humbly loved the Lord and prayed that one of her children might serve Him as a missionary. The Lord called her son, Samuel R. Brown, to be the first American missionary to Japan.

BROWNING, ELIZABETH BARRETT (1806-1861), a British poet, best remembered for her *Sonnets from the Portuguese.* Born in Durham, England, her father was a wealthy sugar plantation owner with investments in Jamaica, West Indies. Her childhood and teen years were spent near Ledburn, Herfordshire. Little is known about her mother, but it was well known that her father was strict about his family and did not want any of his three daughters to marry. Her education was private with a stringent study schedule. At the age of six she studied Greek and at nine made translations in verse. All of that contributed to her frail health, as did the shock of seeing her brother accidentally drown in 1838. Then a spine injury in her teen years further debilitated her condition, and she was forced to spent much time in bed. Expressing her thoughts in poetry was the outlet she needed. Her best works of that period included *The Cry of the Children* and *Lady Geraldine's Courtship.* Her life took on new meaning when she read of Robert Browning, and she complimented him in one of her poems. This prompted his personal reply of thanks. That introduction began a friendship that later led to their courtship and marriage. Not only did her health improve but so did her poetry; yet in the background was the opposition of her father, whom she respected and loved. *Sonnets from the Portuguese* was written during this time of engagement and is considered her finest work. In 1846 Elizabeth and Robert Browning were secretly married in the parish church of St. Marylebone. She remained in her father's home for a week afterward, then joined her husband and left for Italy. Some biographers say that she took with her a maid and her pet dog. Never again did she return to her childhood home or see her father. He did not forgive her for marrying in spite of her many letters to him expressing her love and asking his forgiveness and blessing. In fact, he did not even open her letters, which were returned to her later. Her first book of poetry, *The Battle of Marathon,* was published in 1819; her second book, *An Essay on Mind and Other Poems,* was published in 1826. *Sonnets from the Portuguese* was published in 1847. In 1849 she had a son, Robert Wiedemann Barrett. Her life and writings reflected a spiritual depth and have influenced many. She died in Florence, Italy.

BRUNK, ADA ZIMMERMAN (1908-1954), author, school administrator, and dean of women at the Eastern Mennonite College, serving ten years (1939-1949). She was co-author of a helpful book, *The Christian Nurture of Youth.*

BRUNNER, MARIE ANNA (1800-1836), mother of Francis de Sales Brunner. She founded the Sisters of the Precious Blood Catholic Community in 1833 in Switzerland. Such a community was established in the United States in 1844 with a threefold purpose: educational, medical, and charitable work.

BRUNONA, MARY, appointed as the first provincial superior established in New York of the Felician Sisters of the Order of St. Francis. This Catholic community originated in Poland in 1855. It began in the United States in 1874 for the purposes of education and charitable work. It became the largest group of Franciscan sisters in the United States.

BRYENNIUS, ANNA COMNENA (c. 1038-c. 1150), historian and writer, and the oldest daughter of Emperor Alexius Comnenus by his second wife, the empress Irene Ducoensa. Born in Constantinople, she had a superior education in the classical disciplines. She wrote in praise of her father's leadership, accomplishments, and influence. In spite of his participation in the First Crusade, he is said to have taken a reverse position later for selfish and political reasons. In 1097 Anna Comnenus married Nicephorus Bryennius, leader of Bryennium. She, along with her mother, tried to persuade her father to appoint her husband successor instead of her brother. Her plot to do this failed in 1811, and she entered a convent and wrote extensively. It is her writing for which she is remembered, especially for *Alexiad,* which was written in Greek and presented a historically valuable treatise on the theory of the Byzantine government and the general intellectual and religious concepts of that period. Her presentations enhance the rulership of her father but reflect the history of the church during the early Crusades.

BUCHAN, ELSPETH SIMPSON (1738-1791), a mystic of Scotland who influenced a minister and others with her "special biblical revelations." She founded a sect labeled 'Buchanites' and set up a kind of communal community as they all waited for judgment day. The sect lasted only a few years after her death.

BUCK, THERESA R. (1912-1964), pioneer missionary nurse who helped introduce modern nursing to African nurses. Born in Connecticut, she attended Rollins College in Florida; received a B.A. degree from Bates College, and became a registered nurse, completing her nurses training at a hospital in Boston. She attended the Kennedy School of Missions, and in 1938 went to Mt. Silinda Hospital in southern Rhodesia. In 1949 she became administrator of the Willis F. Pierce Memorial Hospital, Mt. Silinda. From 1959 to 1964 she was administrator of the Chikore Hospital and Dispensary where she retired. She served under the American Board of Commissioners for Foreign Missions.

BUELL, HARRIETT EUGENIA PECK (1834-1910), author and hymnist, a native of New York state, and for fifty years was a regular contributor to the *Northern Christian Advocate* periodical. Only one of her hymns remains a favorite of many Americans today, "My Father Is Rich in Houses and Lands," set to music by John B. Sumner.

BUHLMAIER, MARIE (1859-1938), a remarkable pioneer missionary to German-speaking immigrants in the United States. Born in Heilbronn, Germany, Marie came to the United States with her parents in 1868. She did outstanding work as a "home" missionary; because she herself was an immigrant, she knew their frustrations and needs. She was a great blessing to many, helping them find a place to live and work and giving them the gospel message. She established centers of evangelistic work in many sections of the city, ministering to foreigners, usually beginning with sewing classes, activities for children, and other means for helping them learn English, such as studying the Bible, and holding Sunday schools and evangelistic services. Working with the Home Mission Board of the Southern Baptist Convention, she is believed to have been the first home missionary to immigrants. Later, she was asked to help establish such centers elsewhere and was much sought after as a speaker and adviser for such projects. In 1918 immigration was halted, and she partially retired, although remained active in stimulating the interest of others to realize the vision of home missionary work. She wrote a book of her experiences, *Along the Highway of Service,* which was published by the Home Mission Board of the Southern Baptist Convention in 1924.

BULLINGER, ANNA (c. 1504-1564), a nun before her marriage to the Swiss Reformer Henry Bullinger in 1529. After the death of her father, she and her mother both went to live in the convent Oedenbach in Zurich. Later she became a nun and cared for her mother. The chaplain of the nunnery took Bullinger with him to visit the convent at one time, and Bullinger met Anna. Anna would not marry until after the death of her mother. The Bullinger home became a welcome haven for many refugees, including Mrs. Zwingli. Later, Bullinger was elected to Zwingli's place in the church at Zurich. Several children were born to the Bullingers.

BULMER, AGNES COLLINSON (1775-1837), author and hymnist, was born in London. Her father was Edward Collinson. In 1793 she married Joseph Bulmer. She wrote the book *Scripture Histories* in addition to several hymns. Perhaps her best-known hymn is "Thou Who Hast in Zion Laid," which she wrote for the ceremony of laying the foundation stone of the Oxford Road Wesleyan Chapel at Manchester in 1825. This hymn was included in the Supplement to the Wesleyan Hymn Book published in 1830. She was a member of the Wesleyan Society.

BUNYAN, ELIZABETH (c. 1630-1692), second wife of John Bunyan. They were married in 1659, three years after the death of his first wife. Not long after they were married he was arrested and imprisoned, leaving her to care for his four children by his first wife. Mary, his blind daughter, seemed to be his favorite. During this time he wrote the classic *Pilgrim's Progress*, which has been translated into many languages. Elizabeth traveled to London to plea for her husband's release. Her pleas were not granted until much later. She left no surviving children by him. He preceded her in death by only four years.

BUNYAN, MARY (c. 1625-1656), first wife of John Bunyan. Little is recorded about this Mrs. Bunyan, although we know she and John were married in 1647 had she four children by him, two sons and two daughters. One daughter, Mary, was blind. It is believed that the Bunyans were married when John was only eighteen or nineteen years of age. She was from a rather poor family but had godly parents. She had a good influence on Bunyan and lived to see him become a Christian. Although little is written about her, surely she was a powerful influence in the conversion and writings of John Bunyan.

BURE, IDELETTE de. *See* **CALVIN**

BURGESS, GEORGIA ANNA BURRUS (1866-1948), pioneer missionary in India for nearly forty years. She went to Calcutta in 1895 as a faith missionary and worked among secluded women of the country as she studied the Bengali language. Along with another missionary, Mae Taylor, she founded a girls school in Calcutta in 1896. In 1903 she married Luther J. Burgess, and they spent thirty-two years working among the Bengali, Hindi, Urdu, and Khasi-speaking peoples with the Seventh Day Adventist church.

BURRUS, NONI (c. 1918-1958), a dedicated national of India who attended a mission school and then worked among her own people. When she accepted Christianity in a Seventh Day Adventist school, she took the name of Burrus, after the missionary who had been especially influential in her life.

BUSBY, BERYL ELIZABETH (1903-1983), outstanding missionary to Indonesia and the Far East. She was born in Kansas but grew up in Seattle, Washington. Miss Busby married a minister and they served for twenty-six years in Indonesia under the Assembly of God church. After they arrived in Indonesia in 1939, they started the largest Assembly of God church in Djakarta in addition to a Bible school. They began several other churches and a Bible school in Medan, Sumatra, as well. In 1967 they became missionaries at large, traveling all over the Far East conducting seminars for national pastors of Fiji, Samoa, Philippines, Indonesia, Singapore, and Malaysia. She was widowed in 1977, but went to Australia where she helped organize another Bible school and set up senior citizen programs and related ministries. Altogether she served the Lord forty-four years as a missionary.

BUTLER, FANNY J. (c. 1837-1899), recorded as the first British woman missionary doctor to India. She was a brilliant scholar finishing second out of 123 in the preliminary examination of the Women's School of Medicine in 1874. In 1880 she was accepted by the Indian Female Normal School and Instruction Society to work among women in zenanas. She began her work at Bhagulpur, India, later went to Kashmir, and worked in Srinagar where she opened a dispensary. Her medical training enabled her to be a Christian testimony among women she might not have reached otherwise.

BUTLER, JOSEPHINE ELIZABETH (1828-1907), author and pioneer social worker concerned with the care and protection of needy women; supported shelters for the destitute and reform measures to protect them. She established the Ladies National Association for Appeal in 1869. Although she was compassionate and described as a woman of prayer, her personal religious convictions were not always dominate; yet her efforts served as an example of evangelical reform policies. Her actions led to the founding of the International Federation for the Abolution of State Regulation of Vice. She wrote a biography, *Life of Catherine of Siena*, published in 1878.

BUTTLAR, EVA von (1670-1717), leader and founder of the Buttlar sect, later founder of the Christian and Philadelphian Society. She was born at Eschwege,

Hesse, and at age seventeen married a French refugee, De Vesias. In 1697 she left her husband to go on a religious speaking tour. It was at Allendorf in 1702 that she founded the Christian and Philadelphian Society, which expelled her within a few weeks. They eventually associated with the Roman Catholic church. It is believed that much later she experienced a true Christian conversion and became affiliated with a Lutheran church.

BUYSE, MABEL EASTON (1882-1977), a pioneer missionary, teacher and author; born in Massachusetts, graduated from Mt. Holyoke College, and served with the African Inland Mission. She went to the Belgian Congo (Zaire) in 1917, which was the first work among the Alur tribe at Kasengu. She later went to the Azandos at Bafuka, and the Lugbrar tribe near the Uganda boundary. In 1928 she married another missionary, John G. Buyse, and they worked at Kasengu. She opened a school at the Opari station, a boys school at Katire Ayom, and then the first boys school among the Lotuka people of Logotok. She was a much loved teacher, establishing schools for the nationals and for missionary children, serving as a school administrator and model teacher. She wrote articles for the missionary periodical, and a book, *Nyilak*.

BYERS, EMMA D. LEFEVRE (1875-1946), significant pioneer educator and the first woman to graduate from Elkhart Institute, which became Goshen College, in Indiana. She married the president of that college. Her role was a definite part of the campus life, and she influenced many young people for the Lord.

C

CABLE, MILDRED (1877-1952), a pioneer missionary who worked with Eva and Francesca French at Hochow in Shansi province and established one of the first schools for girls in China. Because of rules involving self-support, they moved to the northwest part of China at Suchow in 1928. She and the others who worked with her traveled to the main cities of Turkestan where they taught the Word of God, held evangelistic meetings, and distributed the Scriptures.

CABRINI, FRANCES XAVIER (1850-1917), because of her influence, her name is associated with hospitals, schools, and orphanages in many parts of the world. Born to Augustine and Stella Cabrini in St. Anglo Lodigiano, Italy, she desired to dedicate her life to missions and go to China. Before coming to the United States in 1888, she established the Missionary Sisters of the Sacred Heart of Jesus in Codogno, Italy, and later similar groups in Argentina, Brazil, Chili, Nicaragua, France, England, Spain, and the United States, where she became a citizen. Her tremendous enthusiasm encouraged many nuns, and her capable leadership, experience, and compassion had wide influence from the Italian immigrants in American cities to nurses and doctors in large hospitals. She established schools, orphanages, convents, and hospitals in New York, Philadelphia, Chicago, Seattle, Denver, and Los Angeles. She was the first American citizen ever to be canonized by the Roman Catholic church, which was done in 1946 by Pope Pius XII.

CALVIN, IDELETTE de BURES STORDEUR (c. 1499-1549), devoted wife of John Calvin, the most famous French Protestant Reformer. The widow of Jean Stordeur, who was a victim of the plague, she had been left with three children. John Calvin had known the family for some time and was instrumental in their becoming Christians. Information about her youth is obscure, but she and Calvin were married in 1539. She had several children by Calvin, but none survived infancy. Her health was frail, and they were married for only ten years when she died. Calvin was so devoted to her that he expressed no desire ever to remarry.

CAMP, MABEL JOHNSTON (1871-1937), musician and hymnwriter of several familiar hymns: "He Is Coming Again" (lyrics and music), "That Beautiful Name" (music), and "Caleb Saw the Lord (music).

CAMPBELL, JANE CORNEIGLE (1763-1835), a member of the Corneigle family that fled to Scotland from France when the Edict of Nantes was revoked. As a result, she grew up with special appreciation for religious freedom. Her primary contribution to church history was as the wife of Thomas Campbell and the mother of Alexander, founder of the Disciples of Christ Church, commonly called Christian. It was one of the first, if not the first, Protestant church that originated in America.

CAMPBELL, LOUISE (1883-1968), pioneer missionary to South China, who administered for more than forty years at the school she founded. Born in Washington state of missionary parents, George and Jennie Campbell, she attended San Francisco State Normal School, Vashan College, Occidental College, Berkeley Baptist Divinity School, and Gordon Bible College. Supported by the Woman's American Baptist Foreign Mission Society, she was the first single woman missionary to serve at Meihsein, South China. She founded the Kwong Yet Girls School and served there until her retirement. In addition to her administrative work at the school, she coordinated work for women in the Hakka Convention of Baptist Churches.

CANDACE (c. 25-c. 41), first-century queen of Ethiopia believed to have been converted through the testimony of her treasurer. Her conversion opened the way for Christianity to be preached throughout her kingdom. Her treasurer was converted through the evangelist Philip, as recorded in Acts 8.

CAREY, CHARLOTTE EMILIA RUMOHR (1761-1821), missionary and second wife of William Carey. She was the invalid daughter of the wealthy Chevalier de Rumohr and his wife, the Countess of Alfeldt. Charlotte's disability was the result of a fire at the family home, at which time she lost her speech and later the use of her legs. She traveled widely over Europe in search of medical help and went to the warmer climate of India. She stayed at Serampore, and there first met Carey. It was reported that her speech improved as did her ability to move about. To the astonishment of many, only six months after the death of his first wife, William Carey announced his plans to marry Charlotte. They were married in the spring of 1808 by Joshua Marshman. It was not only evident that they were truly in love, but her highly intellectual and spiritual life would be an encouragement and help to him. She learned the Bengali language so she could help native Christian families and was much loved by the Carey children as well. She carried on lengthy correspondence with Carey's family and helped him keep in touch with them. Although her health improved after their marriage, in 1820 it began to deteriorate. After thirteen years of a very happy marriage, she died in 1821.

CAREY, DOROTHY PLACKETT (1755-1807), missionary and first wife of William Carey, and an Englishwoman with a Puritan background. They were married in 1781, before he was twenty years of age. She was six years older. Apparently she was uneducated, whereas he could read the Bible in six languages, so their marriage seemed a contrast in ability and interests. They lived in Hackleton and were very poor, but William began to preach regularly at Earls Barton. Later, when Carey answered the call to missions, Dorothy was not sympathetic and refused to go with him to India until nearly the last minute. She consented on the condition that her sister, Kitty, accompany them to help care for their small children. She found life in India rugged; she and the children often became ill. Twelve years before her death, she was plagued by mental problems. Their poor diet, physical problems, rugged living conditions, and many other matters contributed to her difficult life on the mission field.

CAREY, GRACE HUGHES (1778-c. 1840), this forty-five-year-old widow became the third wife of William Carey in 1823. They were married eleven years before his death in 1834. She cared for him as a devoted companion during his final years. Few details are available about her personal life.

CARMICHAEL, AMY WILSON (1867-1951), author, missionary, and founder of the Dohnavur Fellowship. A native of Ireland, she attended the Wesleyan Methodist school in Harrogate, and in 1893 went to Japan as a missionary. Because of poor health, she was in Japan only fifteen months. From there she went to Ceylon and later to England. In 1895 she went as a missionary of the Church of England Zenana Missionary Society to Tiruneveli, South India, and established a home for children at Dohnavur. She sought to help the girls serving in Hindu temples through this home, which later received boys as well. The Dohnavur Fellowship was formed in 1927 to sponsor her work, which was independent from the Church of England. She wrote a number of books, some of the better known are: *Lotus Buds, Gold Cord, Overweights of Joy, Things As They Are, Rose from Brier, The Widow of the Jewels, Windows from the Forest, Mimosa, This One Thing, Though the Mountains Shake,* and *Toward Jerusalem.*

CARY, ALICE (1820-1871), author and hymnist, and sister of Phoebe Cary and Elizabeth Payson Prentiss. She was born near Cincinnati, Ohio, and later moved to New York. Her poetry and hymns were not as well known as those of her sister, but one poem expresses her devotion and longing to see her Savior in the following opening stanza:

Earth, with its dark and dreadful ills,
Recedes and fades away;
Lift up your heads, ye heavenly hills;
Ye gates of death give way!

In 1850 she published a volume simply titled *Poems*.

CARY, MAUDE (1878-1967), missionary to Morocco for fifty-four years under the Gospel Missionary Union. She was the daughter of Jedediah and Sarah Cary, farmers from Kansas who truly loved the Lord. At the age of eighteen she went to the Gospel Missionary Union Bible Institute in Kansas City. After graduating, she gained practical experience as a city missionary in Leavenworth, Kansas. She first went to Morocco in 1901, learned Arabic quickly, and taught both Moslem and Jewish children. Her long and successful missionary experiences are related in the biography *Miss Terri!* by Evelyne Stenbock.

CARY, PHOEBE (1824-1871), sister of Alice Cary and Elizabeth Payson Prentiss. She was born near Cincinnati, Ohio. While still young, she moved to New York, where she and her sister, Alice, lived a quiet life. Phoebe's best-known hymn was written in 1852, "One Sweetly Solemn Thought," first included in a hymnal compiled by her pastor at the Church for the Strangers in New York City. Her work is included in: *Poems and Parodies* published in 1854, *Poems of Faith, Hope and Love* published in 1868, and *Hymns for All Christians,* published in 1869.

CASE, ADELAIDE T. (1887-1948), the first woman appointed to teach in an Episcopal theological seminary. She received her Ph.D. and M.A. degrees from Columbia University after graduating from Bryn Mawr College. She taught religious education for several years at Columbia University Teachers College and wrote many books in her area of expertise. She was active in interdenominational organizations, some on behalf of racial relations with Jews and blacks.

CASSIDY, BERTHA E. (c. 1881-1963), teacher, author, American missionary to China under the American Advent Mission Society. Details of her education are vague, but much of her early teaching was from her mother and a mission school she attended. Her major work was at Wuhu. She wrote *China Adventure* (American Advent Mission Society, 1962), a book of remembrances relating many of her experiences. What she has to say about her own family and experiences are helpful to any young person contemplating the mission field, especially in the Orient. Her life and teaching influenced many for the Lord.

CATHERINE OF ALEXANDRIA (Tenth Century), details are obscure about this Christian martyr, but apparently she lived in the tenth century. She spoke boldly of her faith and the church of Christ in Alexandria. She became a martyr for her faith.

CATHERINE OF ARAGON (1485-1536), third daughter of Isabella and Ferdinand of Spain. She was married to Prince Arthur of England, and after his death became the first wife of his brother, Henry VIII. She and Henry were married for eighteen years. She had several children, but only one survived, a daughter named Mary Tudor, who later became a reigning queen of England. Largely because Catherine had no male heir for Henry, he had the marriage nullified on the grounds of Catherine's previous marriage to his brother. Her influence in church history was largely because of her circumstances. She was influential for Protestantism in England; yet because of her daughter, Mary Tudor, England was swayed to Catholicism.

CATHERINE OF BOLOGNA (1413-1463), native of Italy and founder of a well-known convent of the Holy Sacrament of the Order of Poor Clares in Bologna.

CATHERINE de MEDICI (1519-1589), art and literature may be considered her contributions to society, yet she exercised her royal power to influence church history as well. Born in Florence,

Italy, her father was Lorenzo (II) de Medici, Duke of Urbino. She was a Roman Catholic, a niece of Pope Clement VII. Little is recorded about her early childhood, but at the age of fourteen, she married Henry, son of Francis I, Duke of Orleans and later Henry II of France. They had four sons, three of whom became kings of France, and two daughters who married royalty. One daughter, Elizabeth, married Philip II of Spain, and the other daughter, Margaret, became the wife of Henry of Navarre. Margaret became a powerful influence favorable to the Reformers. One of the sons of Catherine, Francis II, married Mary Stewart of Scotland. When he died, the throne was passed to his brother, Charles IX, who was only ten years old. That gave Catherine the opportunity to rule as queen regent. It seemed that Catherine de Medici had a passion for influence and power, to which she sacrificed her own reputation and harmed many. As a Catholic, she influenced her son Charles IX to order the Huguenots killed. That massacre on St. Bartholomew's Day in 1572 resulted in the death of an estimated 20,000 Huguenots throughout France. In 1574 Charles IX died, and his brother inherited the throne, again giving Catherine influence behind the throne. She was virtually friendless when she died at the age of seventy. Sadly, her influence was used largely for selfish purposes.

CATHERINE OF GENOA (1447-1510), an Italian mystic and author named Caterinetta Fieschi, after Catherine of Siena. In 1463 she married Giuliano Adorno. After her conversion in 1474 she persuaded her husband to free her of marriage obligations. Later he dedicated his life to God affiliated with the Franciscan tertiaries as she worked with the Ladies of Mercy caring for the terminally ill at a hospital in Genoa. She sought spiritual counsel from Cattaneo Marabotto. Her writings include *The Pure Love of God.* published in Genoa in 1511, *Dialogues on the Soul and the Body,* and *Life and Teaching*.

CATHERINE OF SIENA (1347-1380), a Christian mystic who influenced lives of the great and the lowly of the early Italian Renaissance period. She was born as Catherine Benincasa in Siena, Italy, the youngest of a large family. She and her mother were especially close companions. When she was quite young she committed her life to God and from time to time reported having visions as she communicated with God. At the age of sixteen she became associated with the Dominican Tertiaries. In 1376 she journeyed to Pisa, and there, too, received the stigmata. She exercised primary influence for the return of the papacy from Avignon to Rome in 1376. In 1378 she boldly renounced the clergy on the grounds of immorality and sought to improve relations between the pope and the city of Florence. The final years of her life were spent in Rome attempting to help unite the Roman Catholic church. Any kind of political involvements seemed to be strictly for spiritual purposes. She and Francis of Assisi were designated by Pope Pius XII as Italy's chief patron saints. She wrote *The Book of Divine Doctrine,* which is highly ranked in Italian literature.

CATHERINE OF SWEDEN (1331-1381), daughter of St. Bridget; companion of Catherine of Siena. She succeeded her mother as leader of the Brigittine Order, which was confirmed in 1375. She unsuccessfully tried to procure the canonization of her mother. Although her marriage had been arranged, she persuaded her husband to join her in vows of chastity. She supported the followers of UrbanVI. She died as the abbess of a monastery in Vatzen.

CAVINESS, AGNES ELVIRA LEWIS (1889-1973), pioneer educator and author. She was the first degree candidate at Pacific Union College, a Seventh Day Adventist school. After her marriage, she served with her husband in France, founding the Seminaire Adventiste de Salene. She wrote under the name Mother Naomi, and is remembered for the book *The Way He Should Go.*

CAYLEY, Lady (1748-1828), wife of a prominent British Methodist, Sir Thomas Cayley. She was converted at age fifty-two. They lived in Brompton, where she did some local mission work. She sponsored the building of a Methodist chapel.

CECILIA (c. 141-177), a Christian martyr honored by musicians and artists. Incomplete records refer to her as a virgin who resisted marriage, but her parents planned to force her to marry a Roman of high birth. Only hours before the marriage, the groom, Valerianus, and his brother, Tibertius, were converted to Christianity. Both were beheaded for their profession of Christ, and Cecilia's life was threatened. She was martyred later in Sicily, and these three Christian martyrs were buried in the catacombs of St. Callister. About 821 Pope Paschal had her remains taken to the church of St. Cecilia at Trastevere at Rome. A church in Rome was dedicated to her, and artists have portrayed her as a patron of music. She is portrayed in "The Second Nun's Tale" of *Canterbury Tales*. Raphael painted her sitting at an organ.

CHARLES, ELIZABETH RUNDLE (1828-1896), a British author, hymnist, and translator. Born in Devonshire, England; daughter of John Rundle, a member of Parliament. She was educated at home and began writing while quite young. She wrote nearly fifty books, several historical, the most popular was *Chronicles of the Schonberg-Cotta Family*, which depicted the life and times of Martin Luther. Some of her short works were published by the Society for the Promotion of Christian Knowledge. Her Christian faith is expressed in *The Mystery of Thy Holy Incarnation*. Her other works include *Tales and Sketches of Christian Life in Different Lands and Ages*, and *Martyrs of Spain and Liberators of Holland*. Several of her hymns and translations were published in *Voice of Christian Life in Song*, which was published in 1864 and in *Songs Old and New*, published in 1882. It is believed that her best-known original hymn is "Praise Ye the Father for His Loving Kindness." She married Andrew Patton Charles in 1851. He died in 1868. They provided funds for a number of philanthropic projects, and in 1885 she established Friedenheim, a home for the terminally ill.

CHEN, MRS. C. C., a graduate of Mount Holyoke who became a teacher and school administrator in the Bridgman Girls School in Shanghai. She married the Dean of Shanghai Baptist College. She was selected by the Chinese Christian Council as a delegate to the Jerusalem International Conference.

CHESTNUT, ELEANOR (1868-1905), a medical missionary to China. A native of Iowa, went to Park College before going to Chicago for medical school. She studied medicine at the Women's Medical College, then at the Illinois Training School for Nurses for two years. She attended Moody Bible Institute and was appointed as a medical missionary to South China in 1893. She first went to Canton, then inland to Samkong, near the Hunan border. Dr. Chestnut worked in a hospital at Lien-chow and studied the language. The Boxer Rebellion forced her to move, and in the spring of 1902 she returned to the States briefly. She then went back to Lien-chow, which was attacked, and she was martyred along with several others.

CHING, TING SHU (1889-1938), the first YWCA secretary in Peking, China. She grew up in the Chinese village of Lintsing and went to the mission school there. Later she attended Bridgman Academy in Peking and graduated from Yenching University. She became a teacher involved with the Chinese branch of the Young Women's Christian Association. A capable administrator, she was in charge of arrangements for the World Student Conference, which was attended by Christian students from thirty-three nations. She was highly esteemed as a Christian leader far beyond the borders of her native China and served on the National Christian Council of China. Like many other prominent Christians, her influence began with her early training in a mission school.

CHOI, PILLEY KIM (1884-c. 1939), the first Korean woman to receive Western education. Born in North Korea of a prominent family, her mother was converted and taught the Bible in their home. Pilley attended a mission school and was in the first graduating class of that school. She came to the United States and received her master's degree from Columbia University. She went back to Korea and became involved with the Young Women's Christian Association. In 1918 she married Dr. Choi, taught, and was later an administrator at the Jennie Speer School for Girls in Kwangju.

CHRISTIANSEN, AVIS BURGESON (1895-1966), author of hundreds of gospel hymns and two volumes of poetry. Born in Chicago, she grew up in a Christian family. She began writing verse at an early age. As a young woman she felt the Lord's prompting to use her talents for Him, especially in writing hymns of praise. She went to Moody Memorial Church, became acquainted with many at Moody Bible Institute and attended some evening classes there. One of her poems was set to music by Dr. D. B. Towner, head of the music department at Moody Bible Institute. That hymn is "That Is Far Enough for Me," still used. Some of her first hymns were introduced by the choir of Moody Memorial Church. In 1917 she married Ernest C. Christiansen, a member of the staff of Moody Bible Institute. Some well-known musicians who have put her poems to music are Harry Dixon Loes, George Schuler, Al Smith, Haldor Lillenas, and Wendell P. Loveless. Perhaps some of her best-known hymns are "Only Jesus," "Jesus Has Lifted Me," "I Know I'll See Jesus Some Day," "Meet Me in the Home-land," "Love Found a Way," "Come, Come Ye Saints," and "Jesus, Wonderful Name!"

CIRO, CATERINO (1501-1557), an Italian Christian of nobility concerned with reform within the Roman Catholic church and saving the order of Capuchins from suppression. As a very young child she became the Duchess of Camerino when she was betrothed to Giovanni Maria Varano, Lord of Camerino. He was twenty years older than she, and they had one daughter, Guilia, born in 1523. Much unrest in Italy was caused when Caterino decided to marry her daughter to the Duke of Urbino. Her uncle, Pope Clement VII, feared more trouble would result, and the next pope, Paul III, wanted the daughter to marry Farnese, condemning the earlier arrangement. Caterino defied this order. Caterino was imprisoned briefly because she had entered into some of the arguments within the church. As a consequence, a new order, the Capuchins, was formed. There was a compromise, but because she was well-educated in Latin, Greek, and Hebrew and knew of Calvin's *Institutes*, it is evident that she became aware of Scripture truths. She considered her spiritual adviser to be Marc Antonio Falminio, who had revised portions of Calvin's work, including the tract "The Benefit of Christ's Death." In 1539 she vowed poverty, obedience, and chastity. There was some indication of her accepting justification by faith. At least her influence and study caused some changes in the Reformation in Italy. Almost nothing is recorded of the last fifteen years of Ciro's life, although it is recorded that her daughter died some time before she did.

CLAASSEN, KATHARINE REIMER (1827-1869), an influential leader in a supportive role of the Mennonite Brethren church in Russia. Her husband was Johann Claassen, by whom she had several children, most of which died in infancy. She was a native of South Russia and had relatives in that area. Much of her life is recorded in her correspondence with her husband when he was away from home on business. They were largely responsible for forming the group that separated from the Kirchliche Mennonite mother church. They organized and met in the Claassen home in 1860. In 1866 legal arrangements were complete for the settlement of Mennonites near Kuban. She died of malaria in Kuban.

CLARE OF ASSISI (1194-1253), the brilliant and dedicated founder of the Franciscan Order of Poor Clares. Born into an aristocratic family, her father was Count of Sasso-Rosso and her mother was Artolena from a noble family of Fiumi. Clare was reared in a palace, taught at home, and knew the life of wealth. At the age of sixteen she heard St. Francis of Assisi and dedicated her life to serving

God. Later when she inherited the family wealth, and that, too, was given to the service of God, primarily in caring for the poor. Both her mother and a sister followed her example, as did many women of nobility, such as Agnes, daughter of King Ottokar I of Bohemia, a relative of the king of Hungary, and others, but her personal influence was significant in the lives of many more. She was much influenced by St. Francis and sought his counsel on spiritual matters. The order she established in 1215 spread extensively with sixty-five houses of Poor Clares in England, France, and Germany, and in Italy, houses at Assisi, Rome, Venice, Siena, Pisa, and Mantua. The first of such orders in the United States was established in 1875. Characteristic of this Catholic community were the rules of strict poverty, fasting, confinement to the convent.

CLARK, GRACE AGNES (1898-1955), born in England and a missionary to East Africa in reestablishing the work of Seventh Day Adventists that was disrupted during World War I. Later in Kenya, she founded a girls school and served as headmistress for twelve years. She pioneered education work at Nyanchwa and later served in Gendia as a translator for the Advent Press.

CLARK, MARY ELIZABETH BROWN (c. 1838-c. 1913), linguist, teacher, and pioneer medical missionary. She was the daughter of a Scottish missionary doctor who spent forty-five years in India. She studied medicine at the university and in hospitals of Paris. She was a recognized linguist with ability in Sanskrit, Urdu, French, German, Italian, Latin, Greek, and Hebrew. In her retirement she studied Russian. Before her marriage to Robert Clark in 1858 at Marylebone Church, she had served as a missionary in India under the Church Missionary Society. She was the first missionary to the Afghans and founded the Afghan Mission at Peshaivar, where she and her husband later served together. She worked with Indian women in the zenanas, and because she was not permitted to take Bibles with her, she memorized large portions of Scripture. Her medical background provided her successful treatment of many Indian women and thus opened a door for evangelism. They opened a caravansary for Christians at Armistar, formed the Alexandra schools, and performed many other special services for fellow Christians and those they wished to win for the Lord. She worked almost tirelessly until her health forced her to return home in 1878. Her husband returned to India, which required that they be apart for the next ten years.

CLARKE, MARY LANE (1872-1970), linguist, missionary, and author, who translated the first book (gospel of Luke) into the Limba language. A native of New York state, she served in Sierra Leone under the Wesleyan Methodist Church of America for twelve years, in addition to many more years as a translator and author, compiling a Limba dictionary published by the British Foreign Bible Society in 1922. She also assisted in translating and preparing the first Limba hymnbook. She and her husband wrote the first mission history of the Sierra Leon field: *American Wesleyan Methodist Missions of Sierra Leone, West Africa,* published in 1911. She served as superintendent of the Young Missionary Workers Band and at the age of seventy-five returned to Sierra Leone for eighteen months, during which time she completed the gospel of John in the Limba language. Mrs. Clarke taught several years at Houghton Seminary and at the age of seventy-eight received an honorary Doctor of Letters degree from that school. She was listed in the first edition of *Who's Who of American Women* and even at the age of eighty-one studied Greek.

CLARKE, SARAH DUNN (1835-1917), native of New York state, teacher and co-founder of the Pacific Garden Mission in Chicago. First she organized a Sunday school at 23d and State Streets in 1869; then with the encouragement of her husband, Colonel George R. Clarke, she found a location suitable for a much-needed rescue mission. She and her husband founded in the area this oldest of rescue missions and one of the best known of such missions in the world, partly because of the well-known people who were saved at the services there.

CLEMENT, LORA E. (1890-1958), editor of *Youth's Instructor* magazine for the Seventh Day Adventist denomination. She later served until 1958 as librarian for the Review and Herald Publishing Association.

CLEPHANE, ELIZABETH CECILIA (1830-1869), a poet remembered for two of her poems that were set to music as hymns, "Beneath the Cross of Jesus" and "The Ninety and Nine." A native of Scotland, she was a quiet woman, sensitive to spiritual truth as she was bereaved early in life by the loss of both parents. She did much charitable work among the poor and suffering. Two of her poems were included in the publication *Family Treasury,* and it is believed that she wrote "The Ninety and Nine" for children, as it first appeared in the children's section of that publication. She wrote both of the above-mentioned poems only a few months before her death, so she never heard them sung. "Beneath the Cross of Jesus" was set to music by Frederick C. Maker, an organist in Bristol. In 1874 the poem "The Ninety and Nine" was seen in a paper by Ira Sankey; he cut it out and placed it in his pocket as he traveled through Scotland. After a sermon by D. L. Moody in Edinburgh, Moody asked Mr. Sankey to sing something appropriate. Because the message theme was the Good Shepherd, Mr. Sankey immediately thought of the poem in his pocket. He simply placed it on the organ, struck a chord, and composed the music for it as he went along. The very tune he was led to write that night is unchanged to this day.

CLOTILDA (c. 475-545), a Christian queen with considerable influence, although details of her early life are obscure. Her father was Chilperic, king of the Burgundians. It is likely that she lived with an uncle as some of her immediate family were massacred. She must have had Christian teaching while quite young. In 493 she married Clovis, king of the Franks, with an agreement that she would continue to practice her Christian faith. She led her husband to the orthodox faith and exercised Christian influence during his reign. She was one of the first to be named a saint in the church. It is reported that after a battle victory over the Alemanni, Clovis and three thousand soldiers were baptized on Christmas Day in 496. His administration is credited with the founding of many churches throughout France. He had built the Basilica to Peter and Paul near his palace, and he and Clotilda built the Church of the Holy Apostles, known as the Church of St. Genevieve in Paris. After the death of Clovis in 511, Clotilda entered the Abbey of St. Martin at Tours and probably lived there until her death. It was her granddaughter, Bertha, who became the wife of King Ethelbert of Kent and introduced Christianity into England, and her great-grand-daughter, Ethelberga, who spread Christianity in the Northumbria area.

COGHILL, ANNIE LOUISE WALKER (1836-1907), Christian educator born in Staffordshire, England; later moved to Canada. Her father was an engineer. She and two older sisters founded a private school for girls. Later she returned to England as a governess. In 1883 she married Harry Coghill, a merchant. Her literary work includes six novels, a book of children's plays, and a collection of poems. One poem set to music as a hymn was "Work, For the Night Is Coming."

COILLARD, CHRISTINA MACKINTOSH (1829-1891), daughter of a Baptist minister in Edinburgh, Scotland, and pioneer missionary to Barotseland, Africa. In her teens she heard Robert Moffat when he was accompanied by Sarah Robey, the African girl whom the Moffats rescued from massacre as a baby. At that time Christina considered missionary work. She and an older sister went to Paris and heard Francois preach and tell of the work in Africa. Before long Christina fell in love with Francois, although he continued with his plans for going to Africa. Later in writing to her, he proposed. She sailed for Africa in 1860, and they were married in Cape Town in 1861. They pioneered the work in Barotseland, but in 1864 were forced to leave because of war, so they went to Natal and worked with the Zulus for two years. Later they returned to the Basutos where they remained until 1874. Their next move was about five hundred miles into Northern Rhodesia, which they reached after a difficult journey in 1878. The following year they returned to France for their first furlough. Their work was sponsored by the Paris Evangelical Missionary Society. After they returned to Basutoland in 1881, they found that much fruit of their previous work was destroyed; they also encountered opposition, and her health was greatly affected. She died in 1891, thirteen years prior to the death of her husband. They had no children.

COLE, HANNAH HUNTER (1919-1951), missionary martyr in China. A native of Ireland, she came to the United States, attended the Philadelphia School of the Bible, and was appointed as missionary to China in 1947. She served with the Conservative Baptist Foreign Mission Society. She and her husband worked in western China in evangelism and church planting, but when the Communists came in, they were forced to walk through China in order to leave the country. With her small children, the youngest six months, she became exhausted and ill with meningitis and died. She was buried in interior Fulin, China.

COLEMAN, ALICE BLANCHARD MERRIAM (1858-c. 1918), home missionary to minorities in the United States. She was a native of Boston, privately educated, and traveled abroad. In 1874 she entered Bradford Academy in Bradford, Massachusetts, graduating four years later. She considered graduate studies but was forced to change her plans because of eye problems. In 1879 she became involved in the Women's Home Missionary Association of the Congregational Church. She traveled within the United States visiting the various fields of work sponsored by this organization. She later transferred her church affiliation to a Baptist group and become involved with their home missionary service. She married George W. Coleman in 1891. Her work continued, and she became president of the Women's American Baptist Home Mission Society. She worked with interdenominational committees for the betterment of minority people, especially immigrants, serving directly with those in a settlement house for women, largely Syrians and Italians. Her administrative techniques helped to coordinate the home mission work of a number of denominations.

COLLINS, ELIZABETH (1755-1831), a minister in the Society of Friends. She was born in New Jersey. In 1779 she became a minister and traveled in many states. She had great concern for the poor and served in a home missionary role.

COLONNA, VICTTORIA (1490-1549), one of the first women to have poetry published. Her writings reflected true spiritual insight and were inspirational to the great painter Michelangelo. She was born in Marino, Italy, to a wealthy, influential family. Her father was grand constable for King Ferdinand II. She was betrothed at age four and while still a teenager married Ferrante Francecio d'Avalos. He was in the military service and spent little time at home. Thus Victtoria used much time for reading, study, and writing. She shared her poetry with other Christians and became well known for her writing. She was part of a group organized to purify the Roman church from within and wrote a sequence of sonnets *The Triumph of Christ*, which expressed her personal Christian dedication. Michelangelo and Victtoria became friends in 1538, sharing many personal religious views. He painted three pieces especially for her. She became friends with Queen Margaret of Navarre, sister of Francis I, and also the Duchess Renee, an avowed Protestant and friend of John Calvin. Victtoria favored the cause of the Capuchins, who were accused by some as being Lutherans, and her ideas were cited as "evangelical" Catholic. She lived in a convent of the Caesarian palace in Rome in her declining years but never took vows. She and Cardinal Reginald Pole were both helpful to each other, and both accepted the doctrine of justification by faith.

COMNENA, ANNA. *See* **BRYENNIUS**

CONNELLY, CORNELIA PEACOCK (1809-1879), born of a wealthy family of Philadelphia, she chose to take vows in the Roman Catholic church. In 1846 she founded in England the Catholic community named Society of the Holy Child Jesus. The purpose of this group was largely educational.

COOK, JENNIE SIEMENS (1902-1975), missionary, teacher, and instrumental in the founding of two colleges. Born in Iowa, she attended the Northwestern Bible School in Minnesota. She served for twenty years in Assam, in northeastern India, before being appointed in 1952 by the Conservative Baptist Foreign Mission Society for further service in India. With her husband, J. William, she founded the Calcutta Bible College in 1955, where she taught for some time. Later she was involved in the founding of the International College in Honolulu, Hawaii, where she taught until her death.

COOK, SYLVIA SOETENGA (1930-1960), an exceptional missionary who shared in founding one of the largest and strongest Baptist churches in the Philippines, the Capital City Baptist. Born in Racine, Wisconsin, she attended Northwestern College in Minnesota. Her effective and fruitful term of service in the Philippines with her husband, James, was shortened because of a blood disease she contracted there.

COPENHAVER, LAURA SCHERER (1868-c. 1939), a native of Marion, Virginia. Her father was one of the founders of Marion College and served as its president for thirty years. She was a missionary leader in the United Lutheran church and taught and spoke at many missionary conferences. One of her hymns, "Heralds of Christ, Who Bear the King's Commands," is included in both the *Presbyterian Hymnal* and *Lutheran Hymnal*. It was through her influence that missionary work was started by the Women's Missionary Society of the Lutheran Church among the mountain people in the southern part of the United States.

CORDELL, BESSIE (1894-1981), missionary, teacher, and author. She served thirty-six years in foreign lands, mainly with Chinese people. She first went to China in 1923, and served as an administrator of a girls boarding school, in addition to having missionary responsibilities for twenty outstations in the large district of western Shantung province. She was interned for approximately six months by the Japanese in 1941. Unable to return to China, she went to Taiwan and worked among the Chinese there. Even during her furlough she worked with Chinese in Omaha, Nebraska, at the Hope Mission. Her earlier work in China was sponsored by the National Holiness Missionary Board, but in Taiwan she was under the sponsorship of the Missionary church. She found time to write two books: *Blossoms from the Flowery Kingdom*, which went through two printings, and *Precious Pearl*.

CORNARO, HELENA (1646-1684), a dedicated Italian linguist and scholar. Born in Venice, she was the daughter of a procurator of St. Mark. She knew Spanish, French, Latin, both ancient and modern Greek, Hebrew, and the Arabic languages. Not only was she learned in philosophy, mathematics, astronomy, and theology, but she was a gifted musician as well. She dedicated her life to God and lived a quiet, devout life. She attended the University of Padua, where she received several degrees, including a doctor of divinity degree.

COUSINS, ANNE ROSS (1824-1906), poet and hymnist especially remembered for "The Sands of Time Are Sinking." She was the wife of a Presbyterian minister and deeply impressed with the life and testimony of Samuel Rutherford. The above-mentioned hymn is part of a poem consisting of nineteen stanzas and is based on the words of Rutherford just prior to his death as a martyr.

COVETTE, AURELIE founder of the Sister Adorers of the Precious Blood in 1861 in Canada. A community of the same order was established in the United States in 1890. She became mother Catharine-Aurelie.

COWMAN, LETTIE B. (1870-1960), author, evangelist remembered by thousands for her inspirational devotional books *Streams in the Desert* and *Springs in the Valley. Streams in the Desert* was written during the difficult time of her husband's illness, but has been published in more than one hundred English printings, several editions, and into approximately fifteen foreign languages. Chiang Kai-shek is said to have requested that his personal copy be buried with him. A native of Iowa, she and her husband, Charles, founded the Oriental Missionary Society in Japan in 1901. She became president of the society in 1928 and led the work until her retirement in 1949. She then became president of a sister organization, World Gospel Crusades. From 1936 on, her life was absorbed by a program called Every Creature Crusades, which sought to place Scripture in every home of a given nation. She patterned it after the OMS Great Village Campaign in Japan (1912-1918), during which teams visited 10,300,000 homes. The program was a tremendous task. She befriended Emperor Haile Selassie and had some contact with King Farouk of Egypt. She traveled over the world speaking to missionaries and others and doing a considerable amount of writing, including a biography of her husband, *Charles E. Cowman—Missionary Warrior,* in addition to other books and articles. The missionary society founded by the Cowmans is today one of the major faith missions, influencing people around the world for Christ.

COX, BLANCHE B. (1864-1940), outstanding valiant pioneer worker in the Salvation Army who worked on three continents. Born in London, she was the daughter of a prominent London jeweler. At the age of sixteen, she heard Catherine Booth present the gospel. She dedicated her life to the Lord's work. She attended Cambridge University and later was given administrative responsibilities with the Salvation Army in London. After training, she went to India and served in evangelism and edited the *War Cry of India*. She returned to England for a while and later was transferred to Canada and the United States. In Michigan and Indiana she stood firm for Salvation Army privileges to openly present the gospel. She was arrested and sentenced to the state penitentiary for conducting street meetings. She won the approval of church groups, newspapers, and others. Soon she was released and the rights of the Salvation Army restored.

COX, ETHELENE BOONE (1890-1965), author who served in several important leadership roles of the Women's Missionary Union of the Southern Baptist Convention. She was one of the first two women to serve on the Baptist World Alliance executive committee, and the first woman to address the annual meetings of the Southern Baptist Convention in 1929. She wrote the book *Star Trails* and a number of articles for denominational publications.

COX, FRANCES ELIZABETH (1812-1897), translator of hymns. She is remembered for the valuable work of translating at least forty-nine German hymns into English. These were included in the hymnal *Sacred Hymns from the German,* published in 1841. In the second edition (1864) she deleted several, modified or altered others, and added twenty-nine new ones. "Jesus Lives! No Longer Now" is one of her best-known translations.

COX, VERCIA P. (c. 1891-1946), author and faithful missionary to Kunming, China. Great was her faith that she served the Lord more than ten years without any promised support from friends, churches, or mission boards. She returned to the States, and her prayer support grew, but enroute from Seattle to Calcutta she became ill and died suddenly. It is apparent that the work she had begun in China became strengthened through organization. She wrote at least two books: *Plumes over Kunming,* a story of God's providential care of His people along the Burma Road in China during the early days of war; a biography of her husband, *Carson W. Cox, A Mis-*

sionary to China. Her work was later associated with the Southwestern Evangelistic Mission.

CREWDSON, JANE FOX (1809-1863), talented hymnist and daughter of George Fox of Cornwall, England. She married Thomas Crewdson in 1836 and is remembered for several widely used hymns: "Give to the Lord Thy Heart," "Looking unto Jesus," and "How Tenderly Thy Hand Is Laid."

CROLL, MARTHA B. (c. 1847-1906), an influential missionary of the United Free Church of Scotland. Although details of her early life are vague, she was sent to India under the United Free Church but soon returned home because of poor health. In 1898 she went to Kingston, Jamaica, to work in a Hindu settlement. After an initial opposition, she made friends with the people, and her evangelistic efforts were fruitful.

CROMWELL, ELIZABETH BOUCHIER (c. 1598-1672), daughter of Sir James Bouchier and wife of Oliver Cromwell. She and Cromwell were married in 1620 at St. Giles Cathedral in Edinburgh, Scotland. Her personal correspondence reflects her life as one of prayer and and devotion to the Lord. Although her role was not a prominent one, she assisted her husband in ways that in turn influenced many others.

CROMWELL, ELIZABETH STEWART (c. 1562-c. 1654), mother of Oliver Cromwell. Her home became a center of activity and retreat for Puritans, both clergy and laymen. Oliver lived at home until his marriage and later brought his wife there to live. Elizabeth Cromwell was encouraging to many, and her spiritual life deepened by sharing, in spite of a tremendous work load.

CROSBY, FRANCES JANE (VAN ALSTYNE) (1820-1915), blind hymnwriter. Few hymns are sung more often in American Protestant churches today than those written by this prolific hymnwriter, affectionately known as Fanny Crosby. More than eight thousand poems and hymns are credited to her, many of which are signed by some two-hundred pseudonyms. Most of her hymns are based on Scripture, as she had memorized many portions, including the first four books of the Old Testament and the four gospels. Born in New York state, she was blinded when only six weeks old because of a mistaken application of a prescription to her eyes. She was educated at the New York City School for the Blind and after graduation taught there for ten years. Even at eight years of age she wrote poetry and a number of secular songs as a youth. In 1896 her first book of poems was published under the title *The Blind Girl and Other Poems*. At the age of thirty she dedicated her life to Christ at a revival meeting. From then on, her writing took on spiritual meaning, expressing deep devotion and inspiration. Not until the age of forty-one was her first hymn written, and that at the suggestion of composer W. B. Bradbury. In 1868 another composer, William H. Doane, shared a tune with her that he had been composing, and immediately she expressed the hymn "Safe in the Arms of Jesus," one of her first hymns to be translated into several foreign languages. In 1858 She married Alexander Van Alstyne, a blind musician and teacher. He composed music for some of her hymns. It is said that one of her most dominate personality traits was cheerfulness. Our knowledge of her blindness helps us to understand better some of her hymns like "God Will Take Care of You." Other popular hymns by her are: "Blessed Assurance, Jesus is Mine," "I Am Thine, O Lord, I Have Heard Thy Voice," "Jesus Is Tenderly Calling Thee Home," "Jesus, Keep Me Near the Cross," "More Like Jesus Would I Be," "Praise Him! Praise Him! Jesus, Our Blessed Redeemer," "'Tis the Blessed Hour of Prayer," "Pass Me Not, O Gentle Saviour," "Draw Me Nearer," "Rescue the Perishing," and "Near the Cross." Some of the best-known Christians of her day who enjoyed her fellowship were Ira Sankey, D. L. Moody, P. P. Bliss, and George Stebbins.

CROWELL, GRACE NOLL (c. 1898-c. 1963), an American poet and author. *Some Brighter Dawn* is a collection of her poems. Her other books include

Meditations, a devotional, *White Fire, Silver in the Sun, Flame in the Wind, Light of the Years, This Golden Summit, Songs for Courage, Songs of Hope, Songs of Faith, The Radiant Quest, Splendor Ahead,* and others. Her work reflects deep spiritual insight and faith.

CU, LU BI (Dr. LU) outstanding Chinese missionary-physician among her own people. Dr. Lu was reared in a Christian home. Her mother, however, had been abandoned in the streets as an infant and rescued and cared for by American missionaries. Lu Bi Cu was unusually bright and sent to America for schooling. She first went to Herkimer, New York, and then to Foltz Mission Institute. After graduation she was admitted to the Woman's Medical College in Philadelphia, from which she graduated with high honors. She was assigned to a hospital in Ngusheng in the Fukien province. Her practice grew, a new hospital was built, and she found a tremendous response to the gospel through her outreach. She was especially known for her success in working with opium users.

CULBERTSON, BELLE CALDWELL (1857-c. 1938), author, translator, and missionary to Indo-China. Born in Wheeling, West Virginia, graduated from the State Normal School of West Virginia in 1876 and the following year from Wheeling Female College. She went to Indo-China as a missionary of the Presbyterian Board in 1879 serving as a school administrator in the Harriet House School for Girls in Bangkok, Thailand. In 1880 she married John Newton Culbertson of the same mission board. They returned to the United States in 1881. At home she was influential in helping women understand missions and take an active part in praying for and giving to missionaries. She served as head of the Woman's Foreign Missionary Society of the Presbytery of Washington, D.C., and organized many such groups throughout the United States. She and her husband served as home missionaries in South Dakota before going to Washington, D.C. She was a correspondent for the religious press and a translator of German. Some of her writing was published in the *Southern Observer*. In 1906 she was elected president of the Woman's Interdenominational Missionary Union of the District of Columbia. She influenced many, especially women, for the cause of missions.

CUNNINGHAM, Lady ANN (Marchioness of Hamilton) (c. 1591-1647), a notable and influential Scotch Presbyterian, and fourth daughter of James, seventh Earl of Glencairn, by his first wife, Margaret, daughter of Sir Colin Campbell, of Glenarchy. Some of her ancestors were among the first Scottish peers and renowned for their courage in the Scotch Reformation. In 1603 Lady Cunningham married Lord Hamilton. She continued to maintain the principles taught by John Knox and other Reformers, even when her husband became a party to the king's interests and betrayed the church in Scotland. He died at the age of thirty-six. She, then Lady Hamilton, encouraged and welcomed ministers of the gospel to her castle, and her name is associated with one of the most remarkable revivals of the time which took place at the church in Shotts in 1630. She welcomed women of rank to church, sometimes services being extended for prayer. When Robert Blair and others in Scotland and Ireland were deposed by the Bishop of Downs because they stirred up the people, Lady Hamilton used her influence at the court in London to vindicate the accused. When it became necessary, she even stood opposed to her son in upholding Presbyterianism.

CUNNINGHAM, BARBARA notable Scotch Presbyterian robbed, falsely accused, imprisoned for her faith. From a family distinguished for their ardent advocacy of the Reformation, her great-grandfather was a member of the memorable Scottish parliament of 1560 that abolished the papacy throughout the kingdom. Her father, Sir William Cunningham, and her mother, Elizabeth Nicolson, daughter of William Nicolson, Commissary of Aberdeen, were known for their strong faith. She was married in 1657 to William Muir, also a Presbyterian. While serving with the army in an attempt to join the Covenanters, her husband was forced to escape, going to Rotterdam. Meanwhile, the case was tried, and their estate was confiscated leaving her with nothing but her children. She managed to join her husband in Holland, but he died soon after in 1670. Now a widow with four children, she returned to Scotland. As a widow, she was not allowed to claim her former home, but rather was forced away without regard for her rights. She refused monetary help and went to find work to support her family. She went to Glasgow, living in very poor conditions but keeping true to her faith. She and her oldest daughter were charged with having a nonconformist minister preach in her house, and put in the loathsome prison, Castle of Blackness, for over three years. Two of her children died. With the coming to the throne of William, prince of Orange, relief came for her and other Scottish Covenanters. She returned to her former home, which was restored. At last, after twenty years of hardship, illness, and imprisonment for Christ's sake, she returned to Caldwell House to live in comfort and freedom to worship.

CURE, APOLLONIE PELISSIER (1809-1869), became Mother St. John and founded the Roman Catholic community in France called Religious of the Sacred Heart of Mary in 1849. Education was the primary emphasis in this order. She was a wealthy widow before taking the vows, and at one time worked with Pierre Gailhac.

CUSHMAN, EMMA DARLING (1865-1930), an unusually heroic missionary nurse largely responsible for saving many lives. She was decorated for her efforts by the Commander-in-chief of Allied Forces in the Near East. Born in New York state, she attended Manhattan State College in Kansas, studied nursing in Paterson, New Jersey. She first served under the American Board of Commissioners for Foreign Missions in a mission hospital in Caesarea, Turkey; then in a mission hospital in Konya. She stayed on when Americans were requested to leave and then joined the Near East Relief in 1919, helping to save remnants of the Christian minority in Asia Minor, among them 300,000 orphans. Shrewd bargains with the provincial governor spared her life and many others. She organized an underground to save many of the 150,000 refugees passing through Konya. General Milne, Commander-in-chief of Allied Forces in the Near East decorated her for this work six months after armistice. She took up residence in Corinth, Greece, but died while visiting Cairo, Egypt.

CUSHMAN, MARY FLOYD (1870-1965), pioneer medical missionary and author working in Africa under the American Board of Commissioners for Foreign Missions. A New Englander from three generations of ministers, she first went to the Maine State Normal School, then Boston University School of Medicine, finishing in 1892. After internship experience and private practice from 1893 to 1922, she went to the Angola Mission, Portuguese West Africa, from 1922 to 1928. From there she went to medical work in Chile from 1930 to 1941, returning to Chilesso after her retirement between 1946 and 1953. Her autobiography, *Missionary Doctor,* went through five printings. She promoted the missionary needs of Africa and encouraged youth. She was described as a dynamic speaker and an excellent physician.

D

d'ALBRET, JEANNE (1528-1572), Christian queen of Navarre and outspoken defender of Calvin and the Huguenots. She was the only child of Margaret of Navarre and her second husband, Henry II. Navarre was a small country just south of France. Jeanne grew up in a royal atmosphere was educated by a tutor, and had a firm Christian mother as her example. At an early age and by custom, her marriage was prearranged for political reasons. Her resistance to marrying the Duke of Cleves required that she be brought to the ceremony by a constable of France. She escaped to Navarre, and because she was only fourteen, that marriage was annulled. In 1548 she married Antoine, Duke of Bourbon. They had five children of which only two grew to adulthood, Catherine and Henry IV. It was Henry IV who declared the Edict of Nantes in 1598 that provided religious liberty for France. Jeanne was a faithful Bible student, had Protestant services in her palace, and had the Bible translated into Bearnnois, the dialect of that area. There had been Christians there since the fifth century, but never before had the Bible been translated into their own language. She did many other things to insure the spread of the gospel and encourage Bible study. She communicated with John Calvin and cherished his counsel. Jeanne endured great opposition from Roman Catholics because of her Christian stand. It was on Christmas of 1560 that she proclaimed Calvinism the religion of Navarre. When enemies threatened her power, she declared: "I would rather be poor than cease to serve God." She resisted the great opposition of Catherine de Medici, especially preceding the horrible Massacre of St. Bartholomew. When Jeanne suddenly became quite ill, rumors were that her enemies had tried to poison her. On her deathbed she requested the reading of John's gospel, chapters fourteen, fifteen, and sixteen. She pled with her son to carry on true to the faith and the Scriptures.

DANFORTH, CLARISSA (1792-c. 1851), one of the first women in America to speak as an evangelist and conduct revival meetings. Although from Vermont, information about her early life is obscure. In 1809 she committed her life to Christ and in 1814 began preaching. She taught the Bible, successfully held revivals that lasted for several days. She was of the Freewill Baptist persuasion.

DAVIDSON, HANNAH FRANCES (1860-1935), an outstanding teacher, writer, translator, and missionary daughter of Henry Davidson. He was a well-known minister in the Brethren in Christ church and first editor of the denomination's journal *The Evangelical Visitor*. Born in Ohio, she graduated from Kalamazoo College in 1884 with a B.A. degree and a masters degree from there four years later. She is believed to have been the first woman in the Brethren in Christ church to obtain an earned college degree. She was teaching at McPherson College in Kansas when she answered a call from her denomination to do missionary work in Africa. She was one of a small party who in late 1897 left as the denomination's first missionaries to that continent. She helped to found the Matopo Mission in what is now Zimbabwe. In 1906, with another woman missionary, she traveled across that continent to found the Macha Mission in what is now Zambia. They traveled by train from Bulawago to Livingstone, the rest of the way by oxen and wagon. She served as an educator, translator, and preacher in the Brethren in Christ missions in Africa until 1923. She returned to the United States and taught at Messiah Bible College (now Messiah College) until 1932. She wrote an authentic account of the beginning of the Brethren in Christ missions in Africa.

DAY, EMMA V. (1853-1894), faithful Lutheran missionary to Africa from America. Emma's mother died while Emma was an infant. She was reared by an aunt. In 1874 she married D. A. Day of the Lutheran Mission of Africa for the Evangelical Lutheran Church. She specialized in presenting the gospel to children and reaching their mothers for the Lord.

de BONNAULT, MARIE MADELENE de BENGY (Madame) (1781-1858), founder of the Catholic order Faithful Companions of Jesus in France in 1820. That order began in the United States in 1896. She was born in Chaleauroux, France, and married Viscount de Bonnault, who died soon afterward. The primary purpose of this order was education.

de BOURBON, CATHERINE (1559-1604), faithful Christian daughter of Jeanne d'Albret. Her marriage was arranged by her brother, Henry of Navarre, for political gain. She submitted to the ceremonial service performed in 1599 with duc de Bar, son of the Count of Lorraine. However, they lived apart for some time, for she would not agree to denounce her faith and become a Roman Catholic. This greatly irritated her brother, and she endured many hardships because of this situation. As a family of nobility, she set an example for other women of less influence and was true to her Christian faith.

de BOURBON, CHARLOTTE (c. 1546-1582), Christian princess of Orange and the fourth daughter of Louis de Bourbon by his wife Jacqueline de Longoic. Although her father was a Roman Catholic, her mother was Protestant, a devout Christian, taught her children Christian principles, and was much opposed to Charlotte's being sent to a convent for schooling. Her mother, the Duchess de Bourbon, died in 1561 while Charlotte was still at the convent in Jouarre. Charlotte knew the Bible well and even taught it to some nuns in the convent. Charlotte fled to the home of her sister, also a believer, and openly renounced Roman Catholicism. In 1575 she married the prince of Orange, also a Christian. They had six daughters, the oldest was Louisa Juliana of the ruling family of the Netherlands. Queen Victoria was a direct descendant of the prince of Orange. Her Christian testimony and faithfulness influenced many, especially royalty.

de CHANTAL, JANE FRANCES FREMYOT (1572-1641), a French mystic and daughter of Benigne Fremyot, once president of the Burgundy parliament. At the age of twenty-eight she was left a widow with three daughters and a son. When she was thirty-two she heard Francis de Sales and sought his spiritual counsel. They became lifelong friends as she promoted the order he had founded to help widows and young girls. He aided her in founding the religious community Order of the Visitation, at Annecy, France, in 1610. The primary purposes of this group were teaching and caring for the sick. Eighty-eight houses of this order had been established when she died. She had special compassion for the terminally ill as was demonstrated by several incidences, such as when she took a leper into her home, dressed his wounds, and gave him her guest bed, and spoke to him of salvation. She did not shirk from difficult cases, especially those afflicted with cancer or other terminal diseases and nearing death.

de COLOGNY, LOUISE (1553-1620), French Christian survivor of the Massacre of St. Bartholomew in 1572. Daughter of French Admiral Gaspard Cologny and his first wife, Charlotte de Laval. Details of her early childhood are vague, but she had an outstanding Christian witness. In 1571 Louise married an officer of the Protestant army, Charles de Teligny. After he was killed in the fighting she went to Geneva, then to Biarn and Heidelberg as a Protestant refugee. She married again and had one child. Her husband was Fredrick Henry, Prince of Orange, a descendant of William, who was directly involved with delivering England and Scotland from Roman Catholic rule. Louise de Cologny lived through the assassinations of her father, her first and second husbands, her good friend Henry IV of France, the execution of many other friends, and the exile of her pastor. She remained steadfast in her faith, and her example and letters influenced many for the cause of the Protestant Reformation.

DEDERER, ANNA (1902-1976), pioneer missionary evangelist and nurse in the Micronesian Islands. Born in Boeckingen, Germany, she took some of her medical training in Lohr, Hagen, and Tübingen, Germany. She was at the Liebenzeller Mission Seminary in Germany from 1925 to 1929. After she came to the United States, she attended the Andover-Newton Theological Seminary, the University of Hawaii, and the Pacific School of Religion. Ordained in 1949, she taught religion in public and secondary schools in five villages on Kusaie; worked with several pastors there; held hospital chapel services; organized programs for youth camps; and taught Bible classes for youth and women under the American Board of Commissioners for Foreign Missions. Her service in the Micronesian Islands included church and school responsibilities on the Mortlock Islands; a girls training school on Truk for eight years under the Liebenzeller Mission; at Majuro of the Marshall Islands; in the Caroline Islands; and elsewhere in the same general area.

DE FOREST, CHARLOTTE (1879-1973), leader in Christian education for women of Japan. Born in Osaka, Japan, of veteran missionary parents, John and Elizabeth De Forest. Her formal education included three college degrees from Smith College: B.A., M.A., and an L.H.D. She attended Oxford University in London, the University of Chicago, and Hartford Seminary. She taught at Kobe College in Nishinomiya, Japan, from 1903 to 1915; then became president of Kobe College, serving from 1915 to 1940. In 1940 the Emperor of Japan bestowed her the Fifth Order of the Sacred Treasure for her educational service to Japanese young women. In May 1951 she received the "peace award" from Kobe, Japan, and in 1960 was listed among others recognized for special contributions to Japan. She wrote several articles for the Kobe paper as well as some poetry. Her work was sponsored by the American Board of Commissioners for Foreign Missions.

de LAMOIGNON, LOUISE ELIZABETH (1763-1825), founder of the Catholic community Congregation of the Sisters of Charity of St. Louis in France. Born in Paris of an illustrious family, she became the wife of Edouard Mathiew Molé in 1780. They had several children. She lived in England for a time; then moved back to France as the widow of a martyr. The order became one of the best known for offering comfort for those in need.

de l' INCARNATION, MARIE GUYARD (1599-1672), a French widow; pioneer missionary to Quebec, Canada; and author and founder of the oldest convent school in North America. Born in Tours, France, as Marie Guyard. Her mother was from an aristocratic family, and her father was a merchant. She married Claude Martin when she was eighteen. Within three years she was left a widow with an infant son. She lived with relatives briefly; then at the age of thirty-two entered the Ursuline convent in Tours and took the name Marie de l' Incarnation. Her son was reared in that convent. In 1639 she went to Quebec as a missionary to the Indians. She learned the Indian dialects of Algonquin, Huron, and Iroquois, writing and translating books for them. Later she compiled a French-Algonquin dictionary. She spent thirty-two years working among the Indians in Quebec and there established the large Ursuline convent school, first of its kind in North America. Her influence lasted far beyond her lifetime.

de MARILLAC, LOUISE (1591-1660), French founder of the Catholic community known as Sisters of Charity, a work in which St. Vincent de Paul was supportive. Her husband died in 1625, and she turned her time and energies into helping the ill and poor. Some of the work she originated in her own home. Approval for the order was granted in 1655. Other such communities from her original group branched in Paris. She was declared a patron saint in 1960.

de MEESTER, MARIE LOUISE (1856-1928), founder of a Catholic community referred to as Missionary Canonesses of St. Augustine. She established this order in Belgium in 1897 for missionary work primarily with orphanages and hospitals.

DEPEW, MARY KINNEY (1836-1892), an effective evangelist with major spiritual influence in the Wesleyan Methodist Church of America. A native of Warren, Ohio, she was converted at age thirty and felt called to preach and hold evangelistic meetings in that area. Soon her meetings were so effective that she was asked to speak elsewhere. Even without credentials or ordination she was a powerful evangelist. In 1885 the Depews moved to Houghton, New York, where she had charge of women students in a college. She conducted daily prayer meetings at 4:00 A.M. Her evangelistic endeavors influenced many far beyond the local campus and local denomination.

de PRAYER, EVA (Dr.) (1866-1928), a distinguished Christian physician working among the women of Telugus in her native India. Her own ancestry was a combination of Indian and Portuguese. In addition to being a capable physician, she established a loan fund to help poor students, and had charge of an orphanage. On behalf of her mission she made two trips to Europe and Canada, speaking and telling of their needs. Acadia University conferred upon her an honorary LL.D. degree.

de ROYE, ELÉONORE (1535-1564), a leader in the Protestant Reformation. Married in 1551 to Prince de Condi (Louis de Bourbon), also a Christian of the Reformed faith. They had several children, and, along with the wife of Coligny, Eléonore ministered to many wounded soldiers. She went to Strasbourg to enlist the help of German Protestants; although faced with much opposition she maintained unusual faith and courage.

de SOUBOISE, Madame (c. 1475) , although little is known about this humble Christian, she is mentioned because of her great and lasting influence on Renee of Ferrara. As a capable governess, she taught Renee the simple faith of the Bible. Quite young when her mother died, Renee was left under the care of Madame de Souboise and thus grew spiritually with faith and courage. Madame de Souboise was British, a cultured person, cherished her Bible and its teachings, the sourcebook for the training and teaching of Renee. The chain reaction of her teachings in the life of Renee cannot be measured, for it reached out to touch the lives of many. No doubt Madame de Souboise exemplified the faith of Renee's mother and the truths she desired be taught to her children.

de XAINCTONGE, ANNE (1567-1621), an influential French nun who founded the Catholic community Sisters of Ursula of the Blessed Virgin in France in 1606. Born in Djon, France, she was the daughter of Jean de Xainctonge and Lady Marguerite Collard.

DICKSON, LILLIAN LeVESCONTE (1901-1983), missionary and founder of The Mustard Seed, Inc., a nondenominational faith ministry. Born in Prior Lake, Minnesota; graduated from Macalester College in St. Paul, Minnesota, in 1924. She taught briefly, and then attended Biblical Seminary in New York. In 1927 she married James Dickson, and they went as missionaries to Taiwan under the auspices of the Canadian Presbyterian Church. Soon she discovered that many missionary wives were not encouraged to participate actively and directly in the work of their husbands. Realizing the potential of such available unused talent, she organized a missionary outreach which later became The Mustard Seed, Inc. This outreach resulted in the establishment of clinics, orphanages, schools, tribal churches, a haven for homeless street children, a chapel in a leprosarium, a crafts center. They have provided means for the patients to find courage and feel needed. Her husband died in 1967, and as a memorial to him, she helped set up a missionary society that sends tribal Christians to Borneo. Also, in Papua, New Guinea and Indonesia, she began providing schools, churches, vocational training centers and community centers in remote areas while working with regional denominations and local leadership. The Lord has greatly blessed the work she began. There have been at least 183 kindergartens established in the mountain areas; nearly two hundred churches; in Taipei: Mercy Door's Clinic, Bang-Kah Mobile Clinic, prison work, rescue home for boys, milk stations in slum areas. Mountain clinics at Kak-Pan, Pin-Tong, Kim-Lun, Tai-Tang, Koan-San, Sin-Khang, Kong-Hok, and Hualien. Also, special clinics for new mothers or "Room for Mary" at Taitung, Ping-Tung, Koan-San, Kwalien, and Pu-Li. Children's homes not only for the orphaned but handicapped children of leper parents, girl prostitutes, and for babies of prisoners. She founded mobile clinics in Kak-pan, Pescadores, Ping-Tung, and elsewhere. Several tuberculosis sanitariums were established; a number of schools as well as milk stations that provided free milk and vitamins, and other such projects. Her faith and works leave a continuing legacy of missions and thousands have received the gospel and been brought to Christ through the work the Lord used her to begin.

DIEHL, NONA M. (1894-1981), author, missionary, and unusually gifted as a competent organizer and leader of the largest U.S. Lutheran women's organization of her time. She was graduated from Goucher College in Baltimore, did graduate work at the University of Pennsylvania and Columbia University; received an honorary Litt.D. degree from Susquehanna University in 1949. Under her leadership the United Lutheran Church of America not only grew in numbers, but it became more aware of the part women have in the entire missionary outreach of the church. Born in York, Pennsylvania, she became affiliated with the Women's Missionary Society of the United Lutheran Church in 1927 as the secretary and climbed to the office of executive secretary. In her twenty-two years of leadership the society supported missionaries, schools, and hospitals in India, Africa, Puerto Rico, the Virgin Islands, and in the United States Appalachian region. She had unique vision to foresee the outreach of the church at home and on the foreign fields and to encourage church giving for missions to more than twenty-five million dollars. She wrote a history of this progress in *United Lutheran Church Women: Heritage and History,* published in 1961.

DILLON, MARGARET NEELY (1865-1913), pioneer evangelist-missionary to Costa Rica and Honduras. She went to Central America in 1893 under the Central American Mission. She was married to H. C. Dillon in Costa Rica in 1896, and they moved to Honduras where he died the next year. She continued steadfastly with the work in Northwestern Honduras, reaching many for Christ. Even during times of persecution and illness she consistently proclaimed the gospel over twenty years without taking a single furlough. During an evangelistic journey she became ill and died, but she left a church firmly established there and a witness in numerous places in Central America.

DIX, DOROTHEA LYNDE (1802-1887), author, teacher, nurse, philanthropist, social worker, and influential leader for reform in hospitals and institutions. A native of Maine and the daughter of a Methodist minister, she became a teacher-administrator of a girls school in Boston from 1817 to 1835. She wrote *Conversations in Common Things,* which had at least sixty printings, *Meditations for Private Hours,* and in 1825 compiled the book *Hymns for Children.* She taught Bible classes for women in East Cambridge House of Corrections, and seeing the poor conditions there and in hospitals for the mentally ill, she championed to reform the plight of the helpless patients. When the Civil War began she volunteered to assist in caring for the wounded and was soon appointed chief of the Union Army nurses. As an able administrator she gained much support and financed some of her reforms on her own. She was one of the first to appeal for government help for the mentally retarded.

DIXON, HELEN CADBURY ALEXANDER (1877-1969), British author, hymnist, and originator of the Pocket Testament League. Daughter of the founder and owner of the Cadbury Chocolate Company in Birmingham, England. She was born in England of a Quaker family. She became acquainted with Charles M. Alexander, an evangelistic gospel song leader and personal worker, during special meetings in Birmingham. They were married in 1904 with a typical Quaker wedding. *A Romance of Song and Soul-winning*, was her biography of Charles M. Alexander and was published in the early twenties. Later a biography of her father, *Richard Cadbury of Birmingham*,and one of her second husband, A. C. Dixon, simply titled, *A. C. Dixon, A Romance of Preaching* (1931). She wrote stanzas three, four, and five of the hymn "Anywhere with Jesus." It was not long after the death of Mr. Alexander that she became acquainted with A. C. Dixon, a writer, evangelist, and one-time pastor of the Moody Memorial Church in Chicago. He had lost his wife and had several circumstances in common with Helen Alexander. They were married in 1924, but he died the next year. Likely her most effective legacy to the church is the on-going ministry of the Pocket Testament League. It is a missionary organization operating in thirty countries, publishing Scriptures in forty-two languages.

d'MATEL, JEANNE CHEZARD (1596-1670), influential founder of the Catholic order Sisters of the Incarnate Word and Blessed Sacrament, which began in France in 1625 and established in the United States in 1853. The purpose of this group was largely educational.

DOANE, MARGARET TREAT (1868-1954), remembered for her keen interest and great generosity to a variety of ministries. She served as a board member for the Woman's American Baptist Foreign Mission Society and the Association of Baptists for World Evangelism. The daughter of hymnwriter William Howard Doane, she gave much time and money to such interests as Denison University, Eastern Baptist Theological Seminary, the Committee on Christian Literature in Foreign Fields, Houses of Friendship, and other such groups, including her own denomination and the Association of Baptists for World Evangelism projects abroad.

DOMITILLA, FLAVIA (First Century), Christian niece of Domitian (Titus Flavius Domitianus Augustus), Roman emperor between A.D. 81 and 91. She and members of her household, including her husband, Titus Flavius Clemens, fled because they refused to worship the emperor. She went to Pandateria in the Tyrrhenian Sea area. Her husband was beheaded for refusing to persecute Christians. Her life was spared for a time, but she was forced to live a martyrdom kind of existence on an island. She witnessed of her Christian faith, read her Bible, helped others, and assisted in burying martyrs. It is believed she was buried among the catacombs near Terracina, on the Via Ardeatine, where a cemetery bears her name.

DOREMUS, SARAH PLATT HAINES (1802-1877), missionary daughter of Elias and Mary Ogden Haines. In 1821 she married Thomas C. Doremus, who encouraged her many missionary interests in her own denomination, the Dutch Reformed, in addition to establishing other missionary endeavors as well. She became the first president of the Woman's Union Missionary Society of America for Heathen Lands, organized in 1860. Her home became the headquarters of this missionary group, with their first missionary going to Burma. In response to the need for missionaries in China, she led in forming the Society for the Promotion of Female Education in the East. Then in 1835, she became president of a group whose purpose it was to promote and help the Grande Ligne Mission in Canada. In 1840, after helping women prisoners, she organized the Women's Prison Association to assist released women prisoners. She worked with that group for thirty-two years, part of the time as president. Sarah also worked for the Greeks who had been suppressed by the Turks. For thirty-six years she served an appointment of manager of the City and Tract Society. Her activity in the City Bible Society of New York was noteworthy, for she was one of the founders of the House and School of Industry, serving as manager for eight years and president for ten. She helped to found the Nursery and Child's Hospital in 1854 and the Woman's Hospital of New York State in 1855.

DOROTHEA or **DOROTHY** (?- c. 313). Little is known about this early martyr, but her Christian testimony was evident to many as she was led to be executed for her faith. Some consider her legendary, as she is mentioned first in the Hieronymian Martyrology and probably lived in Caesarea in Cappadocia. Some evidence notes that she witnessed to Theophilus. She may have been one of those arrested during Diocletian's persecution of the church.

DOUGLAS, MARGARET (Lady) (1592-1678), born of a noble family of Scotland; married Archibald (Lord Lorne), later Marquis of Argyll, a Presbyterian. When Charles II came into power in 1650, the Marquis of Argyll offered spiritual counsel and influence, but later Charles turned against him. Charles had given verbal assent to Presbyterianism, but his moral life did not reflect true conversion. Charles had the Marquis imprisoned, and Lady Margaret pleaded in vain for his release. She was given time with him before he was beheaded; together they prayed and shared Scripture; he gave a personal testimony to those present. Later, Lady Margaret's son was also martyred; yet she did what she could to provide a place of refuge for Covenanters. She was described as a consistent Christian, faithful, and strongly supporting the Covenanters and reforms of Scotland.

DOYLE, MARY (1763-1834), an Irish Christian philanthropist and leader in the Society of Friends. She and her sister opened a shop in Ballytore. Uprisings caused closure of the business in 1798, but it was reopened later. She and her sister worked together in assisting many others, primarily in nursing and relieving the poor through Christian philanthropic means.

DREXEL, KATHERINE (1858-1955), founder of a Catholic order to work among American Indians and blacks called Sisters of the Blessed Sacrament for Indian and Colored People. She was reared in a wealthy family but chose to enter a convent; later she established new educational orders serving the Pueblo and Navajo Indians of the midwestern United States. She assisted in establishing a number of schools including Xavier University, the first and only Roman Catholic university designated for black students at that time.

DRUILLARD, NELLIE HELEN RANKIN (1844-1937), missionary in South Africa; became secretary of the South Africa Women's Christian Temperance Union. Details of her early life are obscure, but she did found the Riverside Sanitarium and was cofounder of Madison College, institutions of the Seventh Day Adventist church.

DRYER, EMMA (c. 1833-1925), influential in home mission work. She established a training school for women in Chicago, which became the forerunner of the women's department of Moody Bible Institute. Born in New York State, she graduated from LeRoy College, taught at the Illinois State Normal University, and became an administrator there. In 1870 she went to Chicago, founded a home for girls, planning to begin a Christian workers training school. She became acquainted with D. L. Moody and encouraged him to establish such a school for training workers. One of the dormitories of Moody Bible Institute was named in her honor.

DUFF, ANN SCOTT DRYSDALE (c. 1805-c. 1889), missionary and wife of Alexander Duff. They went as the first missionaries of the Church of Scotland to India in 1830. He founded a school that later became the University of Calcutta. Details of her life are not readily available, but she was unusually helpful to him.

DUFF, MILDRED (1860-1932), a British author, editor, and leader in establishing literary standards for the publications of The Salvation Army. A native of England, she served forty years in England and Sweden with the highest rank being Commissioner in The Salvation Army. She edited two international publications, *All the World* and *The Young Sol-*

dier. She did general missionary and evangelistic work in addition to her editing and writing.

DUNCAN, MARY LUDLIE (1814-1839), born in England, the daughter of Reverend Robert Lundlie. She married a minister of the Scottish Free Church, William Duncan, and her youngest sister became the wife of the Scotch hymnist Horatius Bonar. Mary composed twenty-three poems, many of which were set to music, including a children's prayer. These poems were published after her death under the title *Rhymes for My Children*.

DUNN, CATHERINE HANNAH (1815-1863), author, hymnwriter, and translator. She was born in Nottingham, England, and the daughter of a bookseller and publisher. She published a volume of thirty-six hymns in 1857 simply titled *Hymns from the German*. The best known of this collection are: "Hilf, Herr Jesu, lass Gelingen" and "Nun sich der Tag geendet hat."

DUNN, GENEVA MILDRED OLDHAM (1911-1969), author, journalist, and first woman to serve as editor at the Brotherhood Commission of the Southern Baptist Convention. A native of Kentucky, she attended New Mexico Normal University and graduated from the Oklahoma Baptist University in 1939 with a B.A. degree. She took graduate studies at the Southwestern Baptist Theological Seminary. She wrote articles published in: *Baptist Training Union Magazine, Window of YWA, Royal Service, Home Life, Brotherhood Journal,* and other Baptist publications. She wrote program materials for Sunday school quarterlies and the book *Courage to Win,* published in 1967. She also served as a newspaper reporter and became editor of the *Ambassador Life* and *Ambassador Leader*.

DUROCHER, MARIE ROSE (c. 1804-c. 1873), founder of the Roman Catholic community of Sisters of Holy Names in Canada in 1844. It was an education order and established in the United States in 1859.

DUTTON, ANNIE (1698-1765), author, hymnist. She was a native of Northhampton, England, and wife of Benjamin Dutton. He was a Baptist minister of Great Gransden Hunts and was lost in a shipwreck on his return from America in 1743. Two of Annie's poems were published in 1734, "A Narrative of Wonders of Grace" and "A Poem on the Special work of the Spirit in the Hearts of the Elect," and approximately sixty other hymns and poems. These were published in poem form in 1833. Some of her work has been translated into Dutch. Her work is described as being prosaic in style but reflecting Calvinistic theology.

DYER, MARY (c. 1604-1660), a martyr for her Quaker persuasion. She was the wife of William Dyer of Somerset, England. She came to America for religious freedom in 1635. In 1638 she helped establish Portsmouth, Rhode Island. She did not become a Quaker until a trip back to England in the middle 1600s. When she returned to America, she was arrested in Boston, then released. In 1658, she was expelled from New Haven, Connecticut, for proselytism and jailed again each time she visited fellow Quakers in Boston. Finally, she was hanged, as she would not promise to permanently leave New Haven.

d'YOUVILLE, MARIE MARGUERITE (1710-1771), founder of the Grey Nuns of Charity in Montreal in 1738. It was a Catholic community of women with branches in France and Germany, devoted to the care of the sick. Besides the usual three vows, these nuns also vowed to devote their lives to the relief of suffering. She was born at Varennes near Montreal; her father was an officer in the Royal Army.

E

EBERSOLE, MELINDA (1860-1933), was the first full-time worker for a city mission of the Mennonite church in Chicago, where she held that position for twenty years. Born in Pennsylvania of David D. and Anna Martin Ebersole, she had Bible classes, home visitation, and numerous other responsibilities, including some nursing.

EDDY, MARY MORSE BAKER, GLOVER, PATTERSON (1821-1910), an author and founder of the Christian Science church. Born in New Hampshire, she received her early education at home and the Sanbornton Academy in Tilton, New Hampshire. In 1843 she married Colonel George Washington Glover who died the following year, leaving her with a son, her only child. In 1853 she married Daniel Patterson, a dentist, who left her. She then married Asa Gilbert Eddy in 1877. Often ill as a child, she was attracted to the teachings of Phineas Parkhurst Quimby. She suffered a long time as the result of an accident, then felt that her health was restored and devoted her life to the doctrines referred to as "Christian Science." She wrote *Science and Health with Key to the Scriptures,* founded the monthly paper *Christian Science Journal,* and the daily paper *Christian Science Monitor.* In 1879 she founded the First Church of Christ, Scientist in Boston and in 1881 the Massachusetts Metaphysical College to train her followers. Christian Science denies the doctrines of the deity of Christ, the Trinity, sin, death, disease, and Satan.

EDWARDS, MARY KELLEY (1829-1927), missionary, educator, and founder of the only mission school continuing for African girls in South Africa. A native of Ohio, she was widowed when she first went to Africa. In 1868 she was the first woman sent out by the Women's Board of Missions of the American Board of Commissioners for Foreign Missions. The next year she founded the Inanda Seminary for Girls in Zululand, South Africa. She spent fifty-seven years at the seminary, refusing all furloughs in the United States except one. The Inanda Seminary has been an effective means for preaching the gospel. Many Christian homes over the land of the Zulus are patterned after the model of orderliness and family virtue demonstrated by her work and the outreach of the seminary.

EITZEN, SARA BLOCK (1840-1917). medical missionary of the Mennonite Brethren church. Born to David and Sara Block in Rudnerweide, South Russia. She became a Christian during a revival that swept across the Ukraine. In 1866 she married Abraham Eitzen, a widower some ten years older than she. While still in Russia, two children were born to them, one of which died in infancy. They moved into a Mennonite village where he worked for the government forestry department. She continued to be a medical apprentice and often was called on to help with common illnesses and as a midwife. Their family joined the Mennonite migration to the United States, arriving in Peabody, Kansas, in 1876. Her parents had come before. Sara continued her medical practice and records show that she delivered more than 1,800 babies. A year after her death a hospital was built in Hillsboro, Kansas, and was equipped with an obstetric department through memorial gifts in her honor.

ELEANOR (1655-1720), Empress of Austria, second wife of Leopold I, daughter of the Duke of Newbourg. She was married in 1677 and widowed in 1705. She demonstrated her faith by her life and by her compassion for the less fortunate; she tried to help the poor in unusual ways, such as paying their bills and giving them food.

ELIOT, ANN (c. 1611-c. 1675), missionary to American Indians and wife of John Eliot. Little is available about her, but it is likely that she was born in Hertfordshire, England. She was very helpful to her husband in establishing the first Indian church in 1660, and the following year in publishing a catechism and later a New Testament in the Algonquin language. She exercised her skill in medicine and dispensary work as needed. Their two sons carried on the work, which led to the formation of the Society for the Propagation of the Gospel in New England.

ELIZABETH I (TUDOR) (1533-1603), Queen of England from 1558 to 1603 and daughter of Henry VIII and Anne Boleyn. She was born in Greenwich palace. Before she was three, her father had her mother beheaded; by the age of ten she was put under the care of Queen Catharine Parr. Elizabeth was well educated with private tutors and able to communicate in French, Latin, and Italian. She also could read Greek and Cyprian. She succeeded the throne of England from her half-sister, Mary, in 1558, bringing courage and calmness to her people and restoring Protestantism and confidence to the monarchy. Her forty-five-year reign was one of the greatest in English history and was known as the Elizabethan age. Her Protestant stand was not easy, for as Queen she was head of the church. The Roman Catholic church constantly threatened her; yet, she was successful in consolidating the Church of England in 1563, bringing peace and sparing the country the kind of Catholic-Protestant wars that had plagued France and Germany. Even Philip of Spain convinced the pope to excommunicate Elizabeth in 1570, the victory over the Spanish Armada in 1588 favored Elizabeth. She never married and was the last of the Tutors to reign.

ELIZABETH, ALBERTINE (1618-1680), daughter of Elizabeth Stewart and Fredrick V, King of Bohemia. She became Countess of Palatinate. Details of her early life are uncertain, but her Christian testimony was evident as she was a noble leader and friend of a number of the early church leaders. William Penn wrote a tribute to her life in "No Cross, No Crown."

ELIZABETH OF BRANDENBURG (1485-1545), a Danish princess with an outstanding Christian testimony and credited with introducing Lutheranism to Denmark. In 1505 she was married to Joachim I, Elector of Brandenburg, who did not favor the Reformers. However, she remained steadfast in her faith. It is recorded that while her husband was away, she had Protestant services in the palace and took communion. When her husband learned of it, he threatened her with "imprisonment" in a nunnery. She disguised herself as a servant and fled from her palace and went to the palace of her uncle, John the Constant, Elector of Saxony, where she knew she would be safe there; later she was given residence in the Castle of Lichtenburg, near Wittenberg. There she could freely study the Scriptures and serve the Lord openly. Martin Luther visited her frequently. Her husband remained a Roman Catholic and died in 1535. Her household servants were all required to attend chapel services daily, and sometimes she would read chapters from the Bible to them. Her son succeeded his father as Elector Joachim II and became a Protestant.

ELIZABETH OF BRUNSWICK-CALENBERG (1510-c. 1548), as the daughter of Joachim I and his wife, Elizabeth, she accepted the evangelical faith of her mother. When fifteen years of age she married Eric I, Duke of Brunswick-Calenberg, a widower much older than she was. They had four children. Although her husband defended Roman Catholicism, he did not prevent others from becoming Protestants. Elizabeth openly declared her faith, and he loved her so that her faith did not interfere with their marriage. She desired to openly proclaim her Christian testimony and thus wrote to the Landgrave of Hesse in 1538. He sent Antonius Corvin, an evangelical minister, to her. When her husband died, she exercised her Christian influence and with the counsel of Corwin sought preachers to instruct people in the Word of God. It is said that she lived a consistent and holy life; her influence furthered the cause of Protestantism and Christianity for many centuries.

ELIZABETH OF HUNGARY (1207-1231), daughter of King Andrew II of Pozsony and Gertrude, daughter of Berchtbld. She came from a long line of Christians and was reared in Wartburg Castle near Marburg in Hesse. As a young child she was betrothed to Louis IV of Thuringia; they were married when he was twenty-one and she was fourteen. He died during a crusade about six years later, and she was left a widow with three children. She is especially remembered for her dedication to God and her compassion for the ill and poor. She literally gave away her wealth for benevolent causes. She built a home for lepers near Wartburg Castle; during famine, opened soup kitchens; and sold many of her own jewels to provide necessities for the needy. Louis had requested his brother care for her should he be killed in the war. But the brother took advantage of the situation and even requested her to leave the palace. The Crusaders came to her rescue and required her brother-in-law to return power to her son that he might succeed his father. On Good Friday in 1228, she took vows of the third Order of St. Francis and became the first Franciscan tertiary in Germany. She served the lepers and the poor, denying herself. She died of exhaustion within four years. A chapel was erected in her honor.

ELIZABETH OF PORTUGAL (1271-1336), granddaughter of Voilante, sister of Elizabeth of Hungary, after whom she was named. She was married to Denis, King of Portugal; they had two children, Alfonso and Constantia. She was taught at home, as were their children. She founded two hospitals, one near her palace at Coimbra, another for small children elsewhere. She is remembered for her testimony through sharing and compassion for the women and children of the time. After her husband died in 1325, she lived in a convent of Poor Clares, although she did not take vows.

ELIZABETH OF THURINGIA (1207-1235), daughter of Andrews II Hungary, remembered for her testimony through sharing. She had great compassion for the poor, and fed as many as nine hundred of them daily. Her palace became a mission.

ELLIOT, CLARA ELIZABETH LUGINBUHL (1895-1981), an influential Christian, mother of missionary martyr Jim Elliot and another missionary son in Peru. Born in the state of Washington, she lived much of her life in Portland, Oregon, where she was a chiropractic physician. Her husband was an itinerant evangelist. She completed her training at the Pacific Chiropractic College and had her practice in her home. She was active at the Grace and Truth Chapel of the Plymouth Brethren. Described as a truly godly woman, she is remembered by many for her warm Christian hospitality, for she opened her home to many, especially missionaries.

ELLIOTT, CHARLOTTE (1789-1871), hymnwriter. Many are the souls who that have been saved when responding to the invitation hymn "Just as I Am, Without One Plea," written by Miss Charlotte Elliott. She wrote it as her own response to God's invitation to accept Him as Savior. A visiting evangelist, Dr. Caesar Malan, talked with her. She resisted the gospel at first, because she had become an invalid and was discouraged. At last, she responded for the Lord to accept her, "just as I am" and wrote all four verses. Born in Clapham, England, she suffered from an illness that left her an invalid in 1821. After her conversion, she did much to help others and assisted in the compilation of *The Invalid's Hymn Book*, published in 1834. The sixth edition (1854) contained over one hundred of her hymns. Over one hundred of her hymns were included in the book *Psalms and Hymns for Public, Private and Social Worship*, edited by her brother, Henry Elliott. Other hymnals have included her work, but she is remembered most for her familiar invitation hymn, "Just As I Am, Without One Plea."

ELLIOTT, EMILY STEELE (1836-1897), a British hymnist and niece of Charlotte Elliott. She is remembered for a hymn published in *The English Hymnal*, "Thou Did'st Leave Thy Throne and Thy Kingly Crown." Details of her early life are obscure.

ENG, Dr. HÜ KING (1865-c. 1949),

medical missionary among her own Chinese people. She lived in the Foochow area and her family, Dr. and Mrs. Hu, were Christians. Her grandfather was one of the first converts in that part of China. She graduated from the Foochow Boarding School for Girls and in 1884 came to America with American Methodist missionaries to attend Ohio Wesleyan University. She graduated in 1888 and entered the Woman's Medical College of Philadelphia. After her father became ill, she returned to China to care for him; then in 1892 she returned to the United States and completed her medical training and graduated in 1894. That was followed by internship. She returned to Foochow in 1895 and served at the Foochow Hospital for Women and Children, becoming its administrator in 1899. As that work grew she proceeded to provide a nurses training program. In 1902 the first students received diplomas from the nurses training program at Woolston Memorial Hospital, where Dr. Eng and her sister, Hu Seuk Eng, served together. All the work of Dr. Eng was definitely Christian-centered, and many patients became Christians through her faithful witnessing. Her service was recognized one commencement when her Alma Mater, Ohio Wesleyan University, conferred on her an honorary degree.

ENSS, AMY EVELYN GREAVES SUDERMANN (1878-1975), a Mennonite educator who grew up in England. After her marriage to Jacob Sudermann, she taught at the first Mennonite Russian college at Halbstadt. She was left a widow with several small children. In 1912 she married Gustase Enss and emigrated to the United States. She first taught French at Bethel College in Kansas and later served in teaching positions in both Hesston College and Goshen College. In 1969 she wrote the her life's story, which is in the Mennonite memorabelia archives of the Mennonite church in Goshen, Indiana.

EO-ING, MARY (c. 1807), a Chinese-trained nurse serving as a missionary to her own people. She was reared in a Christian family, and her Chinese parents worked with the American-based China Inland Mission. She graduated from the medical course at the Danforth Hospital in Kuikiang and joined the staff of the Presbyterian Missionary Hospital at Chengchow, Hunan. After she married, she moved to Liling and served in the Liling Missionary Hospital.

ETHELBERGA (c. 601-c. 673), daughter of Bertha, who established the first Christian churches at Canterbury and Ethelbert of Kent. She married Edwin, King of Northumbria, for whom Edinburgh, Scotland, is named. Her Christian influence was distinct. She had her own chaplain, and her husband accepted Christ and was the first Christian king of Kent.

EUDOCIA (c. 401-460), wife of Theodosius and daughter of Leontius, a philosopher in Athens. Her name was Athenais, but when she became a Christian she changed it to Eudocia. Pulcheria, the sister of Theodosius, had arranged for their marriage, but they differed in views on religious matters. She is credited with having paraphrased in poetry the first eight books of the Old Testament, prophecies of Daniel, and other Old Testament books. She wrote *The Life of Christ,* believed to be taken from Homer's writings and translated into Latin.

EUDOXIA (375-404); details of her early life are not clear, but she was the wife of Emperor Arcadius, mother of Theodisius II, and she exercised her influence to criticize Chrysostom. She is reported to have disliked his teachings, because she believed he was singling out her in condemning evildoing and evildoers.

EUSTOCHIUM, JULIA (c. 370-418), daughter of Paula and believed to be the first Roman woman to take a vow of perpetual virginity and dedication to God. Although details of her early life are obscure, Jerome wrote of her as a friend, addressing to her his famous letter on the motives required to actuate a life of virginity and rules to govern such a life. In 386 at Bethlehem, a monastery was built with Jerome in charge and for the women was built a convent, which Eustochium had charge of after the death of her mother in 404. Many of Jerome's writings credit her for the message because of her great thirst for knowing God's Word.

EVA OF FRIEDENSHORT (1865-1921), a German author and missionary born in wealth, but after becoming a Christian renounced wealth, comfort, and pleasure to help relieve suffering among the poor. Her mother died when Eva was thirteen and soon afterward her father remarried. She became a Christian by reading the Scriptures and had great compassion for the needy. She gave out soup and food from their castle, until her father refused to let her continue. She studied nursing, and helped many, and was a testimony for Christ whenever she worked. She led several of her relatives to the Lord. Her father agreed to build a refuge for poor people, and so the work at Friedenshort began. After the wealth of estate was spent, the work continued as a faith mission, for she was encouraged by Hudson Taylor. She did some writing for children.

EVALD, EMMY CARLSSON (1857-1946), described as the single most influential woman among Swedish Lutherans in the United States, she was the daughter of a founder and president of the Augustana Lutheran Church, Dr. Erland Carlsson. After attending public schools in Chicago and in Sweden, she received a B.A. from Rockford College, an M.A. degree from Augustana College, and later an honorary L.H.D from Upsala College. She seemed to be a tireless organizer for the causes of women, Swedish Lutherans, and world missions. Perhaps she is best remembered for her organization and forty-three-year presidency of the Augustana Lutheran Women's Missionary Society, which was predecessor to the present Lutheran Church Women, Lutheran Church in America. Under her leadership, Augustana women raised hundreds of thousands of dollars to support missions, schools, and hospitals in India and China. An example is the Emmy Evald Girls School in Hsuchang, China, which later became the Hsuchang Hospital. Her influence was involved in the founding of the Augustana Hospital in Chicago in 1884, the Lutheran Women's League of Chicago, and the World's Columbian Exposition executive committee appointed her president of the First World's Congress of Lutheran Women held in 1893. She had opportunity to address the Illinois legislature and appear before the U.S. Congress. In later life, she was superintendent of the Lutheran Home for Women which, she founded in New York City.

F

FABIOLA (c. 143-199), a Christian mentioned in the writings of Jerome as being a student of the Bible and believed to have founded the first hospital in Europe. She was from a prominent family, and her compassion for the sick along with her personal care for some of them left an impression on the Christians and pagans of Rome.

FALCK, ELIZABETH (1894-1980), born in Pennsylvania and appointed a missionary to China in 1921. She first worked as a nurse at St. Luke's Hospital, Shanghai, and later in the Union Hospital at Chengtu. Miss Falck taught in the English department of St. John's University, Shanghai, and at St. Paul's University in Tokyo from 1951 until she retired and returned to the United States in 1959. She affected many lives for the Lord.

FALCONIERI, JULIANA (1270-1341), founder of the Roman Catholic community of Mantellate Sisters in Italy in 1285. Their primary purpose was one of prayer. Falconieri was born in Florence, Italy, but little is known of her family.

FARRELL, MONICA (1898-1982), an outstanding Bible teacher, evangelist, author, and missionary in Ireland, Australia, in addition to having a speaking ministry in the British Isles, New Zealand, and Europe. Born in Dublin, Ireland, she was orphaned young and reared by a sister. As a child, she was placed in a convent boarding school while her sister was away for nearly three years. Later she attended a public school mixed with Protestant children. Sincerely concerned with the differences between Roman Catholicism and Protestantism, she studied out the truth for herself and became a deep Bible student. The result was that she bravely stepped out in faith, seeking to live for Christ, and denounced the doctrines taught her by the Roman Catholic church. In spite of family opposition, she was mightily used of the Lord to help others with similar background struggling with Catholic doctrines. Her testimony is clearly presented in her book *From Rome to Christ*. She ministered in the Society for Irish Church Missions in Dublin for fifteen years. Then she answered an invitation to speak and minister in Australia. She began a teaching mission, a work sponsored by the Church of England, in the Sidney area. During her ministry in Ireland and Australia, thousands of invitations poured in asking her to speak to gatherings in New Zealand, the British Isles, and Europe. Literally millions have been blessed by her speaking, her testimony, and writings in which Christ is uplifted. Needless to say, she encountered opposition, which she considered a true indication of her effectiveness for Christ.

FAY, LYDIA MARY (c. 1802-1878), a remarkable American missionary to China. Born in Essex County, Virginia, she became one of the first single women missionaries to China, having been sent in 1850. She founded a school in Shanghai, where many teachers and preachers were prepared to carry on the work of spreading the gospel. In addition to teaching and administering the program, she developed a training school, managed the finances, and even provided clothing and other necessities for some of the students. After twenty-five years she turned her school over to the Episcopal board and it grew from her efforts a theological school with a capable faculty to carry on the widening ministry.

FEDORORNA, MARY (c. 1759-1828), Princess of Wurtemberg, then Empress of Russia, a noted Christian leader with remarkable administrative abilities. She married Paul, son of Catherine II, in 1796 became Empress of Russia, and was widowed in 1801. Her husband recognized her faith and talents and had given her leadership responsibilities in education and in the administration of hospitals for children in Petersburg and Moscow. She established various schools, agricultural colonies, and institutions, including a school for the blind and a school in Pavlovsk for the mute, the first of its kind in Russia. She established hospitals and a home for veterans, and in 1798 she founded the Institution of the Order of St. Catherine for the education of women. At Alexandroski she established a large cotton-spinning factory that employed 750 people; a society called Widows of Charity; and she initiated a boarding school that included a Sunday school and library. Her expertise in administration caused her to insist that all of these schools and hospitals be self-supporting.

FELICITAS (c. 107-164), a brave martyr, described as an illustrious but devout Christian Roman woman of great virtues. She had seven sons, all of whom upheld their mother and their own personal Christian testimony. She was interrogated by Publius, then threatened, but she and all her family stood firm in their Christian faith and thus were all martyred.

FELICITAS (d. 203), a Christian martyr from Carthage, North Africa. She was a slave girl martyred along with Perpetua. They were both arrested and imprisoned because Septimus Severus had forbidden conversions to Christianity. She had a child born in prison and placed in care of a Christian relative. Felicitas and Perpetua were tried and then taken to be martyred for refusing to denounce their Christian faith. They were led into an arena, gored by a mad cow, and later put to death by the sword.

FELL, MARGARET (1614-1702). *See* **FOX, MARGARET**

FELLER, HENRIETTA (1800-1865), Swiss Protestant immigrant to Canada largely responsible for founding the Grande Ligne Mission in 1836, the first Canadian French Baptist church. A missionary and educator, she arrived in Quebec from Switzerland in 1835 and began a house-to-house campaign of spreading the gospel. A colleague, Louis Roussy, helped her. She started a school for local children. The 1837 Rebellion required Mrs. Feller, Louis Roussy, and sixty-three converts to go to New York for refuge, as they were being persecuted for their Protestant faith. After peace was restored, they returned to Quebec to continue their pioneer evangelistic work and built a building of what was to be the beginning of Feller College.

FERGUSON, MANIE PAYNE (1850-c. 1927), author, hymnist, home missionary, and founder of Peniel Missions. Born in Ireland, Manie came to North America with her parents. In 1883 she married Theodore Pollock Ferguson, a native of Ohio. He preached and was much involved with inner city needs. She was especially concerned with girls on the streets and those who needed the gospel. The Peniel mission in Los Angeles began in 1886 and as help and financial needs were met, branch missions were organized in San Bernadino (1896), San Francisco (1897), and Oakland (1897). Missions were later established in Vallejo, Long Beach, Pasadena, and elsewhere in California. Peniel Missions have spread into areas beyond California, including Seattle. Mrs. Ferguson is remembered as well for her hymn "Blessed Quietness," although she wrote many poems and an account of the Peniel Mission work.

FIELD, ADELE (1839-1916), a teacher, author, and missionary of the American Baptist Foreign Mission Society. She was a native of New York state and taught before going to Siam, where she ministered from 1865 to 1872. She then served in South China between 1872 and 1890. She established a school for national evangelists and one for training Bible women. Besides writing a number of mission study books, she prepared a dictionary in the Swatow dialect.

FIESCHI, CATHERINE (1447-1510). *See* **CATHERINE of GENOA**

FINDLATER, SARAH BORTHWICK (1823-1907), a translator of hymns. She was a native of Edinburgh, Scotland, and remembered for her work with her sister, Jane Borthwick, in the translation of German hymns into English. She is recognized for her work in compiling *Hymns from the Land of Luther,* published in four series in 1854, 1855, 1858, and 1862. She did fifty-three of the translations.

FISHER, MARY (c. 1623-c. 1698), Quaker activist imprisoned several times for her preaching. She attempted to preach at Sussex College where John Milton and Oliver Cromwell had studied, but she was interrogated and whipped in public. In 1655, she and another Quaker, Ann Austin, came to America. There were attempts to prevent them from introducing Quakerism to the New World. Their Bibles were confiscated, and they were put in prison. In 1657 Fisher returned to England and then went to Turkey with other missionaries. After several years of preaching and traveling she returned to England and married William Bayly, a marine and preacher.

FISKE, FIDELIA (1816-1864), American author and missionary to the Nestorians of Persia, primarily women and girls. She was from a family whose ancestors left England in 1637 to find religious freedom in the new America. She graduated from Mount Holyoke Seminary and taught, but when a missionary to Persia visited the campus and appealed for help, she volunteered. In 1842 she reached Trebizond on the Black Sea. Her station was Oroomiah, where she found about 1,000 Nestorians, in addition to 24,000 Mohammedans and Jews. She found the condition of the women especially sad, began a school for them, but found that she had to bathe her pupils as well as teach them. Women had lost self-respect, and it took some time to motivate them to learn. She formed prayer circles and enlisted the help of many. Her school became so popular that she had to restrict attendance to the women more seriously concerned with prayer. The gospel was taught to many parents as well, many of whom became Christians. She wrote the book *Woman and Her Saviour in Persia.*

FLEETWOOD, BRIDGET CROMWELL (1624-c. 1701), daughter of Oliver Cromwell and Elizabeth Bouchier. She committed her life to Christ and was baptized at the age of twenty-two. She married Henry Ireton, but was unhappy; she was left a widow with five children. She then married Charles Fleetwood, a widower. She had prayer meetings in her home, especially for officers of the army.

FLEMING, LULU CECILIA (1862-1899), born in Florida. This remarkable missionary physician was the daughter of a slave who had died at the close of the Civil War when Lulu was only three. Apparently her mother remarried. She finished the Estey Seminary Course in 1885 and taught for some time. She was the first black person to be commissioned for career missionary service by the Woman's American Baptist Foreign Missionary Society. Her first appointment was to the Congo (Zaire), where she taught for her first term. When she came home on furlough, she enrolled at Shaw University and took the full medical training program in the Woman's Medical College of Pennsylvania. She completed her work and received her M.D. degree in 1895. She then returned to the Congo as a medical missionary at Irebo in Upper Congo. Her term of service was shortened when she contracted African sleeping sickness from which she died at age thirty-seven.

FLOWER, ELIZA (c. 1801-1846), sister of Sarah Flower Adams, who composed the music for most of the hymns written by her sister.

FLOWERDEW, ALICE (1759-1830), an English teacher, author, and hymnist. She lived in Islington and wrote a volume of poems, *Poems on Moral and Religious Subjects* (1811). Her best-known hymn is "Fountain of Mercy, God of Love."

FOX, MARGARET (1833-1893), claimed to be a spiritualist medium along with her sister, Catherine. A native of Canada, she moved to the United States while young. She reported supernatural messages and devised a code to communicate with the spirit world. She held seances and was paid for such. Several well-known people showed interest in her claims, even Elizabeth Barrett Browning. Margaret claimed a common-law marriage to an Elisha Kane, an Arctic explorer. In 1888 she became a Roman Catholic confessing her spiritualism claims were false. She changed her claims again to make a living by holding seances. She died in obscurity.

FOX, MARGARET FELL (1614-1702), remembered for her leadership in the formation of the Society of Friends, as the wife of George Fox, its founder. A member of English nobility, she was married to Thomas Fell, a judge, when she was seventeen. They had a son and seven daughters. Judge Fell died in 1658. He never joined the Quaker movement, although George Fox had visited their home and was widely accepted. She and George Fox were married in 1669 and her estate, Swathmore Hall, became a center of Quaker activities. She was arrested several different times for holding Quaker meetings in her home. Her son turned against her because of her acceptance of Quakerism, but both Margaret and George Fox were devoted to each other and the cause of their movement. In her later years and even after she was widowed and in her eighties, she went to London to appeal to authorities concerning the sufferings and persecutions of the members of the Society of Friends or Quakers.

FREY, AMANDA (1890-1975), distinguished both as an educator and business woman. Her parents were Jacob C. and Mary Burkholder Frey of Ohio. She began teaching in 1908 before a college degree was a prerequisite. She attended seminars and later Goshen College and taught home economics and other subjects in the Elkhart, Indiana, area. Because of an automobile accident in 1933, she turned from teaching to merchandising. She opened a store in 1939, which she operated until retirement. During that time she was active in local church work and served in a national office for the Mennonite Womens Missionary Society.

FROMMAN, ERMA VALENTINE (1904-1976), a pioneer missionary in Central India, who opened the first mission field of the Conservative Baptist Foreign Mission Society. Born in Ohio, she went to Toccoa Falls Institute in Georgia, then to Nyack Missionary Institute, and took further training at the Booth Memorial Hospital in New York. Her work in Central India was directly with the tribes people, setting up Bible classes and later Sunday schools and churches. Even after her retirement she returned to India to serve in evangelism and church planting until her death.

FRY, ELIZABETH GURNEY (1780-1845), a Quaker minister noted for her pioneer work in prison reform, especially for women and children. Born to a wealthy family in Norwich, England, she accepted Christ when she was quite young. Her mother died when Elizabeth was twelve. When she was eighteen she heard a sermon by an American Quaker, William Savery, and rededicated her life to the Lord. Her special interest in improving the conditions of prisons that held women and children not only included physical improvement, but also that they be given opportunity to further their education by learning domestic skills as well as Bible study. In 1800 she married Joseph Fry, of a prominent, wealthy Quaker family. Ten years later she went into the Quaker ministry. In 1813, after eight of her eleven children were born, she revived her prison reform ideas, took on greater activity, and in 1816 spearheaded a movement forming the Association for the Improvement of Female Prisoners in Newgate. She also established a rescue mission in London, organized libraries for the military, and promoted the establishment of the Sisters of Devonshire Square, a school for training nurses. She was invited to Paris by the French government to visit their prisons and make recommendations. She went to Belgium, Holland, and Germany for the promotion of improved prison conditions. She also visited the Duchess of Kent and her daughter, Victoria, reminding them of prison needs.

FRYKENBERG, DORIS SKOGLUND (1909-1981), memorable pioneer missionary in India among the Telegu people. In 1943 she and her husband, Eric, were the first missionaries appointed by the Conservative Baptist Foreign Mission Society. She attended the Dudley Bible Institute and Bethel Seminary. After a long and outstanding missionary career, she had a special ministry of encouragement in visiting missionaries around the world.

FULLER, GRACE L. PAYTON (1886-1966), author, speaker, and affectionately remembered as "Honey." She assisted her husband, Charles E. Fuller, on the "Old Fashioned Revival Hour" radio broadcast. Born at Drain, Oregon, she was the only child of Daniel and Eliwa Kinney Payton. Her father was a physican. The family moved to Redlands, California, when she was five. It was at Redlands High School that she met her future husband. She attended Western College for Women in Oxford, Ohio, the University of Chicago, and the Cumnock School of Expression in Los Angeles. She was a vital part of the large and successful radio ministry beginning in 1937. The program was first heard on MBS and then CBS on more than one thousand stations in North America and several stations abroad. On each broadcast of the hour-long program, she was given five minutes to read excerpts from some 30,000 letters received weekly from listeners. When Dr. Fuller founded the Fuller Theological Seminary in Pasadena, she organized the Women's Auxiliary for the school, counseled student wives, and helped in endless ways. Her picture hangs alongside that of her husband's in the main reading room of the seminary. She wrote regularly for the monthly publication *Heart to Heart Talk*. Their one and only child, Daniel P. Fuller, continues the work of Fuller Seminary. She preceded her husband in death by only two years.

G

GARNETT, CHRISTINE MARGARET (1886-1972), author and missionary for forty-six years in Cuba under the Southern Baptist Home Mission Board. Born and reared in Georgia, she attended the Georgia State Normal School, then graduated from the Women's Missionary Union Training School in Louisville, Kentucky. Her missionary responsibilities included originating a training school for girls, organizing an orphanage, and establishing a home for the aged, in addition to a leadership position in the women's Missionary Union. She wrote the book *Through a Cuban Window* and took on other writing projects, including Sunday school lessons and vacation Bible school materials.

GARRETT, ELIZABETH CLARK (1805-1855), by providing the initial gift to begin the Garrett Biblical Institute, part of the Northwestern University at Evanston, Illinois, she helped to train Methodist ministers. She gave $250,000, at that time the largest amount given to Methodism by a woman. A native of New York state, she had Christian training as a youth and in spite of many difficulties, including the death of her husband and children, she wanted her money to be used to further Christian education.

GAUNT, ELIZABETH (c. 1649-1685), a Christian martyr falsely accused of protecting traitors. Little is known about this woman, except that she was the wife of William Gaunt, an Anabaptist. She was convicted of treason and burned alive because of her beliefs. She testified of her faith in Christ to the very last. William Penn was present when she was martyred and told of her courage.

GENEVIEVE (GENOVEFA) (c. 422-c. 500), is credited with twice saving Paris from destruction and famine, as she formed groups of women to pray for victory and help. One of those times was when Attila and his Huns invaded in 451. A native of Paris, she proposed building a church in honor of Peter and Paul. It was built by Clovis I and his wife Clotilda, a Christian. Genevieve was also known for her fasting as she prayed and made a habit of eating only two times a week, except as absolutely necessary, when she added fish and milk to her diet.

GEORGE, ELIZA DAVIS (1879-1979), an outstanding American missionary to Liberia, a teacher, school founder, and faithful servant. She was born in Texas as Eliza Loretta Davis. Her parents, Litt and Jane Burdick Davis, were former slaves and had been married before the Emancipation Proclamation. Brought up in a Christian home; her father was saved under the preaching of Ira Sankey. As a slave, her father was required to drive his master's wife to a Sankey meeting, and as he waited outside he would hear the preaching. He came under conviction and responded for salvation. Later he became a Baptist minister. At age twenty Eliza went to Guadalupe College and fulfilled the requirements for a teaching diploma, later completing work for a teacher's certificate at Central Texas College, where she served on the faculty for five years. It was during a chapel service at Central Texas College in 1911 that she felt called to be a missionary to Africa. Two years later she resigned her position and left for Liberia, sponsored by the Baptists. After she had spent two years in Africa, the National Baptists and Texas Convention split, and her direct support ended. She had established a school and continued her work by faith, later assisting a missionary couple to carry on the work while she pursued the Lord's direction in beginning a similar work in another area. In 1918 she married C. Thompson George, and together they established a successful program for training national pastors and missionaries. She was widowed in 1939 but continued her work, establishing more schools outside of Kelton. Most of the work she was directly responsible for originating included: the Baptist Industrial Academy, now a Liberian Baptist boarding school; the National Baptist Mission, which included ten churches; the Liberian Baptists in Sinoe, which is the Eliza Davis George Pastor's Training School with fifty churches assisted by Southern Baptists; the Elizabeth Native Interior Mission, which includes five primary schools, a high school, and a technical school; the Independent Churches of Africa consisting of one hundred churches. William Tubman, president of Liberia, and other distinguished people of that day honored Eliza George on her one-hundredth birthday.

GERTRUDE THE GREAT (1256-1302), a mystic and theologian of the Middle Ages and author of *The Herald of Divine Love*. Her book was not well known until it appeared in the vernacular in 1503. Later, a Carthusian monk made it available to the world. Although her early life is not well documented, we do know that she wrote in Latin, and there are other evidences that she was well educated. Her book changed the lives of many and left a legacy of challenge in stressing the mercy of God.

GILBERT, ANN TAYLOR (1782-1866), British hymnist born in London, daughter of Isaac Taylor and sister of Jane Taylor, also a hymnist and with whom some of her hymns are published jointly. In 1813 she married Joseph Gilbert of the faculty of Masborough. In addition to those hymns appearing in works with her sister, some of her work was included in a collection by Collyer in 1812, and approximately 100 of her hymns appeared in 1842 in *Original Hymns* and some in the *Nottingham Hymn Book*. She independently published *Hymns for Sunday School Anniversaries, Hymns for Infant Schools,* and *Wedding Among the Flowers* in 1827. A few of her hymns are: "When I Listen to Thy Word," "How Long, Sometimes a Day Appears," "Father, My Spirit Owns," "Hark the Sound of Joy and Gladness," "The God of Heaven Is Pleased to See," "Jesus, the Condescending King," and "Lord, Help Us as We Hear."

GLENORCHY, Lady WILHELMINA MAXWELL (1741-1786), grew up in Scotland and is remembered primarily for her faithful witness for Christ and benevolence in providing funds to train ministers. In 1774 she opened a chapel in Edinburgh referred to as Lady Glenorchy's Chapel. There it was that a Mr. Jones of Plymouth preached for more than fifty years.

GODOLPHIN, MARGARET BLAGGE (1652-1678), a reserved Christian witness among the elite of England. Her father was Colonel Thomas Blagge, and although she had friends among royalty, she took a definite Christian position. She married an English statesman and businessman, Lord Sidney Godolphin, but left society circles for a life of prayer and study. In 1678 she had a son, but she became ill and died soon afterward. Her husband survived her many years but did not remarry. The journal of Lady Godolphin reveals her spiritual depth in a position where such a Christian witness was difficult.

GOFORTH, FLORENCE ROSALIND BELL-SMITH (1864-1942), missionary, author, relief worker, and wife of missionary Jonathan Goforth. She was born in London but grew up in Canada. Her education was mainly as that of an artist, and she graduated from the Toronto School of Art. In 1887 she married Jonathan Goforth. They went to Honan, China, later opening a mission station at Changte where they worked until they were forced to move because of the Boxer Rebellion. When the Church Union Movement in Canada divided in 1925, the Goforths chose to remain with the Presbyterian Church of Canada. Thus, they left their mission in Honan and began a new work in Manchuria where they stayed for several years. They had eleven children, five of whom died as infants. She was awarded a medal by the Chinese government for her articles about famine in China, which promoted donations for relief work. Her husband preceded her in death by six years.

GOOD, MARY M. (1890-1982), faithful

but humble missionary educator who served more than thirty years in India under the Mennonite Board of Missions in Elkhart, Indiana. She graduated from Goshen College in 1919 and went to India the following year. She taught in a girls school, training her students in home life responsibilities and in teaching others. She was a mother figure for many young Indian women, and her Christian influence penetrated into the home life of many.

GORDON, ANNA (1835-c. 1926), author, served as vice-president of the Women's Christian Temperance Union in the United States and in the world WCTU as well. She first met Frances Willard, founder of the WCTU, at a D. L. Moody revival meeting in Boston in 1877. Miss Gordon received her formal education at Boston High School, Lasalle Seminary, and Mt. Holyoke College. Her writings include: *The Life of Frances Willard, What Frances Willard Said,* and *The White Ribbon Hymnal.*

GORLE, RUTH THOMAS (1899-1971), born in Rhodesia and served for more than thirty years with a college training program of the Seventh Day Adventist Church in the trans-Africa division.

GOVONA, ROSA (1716-1776), founder of the Rosines, a special ministry that helped needy single women. Born in Mondovi, Italy, she became an orphan while quite young and needed to support herself. She found a young girl in a worse condition, so she tried to help the girl help herself. So successful was this venture that she proceeded to find a suitable house and set up a place to offer such help and counsel. Charles EmmanuelIII saw the good that could come from such a project and gave her several large buildings that once belonged to the Friars. She organized the Rosines with branches in Novara, Fossano, Saluzzo, and elsewhere. Although a Christian element was involved, it was not a group that took vows, but a cooperative project that helped destitute women between thirteen and twenty years of age, who were healthy, active, and willing to work. Some of them sold their handiwork.

GRAFFAM, MARY LOUISE (1871-1922), a missionary educator and social worker in Turkey. A native of Maine, she graduated from Oberlin College in 1894 and went to Turkey in 1901 under the American Board of Commissioners for Foreign Missions. She taught mathematics and Bible, then became principal of the girls school in Sivas. She also did outreach visitation in the surrounding villages. In 1914 she went with Dr. Charles E. Clark to the Erzurum front as a nurse. She was able to take girls and teachers east to the Euphrates River and on into exile. Thus, she kept the Armenians safe in Sivas under the American flag while she aided others. She started a factory that employed at least 200 women to manufacture needed clothing for the Turkish army; leased farms; started grist mills, a foundry, shoe shop, and other shops. Her leadership skills were both unusual and outstanding. She was awarded the Decoration of the Red Crescent for her outstanding bravery in saving many people during the war. Miss Graffam died in Turkey of typhoid fever.

GRAHAM, ISABELLA (1742-1814), daughter of a Mr. and Mrs. John Marshall in Scotland. Information about her early childhood is obscure. In 1765 she married a surgeon of the British Army, Dr. John Graham. He was stationed at Fort Niagara, New York, and the family lived nearby. They later went to Antigua. After her husband's death in 1773, Isabella returned to Scotland with their children and taught primary school to support the family. Sixteen years later she returned to New York and organized a school and founded a group called The Society for the Relief of Poor Widows with Small Children, which later became the New York Orphan Asylum. She encouraged widows to open schools in various parts of the city to help the children, and she established two Sunday schools herself. Her daughter, Joanna, married a Mr. Bethune, and they worked together in establishing Sunday schools, Bible studies, and classes for illiterate adults. She wrote a book, *Life and Letters,* and the Tract Society distributed sketches of her life and work. Soon after the death of Isabella Graham, her daughter, Joanna Graham Bethune was instrumental in founding the American Sunday School Union, the first such organization in this country.

GRAHAM, MARY JANE (1803-1830), born in London. The details of her childhood are uncertain. She was well educated but went through a traumatic time of depression, even to the point of doubting her salvation. She returned to her Christian faith, realized that many others went through similar circumstances, and wrote to help them. One of her publications, *Test of Truth*, related her own experience in helping others who were discouraged. Her writings also included *The Freeness and Sovereignty of God's Grace*.

GRAHAM, MORROW COFFEY (1892-1981), an influential Christian and mother of American evangelist Billy Graham. She was reared in a Christian home; her father was disabled during the Civil War. She attended Elizabeth College in Charlotte, North Carolina. In 1916 she was married to William Franklin Graham, and they lived on a 300-acre farm, which he had inherited. William Franklin was their firstborn. Bible study and prayer were vital in the life of this great mother.

GRAMMER, KATHARINE ARNETT (1902-1980), a graduate of Goucher College with a masters degree in Christian education from Columbia University. She served as dean of women at the Philadelphia Divinity School. In 1945 she became dean of St. Margaret's House in Berkley, California, serving there for twenty-one years. She influenced many women of her denomination involved in Christian education and the ministry.

GREEN, HARRIET MARIA (c. 1839-1905), a pioneer missionary among the Kafirs of Africa; supported by the Episcopal church in Scotland. She went to the field with her husband in 1873, and their home became a center of missionary activity. Her missionary work spread over eighteen years.

GREENE, OLIVE (1883-1966), author and missionary educator born in Maine. She graduated from Wellesley College in 1906 and completed her M.A. degree at Radcliffe College in 1927. She also attended the Kennedy School of Missions and earned another master's degree in 1957 in addition to doctoral studies. After teaching at Wellesley briefly, she went to Smyrna (now Izmir), Turkey, where she taught and served in school administration. She founded the Turkish section of the American Collegiate Institute after the burning of Smyrna in 1922 and spent two years working with Armenian and Greek refugee students in Athens who were forced to leave Turkey. She experimented with methods of teaching English to Turks and devised a successful method. She wrote *Convention and Faith*, her philosophy of teaching, which was published posthumously in 1970. Her work was sponsored by the American Board of Commissioners for Foreign Missions.

GREGG, ALICE H. (1893-1978), a missionary to China for nearly thirty-five years. She received bachelor's, master's, and doctoral degrees from Columbia University. She supervised missionary schools of the Diocese of Anking and was a member of the faculty of St. John's University in Shanghai. In 1942 she received Columbia University's Medal of Excellence for exceptional professional service as a missionary. She was the author of two major works, *China and Educational Autonomy: The Changing Role of the Protestant Missionary in China, 1807-1937*, and *The Anking Pagoda*.

GREGG, JESSIE (1875-1942), faithful British missionary evangelist to the women of China. At the age of twenty-two she enrolled in the training school of the China Inland Mission and later in language school at Yangchow. She worked in the northern province of Hopeh in the city of Hwailu. The Boxer Rebellion forced Jessie and other missionaries to flee to inner China, sometimes having to hide in caves or secret places. Yet, the Boxers found them, shot one of the missionaries, and took Jessie and others to the Yamen prison, where they were beaten and tortured. It was reported that during the Boxer Rebellion, 117 Protestant missionaries were killed, approximately half of them serving with the China Inland Mission. Besides her teaching in a school in Hwochow after the Boxer Rebellion, much of Jessie's work was evangelistic, as she traveled to fifteen provinces and had well over five thousand accept Christ as Savior. Her life demonstrated one miracle after another as the Lord used her to reach many Chinese for Him.

GREY, Lady JANE (1537-1555), England's nine-day Christian queen was martyred for her faith. She was the oldest daughter of Henry Grey, third Marquis of Dorset, by his second wife, Frances Brandon. Her mother was the daughter of Charles Brandon and Mary, youngest sister of Henry VII and widow of Louis XII of France. Because of the original will of Henry VIII, she was fourth in line of succession to the throne. Jane was an excellent student and became proficient in Latin, Greek, French, and Italian. She corresponded with Bullinger about studying Hebrew. Her Protestant convictions were received mostly from her reading and the teachings of her tutor, Alymer. When the palace chaplain, a Protestant, turned Catholic with the accession of Mary, Jane sent him a letter of harsh reprimand. Her testimony was well known as was her scholarship. She married Guliford, who wanted her to declare him king, but she refused. However, at the death of Edward, who had succeeded his brother, Henry VIII, Mary and Elizabeth were declared legal heirs and the succession of Lady Jane Grey was changed. Even many of the Protestants were in favor of Mary as she had been somewhat protective of them. However, when Mary was declared queen after the nine days of rulership by Jane, Mary deceived the Protestant cause. Immediately Mary had Jane, her husband, and her parents all put in prison in the tower. Later Jane's parents were released, but Jane and her husband were martyred. It is recorded that even on the scaffold, at the age of eighteen, her Christian testimony was outstanding and moved many to tears.

GRIFFITHS, ANN THOMAS (1776-1805), hymnist from Wales and wife of John Griffiths of Meifod. In 1797 she became a Christian and joined the Methodist group at Pontrobert. She married in 1804 but died the following year after giving birth to a child. Hymns composed by her were shared with her servant girl, Ruth Evans, who married John Hughes, a Methodist minister. The hymns of Ann Thomas Griffiths were published posthumously and reflected literary strength, biblical allusions, and a kind of Christ-centered mysticism.

GRIJALVA, DOROTHY CLINKENBEARD (1920-1970), missionary, author, teacher among the Spanish-speaking people of Texas and Colorado, serving under the Home Mission Board of the Southern Baptist Convention. A native of Missouri, she attended Jefferson City Junior College and graduated from William Jewell College in Liberty, Missouri. With her graduate studies at the Women's Missionary Union Training School in Louisville, Kentucky, she earned an M.R.E. degree. She served in several church leadership capacities and taught English at the Mexican Bible Institute, which trained Spanish-speaking ministers and missionaries. She married in 1947, and for a time her husband served as dean of the Mexican Bible Institute. She and her husband wrote *Heirs of the Soil*, published in 1950 by the Home Mission Board as the year's mission study book for young people. She served on the board of trustees for the Mexican Baptist Children's Home in Texas and was an active church leader.

GRIMKE, EMILY (1805-1879), a Quaker abolitionist and sister of Sarah Moore Angelina Grimke, also a Quaker abolitionist. They worked together in freeing families of slaves, and became Quakers in 1823 after moving to Philadelphia.

GRIMKE, SARAH MOORE ANGELINA (1792-1873), author, Quaker, and active abolitionist. She was born in Charleston, South Carolina. She and her sister freed their family slaves after the death of their father. They moved to Philadelphia, joined the Quakers in 1823, and worked to free all slaves. She wrote *Epistle to the Clergy of the Southern States* and *Letters of the Equality of the Sexes and the Condition of Women.*

GRUEN, OLIVE (1883-1963), a missionary and teacher in China under the Lutheran church, Missouri Synod. A native of St. Louis, Missouri, she attended the St. Louis Extension College, Moody Bible Institute, and received an M.A. degree from Valparaiso University. She taught several years at Madison School, St. Louis, and in 1922 went to Shihnanfu Hupeh, China, and later to Hankow. In 1927 she was sent to Shanghai because of war conditions. In 1937 she again went to China and later had to evacuate to India, but returned in 1945. Later she also served in Taiwan. She pioneered the Lutheran work in Taiwan after the Communist takeover in China.

GUÉRIN, ANNE THERESE (1798-1856), born in St. Briuc, Brittany, and in 1822 joined the Sisters of Providence. Although she studied medicine, her chief ministry was among poor children, teaching and counseling them as needed. In 1840 she founded a branch of the Sisters of Providence in America in St. Mary's of the Woods in Vigo County, Indiana. Her work among children is especially remembered.

GUERIN, EUGÉNIE DE (1800-1848), a French lady remembered as an author, especially for her *Journal*, a biography of her brother, Maurice. Her *Journal and Letters* is composed of two 400-page volumes. Her writings were such a spiritual blessing to others that they went through many printings in French and later were translated into English.

GUILDING, CLARA WIGHT (1886-1974), a Canadian-born translator, teacher, and missionary with the African Inland Mission. She served in Kenya and worked at Machakos among the Akamba. She was on the language committee and helped to write the Kamba Bible translation while also operating a bookshop and translating Kamba textbooks. Her work in Sunday school and Bible studies for women also left a lasting testimony of Christian influence. The Mau Mau uprising forced a change in her plans, and she and her husband retired in the United States.

GURNEY, DOROTHY FRANCES (1858-1932), a poet and hymnist, daughter of Frederick G. Blomfield. She wrote two volumes of verse and a devotional work, *A Little Book of Quiet*. The hymn for which she is most remembered is "O Perfect Love, All Human Thought Transcending," considered by some to be the finest and most impressive wedding hymn ever written.

GUYARD, MARIE (1599-1672), author and pioneer Roman Catholic missionary in Quebec, Canada. She was born in Tours, France, and while quite young decided to become a nun. Her parents objected, insisting that she marry, which she did. After four years of marriage, she was widowed with a son. In 1631 she entered the Ursuline Convent in Tours. After eight years her archbishop requested that she go to Quebec with two other nuns to establish a Catholic community for women. This she did and became the first superior of this Jesuit mission community. The work of that mission was educational and social directly with native Indians and French immigrants. In France and later in Canada she reported having visions. She was requested to record these, which she did in the form of letters. They were published in several French editions. Pope Pius X officially recognized her in 1911.

GUYON, JEANNE MARIE BOUVIER de la MOTTE (1648-1717), a French mystic known for her writings and for introducing *quietism* to France. Born in Montargis near Orleans, her early schooling took place in convents. Her mother arranged for Jeanne to marry a disabled man much older than Jeanne. After twelve years of marriage, she was left a widow with three small children. She declared that she would not marry again and devoted her life to spiritual meditation, study, and writing. She was much influenced by the writings of Molinos and Lacombe. She claimed to have visions and wrote about them and her contact with the spirit world. She went about speaking and organizing groups, met with much opposition by the Roman Catholics, and was condemned. Several times she was put in prison because of her teaching; her last imprisonment in the Bastille in Paris lasted for four years. While in prison she wrote some forty books and several hundred hymns. Her best known hymn is probably "O Lord, How Full of Sweet Content," written 1681 and translated from French by William Cowper. Several volumes of her books were said to have been commentaries on the Bible, yet John Wesley criticized her for not being guided by the Scriptures.

GWINN, ALICE E. (1896-1969), a missionary educator who served in Japan under the American Board of Commissioners for Foreign Service and later the United Church Board for World Ministries. A native of Nebraska, she graduated from the University of Washington with both B.A. and M.A. degrees. She attended the Kennedy School of Missions, the Hartford School of Religious Education, and Union Theological Seminary. After she went to Japan in the early 1920s, she first taught in Tokyo, then at Doshisha University in Kyoto (1924-33), from which she was the first woman to receive an honorary doctorate. She taught one year at Anatolia College at Thessalonika, Greece, and in 1942-45 she returned home to teach Japanese Americans at a relocation center in Idaho. She wrote a number of books and articles on Christian faith that were published in Japanese. The first institution for handicapped children built in Kobe, Japan, was named Gwinn Home in honor of her, and she was awarded Japan's Fifth Order of Merit posthumously.

H

HABERSHON, ADA R. (1861-1918), author, teacher, and Bible scholar. She was the daughter of a gifted London minister and was taught the Bible from early childhood. She wrote pamphlets and books and is probably best remembered for three books: *The Study of Types*, *The Study of Parables*, and *The Study of Miracles*, the latter coming out with an American edition in 1957.

HALE, MARY WHITWELL (1810-1862), hymnist and poet with several pieces, including the *Cheshire Collection*, published in 1844. A native of Boston, her education was better than usual and she contributed to the *Christian Register* periodical but signed her articles with only the initials YLE, the final letters of her first, middle, and last names.

HALE, SARAH JOSEPHA BUELL (1795-1879), author, editor, hymnist, a native of New Hampshire. In 1822 she married David Hale, an attorney. She became editor of *The Ladies' Magazine* and later *Godey's Ladies' Book*. Her most-remembered hymn was based on the Lord's Prayer and appeared in 1831 in the *Church Psalmody*. Her denomination affiliation was Protestant Episcopal.

HAMER, LILIAN (1912-1959), English nurse and devoted missionary with the China Inland Mission to Southeast Asia. After completing requirements for nursing, she attended Redcliff Missionary Training College and completed Bible and other requirements. Although she felt the Lord wanted her to become a missionary to China, World War II conditions delayed her going except with the British Red Cross. After her original assignment she was transferred to a Canadian hospital in the province of Szechwan, which included the wartime capital of Chungking. It was here that the emergency headquarters of the China Inland Mission was established. As soon as she fulfilled her contract with the Red Cross she became part of the China Inland Mission and worked in a hospital in Tali near the Burma border. Because of the war, even the hospital at Tali had to be turned over to the Chinese authorities. She then spent time in northern Thailand. Later she went to Tsaba to live and work among the tribe there and had to live alone for most of the time. In northern Thailand she was killed as she went about her work. Some of the tribespeople were concerned that she was taking advantage of them and did not want her help and influence.

HANAFORD, PHOEBE ANN COFFIN (1829-1921), considered to be the first ordained woman minister in New England. She served largely in Universalist churches and withstood much criticism. Born in Nantucket, she ministered in Hingham and Walthan, Massachusetts, New Haven, Connecticut, and Jersey City, New Jersey. She also did some writing.

HANKE, SARAH EMMA CATHERINE HARER (1897-1959), born and raised in Houston County, Brownsville, Minnesota. She completed a teacher education course at the Normal School in La Crosse, Minnesota, and taught several years in that state. She married Ernest Hanke, an agriculturalist. As a wife, and mother of seven children, she maintained an active life in the ministry of the Evangelical and Reformed church, serving in several elected offices and teaching in the Sunday school. She also worked for the Salvation Army; served four years as president of the Tri-State Women's Guild; organized the Northern Synod Women's Guild, serving as vice-president for four years. She became the only woman lay delegate to the General Synod at Lancaster, Pennsylvania, in 1956, when the Congregational and Evangelical Reformed churches merged to form the First United Church of Christ. Not only was Mrs. Hanke an example of a dedicated Christian in her church life, but she served in several offices and leadership positions in the Farm Bureau; did extension work for 4-H Clubs; worked with the PTA; served on the County Nurse Advisory Board as president for eight years. In 1928 she was honored with the "Master Farm Homemaker" award by the Webb Publishing Company of St. Paul, Minnesota. Mrs. Hanke left a legacy of practical Christian application and stewardship.

HANKEY, KATHERINE (1834-1911), wrote many hymnals in English. Two familiar hymns by Katherine Hankey are "I Love to Tell the Story" and "Tell Me the Old, Old Story." Although sometimes classified as hymns for children, both have become popular with adults. In 1866 she wrote a poem of fifty stanzas about the life of Jesus. While recovering from a serious illness she wrote the section we know as "Tell Me the Old, Old Story," which was set to music by William H. Doane and translated into German, Spanish, Welsh, Italian, and other languages. Her hymns became known to an even wider circle when Major General Russel read the lines of "Tell Me the Old, Old Story" at an International Convention of the YMCA in Montreal in 1867. These were first published in 1872 as part of a book, *Music for Camp Meetings*. Miss Hankey was remembered as well for her missionary interests, which were broadened when she accompanied an invalid brother to South Africa. She sponsored Bible classes for many women in London, including those who worked in shops.

HARKNESS, GEORGIA ELMA (1891-1974), a native of New York state, she received a B.A. degree from Cornell University and in 1923 a Ph.D. degree from Boston University. After teaching in high school, she became a professor of religious education at Elmira College for Women, then a professor of history and literature at Mt. Holyoke College, and later at Garrett Seminary and the Pacific School of Religion. She was the first woman named to a theological professorship. She officially retired from teaching in 1961 but continued to write, lecture, and actively pursue theological studies. Although she declined ordination, she advocated equal clerical status for women in church work and was honored in 1947 as one of the ten most influential living Methodists. She participated six times as a delegate to the general conference of the United Methodist church and twice as a delegate to the World Council of Churches. Dr. Harkness wrote thirty-six books, was awarded several honorary doctorates, and won the award of the Hymn Society of America for the best hymn written on the theme of the 1954 World Council of Churches convention, which was "Christ, the Hope of the World." Her hymn was titled "Hope of the World, Thou Christ of Great Compassion."

HARLEY, BRILLIANA CONWAY (1600-c. 1644), a distinguished Christian with a steadfast testimony in high places. The second daughter of Sir Edward Conway, she was born in Holland, probably near Brill from which her name is derived. Her father was lieutenant-governor in that area. While she was still young, her family moved to England. Her home life reflected Calvinistic doctrine and her ideas evidenced such. Her early education was private, but her life reflected Puritan strictness and regular church attendance. She was much impressed by reading John Foxe's *Book of Martyrs* and the biography of Martin Luther. In 1623 she became the third wife of Sir Robert Harley, the first Earl of Oxford, who headed the Torey ministry in 1710 and was later elected to Parliament. At one time he was Chancellor of the Exchequer and considered one of the most influential men in England. Her letters to their children demonstrate her Christian experience. John Ley, Vicar of Great Budworth, dedicated a book on the Life of Mrs. Jane Ratcliffe to Lady Brilliana Harley in 1640. Later, when she was threatened because of her testimony, she refused to surrender Brampton Castle, explaining that it was an honor to suffer for the cause of Christ.

HARPER, FRANCES ELLEN WATKINS (1825-1911), teacher, poet, pioneer worker with American blacks. Born to free black parents, she was orphaned young and reared by relatives. In 1845 her first poems were published. She went to school, then taught at Columbus, Ohio, and Little York, Pennsylvania. Between 1860 and 1865 she lectured in many states; her home in Philadelphia became a refuge for slaves. In 1860 she married Fenton Harper but was widowed after only four years. She was especially sympathetic with black women in the South who had not been given basic education. She helped to organize a Sunday school and assisted with programs of the African Methodist Church. She later became involved with the Women's Christian Temperance Union.

HARRISON, ALDA B. HAWORTH (1877-1959), a pioneer in the field of youth communications. Although the wife of a distinguished Presbyterian minister, she began a magazine for Pentecostal believers. In 1929 she started *Lighted Pathway,* which was made the official youth magazine for the Church of God in 1937 and today has a circulation of 26,000.

HARTZLER, SADIE (1896-1972), memorable educator and librarian who influenced many young people for the Lord. She served for thirty-six years at the Eastern Mennonite College.

HAVERGAL, FRANCES RIDLEY (1836-1879), a devout Christian writer, musician, and hymnist of unusual talent. She was born in Worcestershire, England, where her father, William H. Havergal, was rector. Her middle name was after Nicholas Ridley, a prominent bishop martyred at Oxford in 1555. Because she was frail in health, her education was at home and in private schools. She attended a school in Worcester and later one in Dusseldorf, Germany, and mastered several languages including Latin, Hebrew, and Greek. She began writing poetry at an early age and had several pieces published in Christian periodicals, including one called "Good Words." She committed her life to Christ at age fourteen and lived an unusually disciplined prayer life. Her father was an accomplished pianist and wrote the music for some of her hymns and chants in addition to other music. One of her best-loved hymns, "I Gave My Life for Thee," was written when she was eighteen, just prior to an extended illness during which she did little or no writing for nine years. One of the most popular of her writings is a consecration hymn written in 1874, "Take My Life and Let It Be." Some hymnals today include her "Like a River Glorious," "Who Is on the Lord's Side," and "I Am Trusting Thee, Lord Jesus." She had a volume of poetry published in 1884, *Poetical Works*. Her prose writings include *Kept for the Master's Use* and *Royal Commandments and Royal Bounty*. After the death of her father in 1870 she published *The Ministry of Song*. Although she and Fanny Crosby were contemporaries and corresponded, they did not meet. Frances Havergal died in Caswell Bay, South Wales. A memorial fund was initiated to assist in publishing and circulating her work and for support for some of the Bible women in India.

HAVILAND, LAURA SMITH (1808-1898), born of Quaker parents in Ontario, Canada, her family moved to New York state when she was quite young. Her education was largely at home. She married a Quaker gentleman, and they moved to Michigan. Especially significant was her leadership in organizing assistance for slaves escaping from the South. In 1841 she experienced a spiritual awakening and became affiliated with the Wolf Creek Wesleyan Methodist Church. She taught her own children and many of the children in the neighborhood, primarily orphans, which led to the founding of the Raisin Institute for orphans in 1836. Later it was taken over by the state of Michigan. In spite of the death of her husband and several other members of her family, she became active in the Underground Railroad movement, and when the Civil War began, she obtained permission to go to Mississippi and minister to wounded soldiers and former slaves. Through her efforts, military hospitals offered better conditions and better treatment for the patients. She helped to found an educational institution for refugees and went to Washington in 1883 to secure financial support from Congress for her efforts to help blacks. She gave spiritual courage to many, and her labors led to the naming of Haviland, Kansas, in her honor. Eleven years after her death, a life-sized statue of her was erected in front of the city hall at Adrian, Michigan, one of the few such commemorations for a woman in our country at that time.

HAWKS, ANNIE SHERWOOD (1835-1918), a native of New York state, she began writing poetry while quite young, some of which was published in newspapers. Later she was urged to write hymns. Of her several hymns, she is remembered for "I Need Thee Every Hour," for which her pastor, Robert Lowery, wrote the tune and words of the refrain. It has become such a favorite that it has been translated into several languages. A Baptist by conviction, she was a recognized hymnist by other denominations.

HAYASHI, UTAKO (c. 1850-c. 1937), outstanding Christian educator and leader in her native Japan. She taught at the Episcopal school for girls in Tokyo; later founded the Osaka branch of the Womens Christian Temperance Union; and established the Osaka WCTU Woman's Home. She visited the United States to observe charitable institutions and was influential in improving conditions for women in Japan. In 1920 she was given a government citation for her work.

HAYES, LUCY WEBB (1831-1889), a faithful Christian first lady and wife of the nineteenth president of the United States, Rutherford B. Hayes. Her father was a physician in Chillicothe, Ohio. She had the prestige of being the first president's wife with a college education, having graduated with honors from the Wesleyan Female College in Cincinnati in 1852. She was married in December 1852 and became active in the Methodist church of their hometown, Fremont, Ohio. While the Civil War raged and her husband was directly involved with it, she assisted in army hospitals and did what she could to relieve the suffering, including helping slaves. Twice she was first lady of Ohio before reaching the White House. Her family life was consistently Christian, including daily family devotions, Sunday evening hymn sings, and prayer services. She was especially firm in her conviction of abstinence. Neither wine nor alcoholic beverages were served in the White House or wherever their home was. Her personal life was plain and in many ways provided an example of Christian family life. They had three sons who died in childhood, but five lived to grow up, two of which lived in the White House. The portrait of Mrs. Hayes that hangs in the White House was presented by the Women's Christian Temperance Union. She served as president of the Women's Home Missionary Society of the Methodist Episcopal Church for nine years. The school for training deaconesses in Washington, D.C., is named the Lucy Webb Hayes Training School for Deaconesses. She preceded her husband in death by only four years, just eight years after they left the White House.

HAYGOOD, LAURA ASKEW (1845-1900), evangelist, missionary, teacher, and school administrator. She graduated from the Wesleyan Female College in Macon, Georgia, in 1894. She helped organize a number of Sunday schools and in 1884 went to China as a missionary. She was forced to return home for war reasons. In 1896 she returned to China as director of all work of the church's women's board of evangelism. There she saw the need for training women and she founded two training schools for Bible women at Soochow and Sungkiang. This became known as the Laura A. Haygood Home and School at Soochow.

HAYN, HENRIETTA LUISE von (1724-1782), a gifted hymnist and daughter of George Heinrich von Hayn. Born in Nassu and educated in a Moravian community at Herrnhaag, Germany, she taught in a school for girls. She wrote over forty hymns or portions of hymns. One was used outside the Moravian hymnbooks. It was a beautiful hymn for children, "Weil ich Jesu Schaflein bin."

HEATWOLE, LYDIA (1887-1932), founder of the Mennonite nurses training program, especially for missionaries.

Her parents were Reuben J. and Margaret Kilmer Heatwole. She attended the nurses training school at LaJunta, Colorado, in addition to doing special work in a tuberculosis sanitarium. Later she returned to LaJunta as administrator of that training program. She helped to make nursing a ministry rather than a duty.

HECK, BARBARA RUCKLE (1734-1804), she is credited with founding the first Methodist church in America. Born in Ireland of German refugee parents, she was influenced by the preaching of Wesley. In 1760 she married Paul Heck, and they came to the American colonies, settling in the New York area. She encouraged her cousin, Philip Embury, a minister, to hold the first Methodist meeting in his home in 1766. This meeting resulted in a congregation that became the John Street Methodist Church in New York. During the American Revolution she and her family were forced to move to Canada because of their Tory views. She was influential in organizing Methodist societies in addition to starting another Methodist church in Canada.

HECK, FANNIE EXILE SCUDDER (1862-1915), a native of Virginia and a long-time leader in the Women's Missionary Union of North Carolina. She was one of the founders of the Women's Missionary Training School of the Southern Baptist Convention. In her early years she attended the Hobgood Seminary and Hollins Institute (now College) and was active in the local Baptist church, teaching, and working in many ways. She wrote the hymn "Come Women, Wide Proclaim" and numerous tracts and articles. Carver School of Missions and Social Work named their chapel the Fannie E. S. Heck Memorial Chapel. It is of interest that she took the name "Exile" in memory of her birthplace, where her mother had sought refuge from the Civil War. In later years Fannie added the name Scudder in honor of her great-grandmother.

HEDRICK, LAURA GOSSNICKLE (1858-1934), a native of Maryland. She taught, spoke to church gatherings, and in 1891 became one of the first women ordained in the Ohio Brethren Church Conference. She served in several churches and was active in promoting a Sister Society of Christian Endeavor, becoming its second national president. She organized several groups within this society and wrote for the *Brethren Evangelist* paper.

HEDWIG (c. 1174-1243), patron saint of Poland, daughter of Agnes and Berthold, Duke of Carinthia. Information of her early childhood is obscure, but she is believed to have been educated in a convent. At the age of twelve, she married Henry, Duke of Silesia. She is credited with originating the Cistercian convent at Trebnitz near Breslau, and helped to build several others. After the death of her husband she entered a convent, although she did not take vows.

HEDWIG, ELEANORA von HAARTMAN (1860-1902) This evangelist and leader was a native of Finland, serving there, in Germany, and Switzerland with the Salvation Army. Born of a noble family, she was instrumental in the establishment of the first Salvation Army work in Finland. She attended the International Training Garrison in London and returned to Finland for a full-time ministry. In 1902 as she was on her way to a German-Swiss province, when at Hamburg, Germany, she became ill and died. She left a legacy of spiritual enlightenment.

HELENA (c. 250-c. 330), mother of Constantine. She was born at Drepanum in Bithynia, Asia Minor. Details of her early life are obscure, but records show that she was converted to Christianity in 313. She married Constantius Chlorus, who later divorced her for political reasons. After Constantine came into power, he recalled his mother to court in 306 and honored her, including giving her the title of Augusta. Her Christian influence was very evident in her son, the first Christian emperor of Rome. She visited the Holy Land in her later years, and today her name is associated with the discovery of the Holy Sepulcher and the

Church of the Nativity. The authenticity of their discovery was never proved and are believed to be tradition.

HELOISE (c. 1098-1164), a learned French woman, niece of Canon Fulbert of Notre Dame in Paris. She and her tutor, the famous theologian-philosopher Peter Abelard, were married secretly. She had a son by him, but her uncle, outraged by all this, had Abelard tortured and disgraced. Heloise entered the Convent of St. Argenteuil. Nevertheless, she and Abelard continued to exchange correspondence. In 1129 she became superior of the Convent at the Paraclete. Abelard spent his final days in a monastery of Cluny, but when Heloise died some twenty-two years after Abelard, she was buried beside him.

HENRY, KATHARINE (1629-1707), wife of Philip Henry and mother of Matthew Henry, well-known biblical expositor and author. Born in Broad Oak, England, she was the daughter of a wealthy family. She apparently became a Christian under the preaching of Richard Steel. She had six children, and all but one son, John, lived to adulthood. Matthew was their second son and was born in 1662. She taught the children well, and their home was a godly one. She was widowed in 1696, and several other family members died of a malignant fever. Matthew took his mother and several of the family into his home. Katharine lived almost eleven years as a widow and did what she could to help Matthew with his exposition of the Pentateuch, which was published the year before she died.

HERSHEY, MAE ELIZABETH HERTZLER (1877-1974), pioneer of Christian education and a missionary to Argentina. She served with her husband in language work, first in Buenos Aires and later in Pehuago. She assisted in establishing primary schools, a training program for Sunday school teachers, and other work for Mennonite women in Argentina.

HEUSSER, META SCHWEIZER (1797-1876), German author and hymnist. Details of her childhood are obscure; in 1821 she married a physician. Her poems grew in popularity and some were developed into hymns. Two volumes published; the first in 1857 and the second in 1862. Some of her songs selected to be translated into English are included in *Hymns from the Land of Luther* and *Christ in Song*.

HEWITT, ELIZA EDMUNDS (1851-1920), American poet and hymnist. She graduated from a teachers college and taught in the Philadelphia area. She was active in her church and served as its Sunday school superintendent. Some of her hymns that have become favorites are: "More About Jesus Would I Know," "Sing the Wondrous Love of Jesus," and "There Is Sunshine in My Soul Today."

HIEBERT, MARY J. REGIER (1884-1970), Christian educator, counselor, and faithful steward. She was born in Boone County, Nebraska, of the Johann J. Regier family, who had come to America from the Molotschna Mennonite Colony in Russia just five years prior. Mary attended public school in Nebraska and the school of the Mennonite Brethren church. In 1895 she went with her parents to Russia to visit relatives and in the village of Rueckenau and completed the first and second grades in German and Russian. In 1906 she enrolled in a Bible Institute at Fort Wayne, Indiana, and later transferred to Tabor College in Hillsboro, Kansas. She taught several years and attended the Bible Institute of Los Angeles (later named Biola University). In 1918 Tabor College experienced a fire that destroyed much of the main building. Mary sold some land she had inherited and gave $15,000 as an annuity to build a women's dormitory at Tabor College. She became the first matron in that dormitory and spent the next twenty years in that important staff position. In 1940 she moved to Emporia, Kansas, and there was able to establish a home for girls attending the state teachers college. In 1961, nearly seventy-seven years old, she married a widower, J. J. Hiebert, whom she had known for a long time. They lived in California, but in 1966 he died suddenly and she returned to Kansas. Her life influenced many others for the Lord, especially young people.

HILDA (614-680), founder of the Whitby Abbey at Streanshalch in Yorkshire, England, where she was the abbess for twenty-two years. Born in Northumbria, she became a Christian through the preaching of Paulinus in 627. In that same year Edwin, King of Northumbria, was converted as well. She served the Lord for a number of years before deciding to enter a convent. She planned to enter a convent in France but received a request from Aidan in 649 asking her to be the abbess of a convent at Hartlepool. Just ten years later she founded the Abbey at Streanshalch, which became well known for its academic program. Several well-known theologians, bishops, and authors went there, including Caedmon, an early English poet.

HILDEGARD (1098-1179), a German Benedictine nun; author, and hymnist founder of a covenant. She was in born in Bökelheim and schooled in a Benedictine convent where she became an abbess. Later she moved to Rupertsberg where she founded another Benedictine convent about 1150, and yet another at Eibingen. She is said to have written at least three books, of which the best known is *Know the Ways of the Lord.* She spent nine years writing it. She is credited with sixty-three hymns. Regarding philosophy, she is described as a mystic. She recorded some twenty-six mystical revelations between 1141 and 1150, which were published by the title *Scivas.* Bernard of Clairvaux became a friend of hers.

HILL, GRACE LIVINGSTON (1865-1947), author. Few authors of light Christian novels have had more influence in young lives over several generations than Grace Livingston Hill. Her books have universal appeal and have been reprinted many times. She was born in New York state and was the daughter of a Presbyterian minister. She was especially interested in art and studied at the Cincinnati Art School and later at Elmira Collage. She enjoyed the company of an aunt who was an author. As a child she enjoyed writing and later contributed occasionally to the *Christian Endeavor* publication. In 1892 she married Frank Hill, a Presbyterian minister who pastored the Wakefield Church in Germantown, Pennsylvania. Two daughters were born to them. In 1899 her husband was stricken with an acute attack of appendicitis and died suddenly. Left with two very young children and the need to earn a living, she returned to her interest of writing. She wrote about one hundred novels in addition to articles and short stories. She was active in church work and was especially interested in missions.

HINDERER, ANNA MARTIN (1827-1870), an influential Church of England missionary to Africa. She was born in Hemphall, Norfolk; orphaned young and lived with her grandfather; then worked for a vicar. In 1852 she was married to a German missionary serving under the Church of England in Africa. Soon after they were married they went to Africa, where she had a ministry with African children. Later they were sent to Ibadan. The nationals resisted interference from white people and the motives for their presence. Anna died in the ensuing bloodshed.

HINZ, HANSINA CHRISTINA FOGDAL (c. 1803-1896), a missionary to Greenland. She was born of a German family in Schleswig. She worked briefly at the Sister's House at Christiansfelt but returned home. A letter arrived from Moravian missionaries asking her to serve on the foreign mission field of Greenland. The significance of such a request was that customarily such Moravian missionaries selected wives to be missionaries. The missionaries who wrote the letter indicated that a fellow worker there needed a wife, and they believed that Hansina would be a good match for him. Both had come from similar backgrounds and attended their mission college. Hansina counseled with her family and Christian friends, felt the call was clear and decided to go. In 1895 she sailed for Greenland to meet her future husband. After a difficult voyage, she met him and they were married as servants of the Lord. Their mission station was

Lichtenau. Her life in the climate of Greenland was short-lived, for the following year she died, only eight days after the birth of a daughter. Complications caused the baby to die as well.

HOBART, Lady (1603-1664), a British Christian of some wealth who gave liberally for Christian causes and to needy people to the extent that after the death of her husband, Sir John Hobart of Norfolk, she deprived herself of her own needs to help others. She believed that all that she had was really not her own, but rather belonged to those in need. Her generosity furthered the cause of spreading the gospel.

HOLECEK, RUTH STEVENS (1921-1968), an outstanding missionary to Japan under the Conservative Baptist Foreign Mission Society. She was a native of Canada and received her education at Northwestern Bible School in Minnesota. Appointed in 1946, she had an unusual ability to adapt to Japanese culture and was especially skilled in reaching the Japanese with the gospel.

HOOTEN, ELIZABETH (1598-1672), considered the first woman minister of the Quakers. She was converted to Quakerism under the preaching of George Fox in Nottingham, England, in 1647. Her husband was Oliver Hooten, who was of a Baptist group that had already divided before Fox came. After the death of her husband, Elizabeth went to Boston but was imprisoned for her preaching. She also went to Rhode Island and later sailed to a Quaker settlement at in West Indies. She returned to Boston in 1622 and was arrested again for preaching. At Cambridge she was tied to a whipping post and whipped with a three-stringed whip, which had three knots at each end. She was also whipped at Watertown and Dedham. She returned to England and traveled, preaching and working for the relief of Quaker prisoners.

HOPKINS, EMMA CURTIS (1853-1925), a journalist and one-time editor of the *Christian Science Journal*. She had studied at Woodstock Academy in Connecticut and later taught there. In 1883 she moved to Boston and enrolled in the Christian Science course of Mary Baker Eddy. However, she and Mrs. Eddy disagreed on many points, especially concerning Emma's consultation with other sources than Mrs. Eddy's writings. Considerable publicity resulted over their split, and Mrs. Hopkins moved to Chicago in 1886, establishing the Christian Science Theological Seminary. She served as president and main writer for the *Christian Metaphysician* magazine, which gained a wide following. Mrs. Eddy denounced Emma Hopkins's teachings and created considerable controversy.

HOPPE, ANNA BERNARDINE (c. 1882-1941), a translator and hymnwriter who began to write verse at an early age. She was the daughter of German immigrants and translated a large number of German hymns and at least one Norwegian hymn into English. Her hymns are included in a number of hymnals, and twenty-three of them are in the 1925 edition of *The Hymnal* of the Augustana Lutheran Church. Anna Hoppe may be best remembered for writing "The Sower Goeth Forth to Sow," "Jesus, O Precious Name," and an epiphany hymn, "Desire of Every Nation."

HORTON, ROSE (1883-1972), a native of Pennsylvania. She attended Moody Bible Institute and served on the mission field of Africa for many years under the African Inland Mission. She was known especially for her translation work as part of the Kikamba Language Committee. She also worked with African leaders in translating the Kikamba Bible and other books and Bible school materials.

HOURANI, ALMAZ (c. 1860-c. 1925), an unusual Syrian educator and translator born of Christian parents in a mountain village. She did so well in the mission school that she was selected to attend Sidon Seminary. She graduated with honors and became a teacher in that seminary. She taught there for forty-seven years and at the American School for Girls in Beirut. Her teaching field was Arabic grammar, and she assisted in the preparation of numerous Arabic books. Her Christian life was an example, and her testimony was heard in North and South America, England, and Egypt.

HOWE, JULIA WARD (1817-1910), a native of New York state, who wrote for leading magazines when only seventeen and is best remembered for her "Battle Hymn of the Republic." The meaningful words that Julia Ward Howe put to a traditional melody were sung by the Union soldiers during the Civil War. It is said that she scribbled the words on a scrap of paper after visiting a Union Army camp on the Potomac River in 1861. This familiar hymn is included in many hymnals today. In 1843 she married Dr. Samuel Gridley Howe, director of the Perkins Institute, Massachusetts State School for the Blind. She wrote three volumes of verse: *Passion Flowers* (1854), *Words of the Hour* (1856), and *Later Lyrics* (1866).

HROSWITHA (935-1002), a German author of nobility and distinction writing, prose, drama, and a poem about the book of Revelation. She received her education in a Benedictine convent, Gandersheim. She was considered to be the first woman poet and playwright of Germany. Many of her writings deal with Christians who meet temptation but are victorious in their faith. Her writings reflect high intellectual and spiritual insight. Her work was in Latin, but some of it was translated into English and German. She expressed the fear that her talent would overshadow her desire for Christlike humility.

HSIEH, WAN YING, a dedicated Chinese Christian author and teacher. She was the daughter of an admiral in the Chinese navy. She was well educated, first attending Bridgman Academy; next Yenching University, where she received her B.A. degree; and then took graduate studies in America at Wellesley College for her master's degree. Her thesis was on Chinese women poets of ancient times. She produced other writings in addition to poetry and used her pen as a Christian influence.

HULL, ELEANOR HENRIETTA (1860-1935), born in Manchester, England, and remembered as the founder and first secretary of the Irish Text Society. She wrote "Be Thou My Vision, O Lord of My Heart" and several books on Irish literature and history. At one time she served as president of the Irish Literary Society of London.

HUME, Lady GRISELL (1665-1746), a brave and steadfast Christian of a noble family; daughter of Sir Patrick Hume, a patriot of Scotland and staunch Covenanter. Sir Patrick was a prominent target of the enemy, and Lady Grisell was extremely faithful in protecting and caring for him. The accounts of how she secretly took food and water to him in prison and in unusual places of hiding make a thrilling story. For example, Sir Patrick memorized much Scripture while hiding in a vault, and she hid food from their table so that the servants would not know that she took it to him regularly at midnight. His escape to freedom and all the events of that close Hume family present an unusual impression of life during the Protestant Reformation. After he was freed and their estate restored, her father was given the high office of Lord Chancellor of Scotland. In 1692 she married George Baillie and three children were born to them. Lady Baillie's husband died when she was seventy-five.

HUNT, HELEN (1890-1975), daughter of Dr. Emory Hunt, former president of Denison and Bucknell universities and of the Northern Baptist Convention. She received degrees from Simmons College in Boston and Denison University and served as a missionary teacher in Rangoon, Burma, under the Women's American Baptist Foreign Mission Society. She taught at Judson College in Rangoon from 1919 to 1948 and influenced countless young Burmese and tribal women though her teaching and as hostel manager of the campus dormitory for women.

HUNTINGDON, SELINA HASTINGS (1707-1791), a benevolent and devout Christian and originator of the Calvanistic Methodist group "Huntingdon's Connection." She was born in Leicestershire, England, and was the daughter of Washington Shirley, Earl of Ferres.

She married Theophilus Hastings, Earl of Huntingdon, in 1728. As a young girl she demonstrated Christian commitment, but mature Christian dedication was the result of the influence of her friend and sister-in-law, Lady Margaret Hastings, wife of a Methodist minister. Lady Huntingdon became a member of the first Methodist Society in Fetter Lane in London, and the first Methodist conference was held in her home in 1744. She lost two sons during the smallpox epidemic in 1743, and her husband died in 1744. She devoted her life and means to promoting the gospel. She traveled to many places in the British Isles, taking clergymen with her to preach while she interceded for them in prayer. At Trevecca College in South Wales she provided funds for a chapel and a seminary for the education of chaplains. She provided for more than sixty chapels; and in the case of Tunbridge Wells, she requested that no collection be taken as the people were very poor; she paid the pastor herself. As part of her personal ministry, she compiled a collection of hymns for use in her chapels. These were simply called *Huntingdon's Hymn Books*. She invited George Whitefield to preach in her home, and among the notables who came there to hear him were David Hume, Horace Walpole, Lord Bolingbroke, and Lord Chesterfield. Although she is credited with reconciling some of the differences between the Wesleys and Whitefield, she favored Whitefield and upon his death became the trustee of his institutions in Georgia. Near the time of her death she requested an association be formed to carry on the work she had begun.

HUNTLEY, AMELIA ELMORE (1844-c. 1920), a leader in Christian work and missions, She was born in New York; her mother died when she was nine years old. She graduated from a women's college in Lima, New York, and married a Methodist-Episcopal pastor, E. D. Huntley, who later became president of Lawrence College in Wisconsin. In addition to her activity with the Women's Foreign Missionary Society, she was much involved with the Women's Christian Temperance Union. Her special interest in missions led her to be sent as a delegate to Edinburgh to the International Conference on Missions in 1910. Her life and work influenced many young people.

HUSSEY, JENNIE EVELYNE, poet and hymnist. She was a quiet, dedicated Christian who spent much of her adult life caring for an invalid sister. Although she wrote many poems, she is remembered for the hymn "Lead Me to Calvary," put to music by William J. Kirkpatrick.

HUSTON, RUTH (1899-1982), missionary, author, and good steward of abundant resources. She was the daughter of a wealthy steel company family of Pennsylvania. Her family roots were deeply planted in Scottish Presbyterian background. Her education was private, and she traveled for a time. She and a friend visited the mission work of a small group in eastern Kentucky, where later she returned to teach music and assist in the work for a "brief time," which turned out to be a lifetime missionary career. She kept busy over many years teaching Bible classes, Sunday school, and in summer camps. She also sponsored a bookmobile library service and helped people in many other ways, often from her own resources. She wrote two books: *Observation of God's Timing in the Kentucky Mountains* and *Acting Like Christians*. Her personal generosity went far beyond the mission she served, for she helped many young people prepare for the Lord's service. A women's dormitory is named for her at Bryan College in Dayton, Tennessee, where she served on the Board of Trustees for nearly twenty years.

HUTCHINSON, ANNE MARBURY (1591-1643), known for her religious activism in the American colonies. She was born in Alford, Lincolnshire, England. Her father, Francis Marbury, a graduate of Christ College at Cambridge, was unfrocked for his controversial religious views. In 1612 she married William Hutchinson, a dealer in textiles, and lived for twenty-one years in Lincolnshire, England, where she had fourteen of their children. The family emigrated to America in 1634, settling in the Boston area of the Massachusetts Bay Colony. As a respected Bible student she formed classes and taught the Scriptures, especially to women, although she became a popular public speaker as well. Her views were highly criticized by the clergy. In 1637 she was brought before a synod and tried; then charged with heresy and sedition. At the trial she defended herself well, but concluded by announcing that God had revealed to her that He would destroy her persecutors. That extrabiblical revelation worsened her respect of the Puritan state. She was requested to leave the Massachusetts Bay Colony. The family then moved to Portsmouth, Rhode Island. Again she was outspoken concerning antinomian doctrines and was respected for her acts of benevolence. After the death of her husband in 1642, she moved to Pelham, New York, a Dutch settlement. It was there the following year that she and eight members of her household were killed in an Indian massacre.

HUTCHINSON, LUCY APSLEY (c. 1620), a British author and devout Christian of nobility. She was the oldest daughter of Sir Allen Apsley, Lieutenant of the Tower of London. It is recorded that Lucy was born in the Tower of London, that by the age of four she could read well, and at seven she had eight tutors in different branches of education. Her mother taught her the Scriptures in their private devotions and by her example. When she was eighteen she married John Hutchinson of St. Andrews in Holborne. She was described as a strict Calvinist, and her husband became one as well. During the fourth year of their marriage the English Civil War broke out, and her husband was stationed at Nottinghamshire, near relatives. He became a colonel and reluctantly fought while Lucy cared for wounded soldiers and their estate. After the war, Colonel Hutchinson was one of those arrested for his opposition to Charles I. She wrote a plea for his pardon and forged his signature. But only two years later he was arrested and placed in a prison, where he became ill and died. She ministered to the last. Later she wrote a biography, *Memoirs of the Life of Colonel Hutchinson,* which portrays him as a Christian gentleman and gives a view of the Puritan contributions to the Protestant Reformation in England. Her final years were so obscure that her death date is not certain.

HYDE, MARGARET (c. 1495-1557), a resident in the county of Essex apprehended for her faith and testimony for Christ. She was sent to London for questioning; then confined to Newgate Prison. After almost three months she appeared before a bishop for further interrogation. She remained a steadfast witness for the Lord but was sentenced to death. Along with others she was burned at Smithfield in 1557.

HYPATIA (c. 375-415), a teacher of the pagan philosophy Neoplatonism. She was born in Alexandria, the daughter of Theon, a professor of mathematics and astronomy in Athens. She studied in Athens, was recognized as a learned lecturer, and later identified as head of the Neoplatonic school in Alexandria. Synesius was one of her students and later became bishop of Ptolemais. The monks became upset by her teachings, rebelled against her, finally murdering her in the street. Her life was the basis for the novel written by Charles Kingsley called *Hypatia.*

I

INGALLS, MARILLA BAKER (1830-1895), an unusual American missionary to Burma. She was married in 1850 and went to Burma the following year, but her husband lived only two years after they were married. She returned to America briefly, then went back to Burma where she established Bible societies and distributed tracts in the languages of the area (primarily French, English, and Burmese) in an effort to reach the Shans, Hindus, and Karens. Marilla had an effective ministry to Buddhist priests, opened a library of Christian books for the employees of a railway company, and later established branch libraries. She trained others to help her and carry on the work. She had the respect of government officials and business people.

INOUYE, Dr. TOMO, considered the first Christian Japanese woman to become a physician. She was converted under the work of American Presbyterian missionaries. She wanted to become a missionary nurse but was refused admission for training because she was not tall enough. She came to America, attended a medical school in Cleveland, Ohio, graduated, eventually became a physician, and returned to Japan as a missionary doctor to women of her own country.

IRENE (752-803), married Leo IV, Byzantine emperor who forbade the religious use of icons in 769. When he died in 780 she assumed power. Through her negative but powerful influence the worship of icons was encouraged. She called the second Council of Nicea in 787, which sanctified veneration but not the reverence or worship of icons.

IRENE (1832-1896), founder the first home for orphans and unwanted children in New York in 1869. It was known later as the New York Foundling Hospital. She was born in England as Catherine Fitzgibbon. She became a member of the Order of Sisters of Charity and given the name Irene.

ISABELLA OF CASTILE (1451-1504), Christian queen of Castile whose father was John II, king of Castile, who was succeeded by his son, Henry, Isabella's brother. When Henry died in 1474, Isabella inherited the throne. Her mother was Dona Isabel, a devout Christian. Even as a child Isabella was religious and spent much time in prayer. She married Ferdinand II of Aragon in 1469, which united the kingdoms of Aragon and Castile. She was crowned queen in 1474. Although her reign was difficult and warlike, one of her most memorable acts was to sponsor the voyages of Christopher Columbus to the New World. Her actions were prompted by religious reasons, and on the second voyage she sent clergymen and materials to establish the first church in America. It was with a Christian objective that she engaged in the crusade against the Moslem Moors, personally taking charge of some of the troops and going to the front lines to administer aid to the wounded. She had large tents designated for wounded soldiers, the first record of any kind of field hospital. Her Christian influence was evident in many of her acts and was definite in the life of her daughter, Catherine of Aragon.

ISHERWOOD, CECILE (1862-1905), British missionary and founder of an orphanage and school in South Africa. While she was young she lost both her parents and was sent to London to be reared by General Sir James and Lady Browne. She was converted and served in a mission house at Vauxhall Bridge Road. In 1883, when Bishop Webb asked for volunteers for mission work in South Africa, she offered herself and went as a deaconess to Grahamstown. She founded the Community of the Resurrection and was its administrator. From this beginning grew a chain of spiritual and educational institutions of special Christian ministry. She originated an orphanage, a kind of industrial school, and a large national school at Keiskama Hock, some distance from Grahamstown. Although from an Anglican church, Cecile worked with those of many other denominations. In 1894 she founded the Grahamstown Training College for women teachers. She was an influential force for extending Christian teaching and served in South Africa for approximately twenty-three years.

IWAMATO, KASHI SHIMADA (1863-1896), influential Japanese Christian educator and author. She was orphaned quite young and placed in Ferris Seminary at Yokohama. She became a teacher, learning English from missionaries. Her keen ability to communicate well in both English and Japanese aided her effective ministry of teaching the gospel to Japanese women. She wrote some of her teaching materials.

IWASA, RIN (1891-1949), one of Japan's first women physicians. She served in the Salvation Army's Tokyo Hospital for the Poor. She was appointed superintendent of that hospital in 1930, which is believed to have been the first time a woman was appointed to such an administrative position. She specialized in the treatment of tuberculosis and won much respect and gratitude. Using her acumen as a businesswoman, she was able to establish and build a tuberculosis sanatorium in Tokyo. She received the Emperor's Order of the Blue Ribbon in 1944 in recognition of her work. Although the Salvation Army in Japan was dissolved by decree of the government during World War II, through her counsel it was kept alive, influencing its reopening there in 1946. She was not only highly respected as a physician but as a firm witness for Christ as well.

J

JACKSON, ALICE (1876-1906), teacher, author, and home missionary. She was born in Cheshire, England, and came to America with her family and settled in New Jersey. She attended Smith College and dedicated her life to missions. She applied for an appointment to China but was turned down for health reasons. She attended the New York School of Pedagogy and taught in Brooklyn. Between 1899 and 1901 she served as secretary of a girls club in Greenfield, Massachusetts. She did home missions work with needy children in New York City, and was secretary for the Young Women's Christian Association in New York. She later taught Bible classes and did some writing, including the song "A Prayer," which became a favorite of children.

JAMES, MINNIE LOU KENNEDY (1874-1963), author, teacher, and leader in the Women's Missionary Union of the Southern Baptist Convention. In 1923 she represented that body at the Baptist World Alliance in Stockholm, Sweden, and held other leadership positions in her denomination. A Christian training school for girls was established in Bucharest, Romania, and was named the James Memorial Training School, in her honor. She contributed regularly to a feature for *Current Events to the Royal Service* publication, wrote program materials for the Women's Missionary Society publications, and was the author of two books: a biography of her predecessor, Fannie Heck, and a *History of Bethlehem Baptist Church* (Chesterfield County, Virginia, 1940).

JAMESON, ANNA (1797-1860), author of the book *Sacred and Legendary Art*. She is believed to have been the first British woman author to deal with sacred art.

JERSEY, MARGARET ELIZABETH VILLIERS (1849-c. 1930), author, hymnist, and daughter of Lord Leigh of Warwick, England. In 1871 she had published a collection of hymns by the Religious Tract Society under the title *Hymns and Poems for Very Little Children*. Another series was issued in 1875 with the same title. Several of her hymns were included in W. R. Stevenson's *School Hymnal* (1880). Her work in included in other collections, particularly *Voice of Praise*.

JOAN OF ARC (JEANNE D'ARC; JEANNE LA PURCELLE) (1412-1431), a national heroine of France on whom much literature is based. She was born in Domremy-on-the-Muse River in northeast France and the youngest of four children. Her parents were Jacques d'Arc, a Christian farmer and leader in the community, and Isabella Romee, a devoted mother who taught her children Bible truths. When Joan was thirteen, she reported hearing heavenly voices and observing visions. As these experiences came often, she felt divinely directed to aid her country in the Hundred Years War, then being waged. She went before the dauphin and shared her message of victory for France and the crowning of the dauphin as king. She was put in charge of French troops with a determination to drive the English out of France. Dressed in snow white armor and riding a black horse, she charged into battle, vowing never to use her sword to kill. The result was considered a miracle with France's victory being divinely appointed. The victorious year of 1429 provided special recognition of her at the coronation of Charles VII. The following year she was taken prisoner by the Burgundians, allies of the British. They sold her to the British, who in turn took her to the ecclesiastical court of Rouen, France. She was tried for witchcraft, heresy, and the wearing of masculine clothing. She was condemned and burned at the stake in Rouen at the age of nineteen. Much later a retrial was ordered by Charles VII, and Joan was declared innocent. She was canonized by Pope Benedict XV in 1920 as the second patron of France.

JOAN OF KENT (c. 1306-1385), one of the first of several noble women to protect and further the cause of the Protestant Reformation. Joan was the only child of the Earl of Kent. Little is recorded about her early life, but it may be assumed that because she was of nobility and wealth, she was well educated for her station in life. Joan was a niece of Edward II, whose first wife had died; he then married Isabella, daughter of Philip of France. The situation was such that Isabella exercised the ruling power, and one of her first acts was to execute anyone who opposed her, including Joan's father. Joan was three years old when her father was beheaded. The prince of Wales desired Joan in marriage, but his mother objected. Joan married Sir Thomas Holland, and they had several children. When Sir Thomas died, the prince of Wales was still waiting, and he and Joan were married. He was known as the Black Prince because of the color of his armor. About this time John Wycliffe was attracting attention with philosophy and preaching. Joan and Wycliffe became friends, and she exercised considerable influence to protect him and his translations of the Scriptures. Joan studied the Bible with Anne of Bohemia, who was later to become Joan's daughter-in-law and the queen. After Joan was widowed in 1376, her young son, Richard II, became the monarch, although Joan was the power behind the throne. Wycliffe was a statesman and political economist as well as a theologian, and Joan was able to protect him so that he could finish his work of translating the New Testament into English by 1380. The pope who had ordered the arrest of Wycliffe died soon after, and the translations were preserved.

JOHNSTON, DOROTHY GRUNBOCK (1915-1977), author and Christian educator born in Seattle, Washington, who lived most of her life in that area. She married Monroe B. Johnston and had several children. She went to the University of Washington, Prairie Bible Institute in Canada, and Moody Bible Institute in Chicago. She wrote a regular column called "Hey Mom" for the *Power for Living* periodical. Another column appropriately called "Kitchen Kathedral" in the *Christian Parent* magazine. She wrote a number of tracts, a series of Christian guidance books for youth titled the Pete and Penny series, a devotional book for juniors, *Bob and Betty Wonder*, another for young teens, *Four Teens*, and numerous articles for Christian periodicals.

JOHNSTON, JULIA HARRIETTE (1849-1919), Christian educator, writer, and hymnist, the daughter of Robert Johnston, pastor of the First Presbyterian Church of Peoria, Illinois. She served as Sunday school superintendent for the children's department for over forty years and was president of the church missionary society for twenty years. She wrote primary teaching materials and several books. Among her published books are: *School of the Master* (1880); *Bright Threads* (1897); *Indian and Spanish Neighbors* (1905); and *Fifty Missionary Heroes* (1913). Although she is credited with more than 500 hymns, only one seems to be included in recent hymnals, "Marvelous Grace of Our Loving Lord."

JOHNSTON, RUBY (1909-1983), registrar for many years at the Canadian Bible College and Canadian Theological Seminary. She was founder of the first North American Chinese Missionary Alliance church; founder of the Canadian Chinese Christian Youth Winter Conference. Converted at the age of twenty-one, she went to college and began her work at Canadian Bible College in 1944. She was a beloved counselor to many students; an active member of the Hillsdale Alliance Church in Regina, where she was a charter member.

JONES, KATHERINE BOYLE (1614-1691). *See* **RANELAGH, Lady KATHERINE**

JUDSON, ANN HASSELTINE (1789-1826), teacher, translator, author, pioneer missionary, and first wife of Adoniram Judson. They were the first American missionaries to establish work in the Far East. Born in Bradford, Massachusetts, Ann became a Christian at sixteen, studied at Bradford Academy, and began to teach when eighteen. She first met Judson when he stayed in their home during a meeting of the American Board of Commissioners for Foreign Missions. He was a Congregational minister. They were married on February 5, 1812, and within a few days departed for India with other missionaries. It was a four month's voyage, and enroute the group realized their differences concerning the ordinance of baptism. The result was that one of that group, Luther Rice, later returned to America to organize a Baptist foreign mission society. From Calcutta, the Judsons went to Rangoon, Burma, arriving on July 13, 1813. Ann proceeded to study the language along with her husband. In January of 1815 she gave birth to a son, the first child born of white parents in Burma; he died in infancy of jungle fever. Ann helped in the translation of the Bible into Burmese. She opened a school for girls, and in 1816 the first printing press was brought to print tracts. Although Ann Judson returned to America briefly in 1822 because of ill health, she wrote a history of the Burmese work titled *American Baptist Mission to the Burman Empire,* published in 1823. After she returned to Burma, war broke out between the Burmese and British, and her husband was imprisoned for several months. She made numerous pleas for his release and took food to him almost daily. He became ill, and she cared for him in spite of her own frailty and the birth of a girl. Had it not been for her care, Adoniram Judson would likely have died in prison. After he was finally released, they moved to Amhearst where she became ill during his absence on a business trip to Ava. She died at the age of thirty-seven; their infant daughter died soon afterward.

JUDSON, EMILY CHUBBUCK (1817-1854), author, missionary, and third wife of Adoniram Judson. Born in Easton, New York, her parents were Lavinia Richards and John Chubbuck. She was a professional writer and used the pen name of Fanny Forrester. Judson had read some of her writings and contacted her to write the biography of his second wife, Sarah. As they worked together on the biography their friendship became serious. They were married in 1846, not quite a year after his return to the United States following the death of Sarah. They went to Burma, and she finished the biography of Sarah, which was published in 1848. Emily and Adoniram Judson had two children, one born after the death of Judson. He died while on board a ship, and Emily did not know of of his death for some time. She returned to America in 1851 with four children. Emily contracted tuberculosis and died in New York.

JUDSON, SARAH HALL BOARDMAN (1803-1845), translator, author, hymnist, pioneer missionary, and second wife of Adoniram Judson. Born in Alstead, New Hampshire. She was the oldest of thirteen children of Ralph and Abia Hall. Her family knew the Judsons well, and when she was thirteen she wrote a poem on the death of the first child of Ann and Adoniram Judson. Sarah and George Dana Boardman were married in Salem, Massachusetts, in 1825, and went to Burma to work with the Judsons. Later they settled at Tavoy to work with a mountain tribe, the Karens, where she founded a school for girls. Her husband died in 1831, and she carried on the work with their small son. Sarah and Adoniram Judson were married in Tavoy in April of 1834, some seven and a half years after the death of Ann Judson. Sarah made new translations into the Burmese language and did some writing as well as having several children. At the time of her death she was translating John Bunyan's *Pilgrim's Progress* into Burmese. She is also credited with translating about twenty hymns and other material in the Burmese and Peguan languages. Exhausted and ill, she died near the island of St. Helena on a ship sailing back to the United States. She was buried beside another missionary grave of a woman who had been a missionary in Ceylon.

JUGAN, JEANNE (MARIE de la CROIX) (1792-c. 1861), born near St. Servan in France and founder of the Catholic community Little Sisters of the Poor in France in 1839. The order came to the United States in 1868. Its purpose was charitable work, especially nursing.

JULIANA OF NORWICH (c. 1342-c. 1413), a nun of the Benedictine order in Norwich, England, believed to had been the first English woman to write a book on personal spiritual experiences. Three of her manuscripts were taken to the British Museum in London, and another is preserved at Paris in the Bibliotheque Nationale. Her book *Revelations of Divine Love* is a record of a series of sixteen visions or revelations she experienced within a few hours in the spring of 1373, but recorded some twenty years later. She was influenced by Neoplatonism; love and unity of soul with God were the dominating emphases. Her writing was read by only a few early researchers until it was printed in book form in 1902. After that, her writing gained some popularity for the first time. Little is known of her early life, and during adulthood she had little contact with the outside world. Her life-style was monastic; she resided at the Norman Church of St. Julian at Norwich.

K

KAHN, Dr. IDA (K'ANG C'HENT) (1872-1932), a Chinese medical missionary physician and surgeon. As an infant Ida was adopted by an American Methodist missionary Miss Gertrude Howe. Thus, Ida's early education was in mission schools. In 1892 Miss Howe brought Ida Kahn and her Chinese friend Mary Stone to America for medical school training at the University of Michigan. They were excellent students; both graduated with honors and returned to China to serve their own people as medical missionaries and were the first Chinese women to become doctors. Dr. Kahn represented the women of China at the World's Congress in London in 1899. She and Dr. Stone shared the work of the Danforth Hospital in Kiukiang in 1900. Three years later, Ida went to Nanchang, a city in Kiangsi, and served as head physician for a large hospital there. Taking a two year furlough in 1907, Dr. Kahn came to the United States and completed a three-year literary course at Northwestern University and the University of Chicago. In 1910, again representing her own people, she attended the Conference of the World's Young Women's Christian Association in Berlin. She spent six months studying tropical diseases in London before returning to China. Dr. Kahn should not only be remembered as a brilliant medical doctor of China but also a faithful servant of the Lord among her own people.

KALOPOTHAKIS, MARY, an outstanding Christian medical doctor in Greece. She was the daughter of the founder and first pastor of the Greek Evangelical Church in Athens. She received her early education in Greece and her professional training at the medical school of Athens University. For some time after she finished, she was the only woman graduate of that school. Dr. Kalopothakis did postgraduate work in both Europe and the United States. She served in several European hospitals and was sponsored by the Greek Evangelical Church of Athens. During wartime she volunteered her services to the Greek Red Cross and gave free medical help to the poor. In addition to being a highly skilled physician, she taught a Bible class, served as the regular church organist, and translated hymns for the Greek hymnal, even composing several herself. She wrote articles on a regular basis for the *Star of the East* evangelical weekly.

KANAGY, MINNIE (1891-1976), a memorable Mennonite missionary to India. Daughter of Joseph and Emma Zook Kanagy, she graduated from Goshen College in 1922 and served in India for several years. Apparently most of her work was in Christian education and presenting the truths of the gospel, especially among women.

KARMARKER, Dr. BUBUBA, a notable missionary physician and evangelist. She was the daughter of the national pastor of a church of the London Missionary Society in Western India and attended a mission school in Bombay. After her marriage she came to the United States with her husband to study. While he studied she entered the Woman's Medical College of Pennsylvania in Philadelphia. Within five years they completed their schooling and returned to India, having been sponsored by an American missionary organization. They were sent to Basslin, near Bombay, where she served as an evangelist and doctor while he served as an evangelist and teacher. Later, in Bombay, she became the physician for a mission school in addition to her medical practice.

KASPER, CATHERINE, founder of The Ancilla Domini Sisters Roman Catholic order in Germany in 1851. Its purpose was threefold: education, hospitals, and charity. It was established in the United States in 1868.

KAUFFMAN, EMILY STRUNK (1873-1960), a remarkable Christian educator in spite of physical limitations. She was born near Mount Union, Pennsylvania, of George and Elmira Fry Strunk. Her hands were accidentally burned, disabling her for life. Nevertheless, she went to college and became a teacher. She married Israel M. Kauffman. She taught in Sunday school for about thirty years, served as president of the women's missionary group in her church for twenty-five years, and carried on an effective ministry for the Lord. As an adult both of her hands became infected and had to be amputated. Her persistent witness for the Lord was unique.

KAUFFMANN, CHRISTMAS CAROL (1901-1969), a memorable author and city missionary for twenty-two years in Hannibal, Missouri. She was the daughter of Abraham R. and Selena Bell Wade Miller who named her appropriately, as she was born on Christmas Day. Her books have become popular Christian reading, and her name is included in the *Contemporary American Authors* and the *Index to Literary Biography*. Several of her books have been translated into German, Norwegian, Finnish, and French.

KAWAI, MICHI, a Christian educator, author, and missionary among her own people of Japan. Her family became Christians. She graduated from the Presbyterian school in Sapporo, receiving a scholarship to Bryn Mawr College in the United States. Afterward, she returned to Japan as a teacher and official of the Young Women's Christian Association. She had a deep conviction for the need of Christian leadership. She became a popular public speaker and accomplished writer.

KELLER, FLORENCE ARMSTRONG (1875-1974), a missionary physician for forty-seven years. She was the doctor of the Maori royal family in New Zealand. She became the first woman and first physician to be elected to the board of management of all hospitals in Auckland, even though she was not a citizen of that country. She was a Seventh Day Adventist.

KEMPE, MARGERY (c. 1373-1433), a mystic, a daughter of John of Burnham, mayor of Lynn. She became the wife of John Kempe. She and her husband took vows of chastity before the Bishop of Lincoln after they had a number of children. She went to Palestine on a pilgrimage about which she wrote in the *Book of Margery Kempe*. This book contained not only her travel experiences but also some of her mystical ideas as well.

KENNETT, Dr. GRACE a physician among her own people in Madura, India. Orphaned in lowly circumstances, she was brought to the mission hospital by a relative when she became ill. An American woman physician and head of that hospital by the name of Dr. Parker, treated Grace, but an eye infection made it necessary to take her elsewhere for treatment. With the consent of the Grace's grandmother, Dr. Parker adopted her and took her to the government specialist in Madras. However, it was found necessary to remove the infected eye. She finished school at the mission and had a great longing to become a doctor. She attended the Government Medical College at Madras so that she might return to Madura to become a medical assistant in the Woman's Hospital. She also became the medical officer of Capron Hall, giving regular physical examinations to several hundred children.

KERSEY, RUTH MAY (1889-1958), medical missionary to Nigeria under the Southern Baptist Convention. A native of Virginia, she spent nearly thirty-five years in Ogbomosho, Nigeria, where she founded and directed the orphanage known as the Kersey Children's Home. She also did medical and evangelistic work at the Baptist Hospital there and at the Baptist Academy in Lagos, Nigeria. Her preparation included graduated from the Women's Missionary Union Training School in Louisville, Kentucky, where she earned a Bachelor of Missionary Training degree and later took nurses training in Richmond, graduating in 1920. Her work on the mission field brought great blessing, and many children were grateful for her physical care and spiritual influence.

KILBOURNE, HAZEL WILLIAMS (1894-1955), an exceptional teacher, evangelist, author, and missionary to the Orient for forty years with the Oriental Missionary Society International. A native of Ohio, she went to the College and Missionary Training Home in Cincinnati, Ohio, before being assigned to Japan along with her husband in 1915, They had three sons, who have also served with the Oriental Missionary Society. She was an excellent speaker and her writing for children of constituents of the Missionary Society influenced their interest in missions and giving to missionary work. She published a magazine for children called *Children's Own Magazine.*

KIM, HELEN KIDUK, noted for her service with the YWCA in her native Korea; she was general secretary of the National Committee. After graduating from Ewha College she attended Ohio Wesleyan and Boston universities. In 1924 she was chosen to represent Korea at the international convention of the YWCA in New York.

KING, MARGARET (c. 1884-1930), a native of Canada. She was brought up in wealth and culture. Her life changed when she heard J. Hudson Taylor speak. Later, she attended a Keswick conference and returned to Montreal to do missionary work in the slums, especially with girls. Eventually she went to China as a missionary under the China Inland Mission and served as a teacher-missionary; she worked also with the Door of Hope Mission.

KLUDT, ALMA (1918-1976), a distinguished Christian education specialist, missionary, and founder of the Girls Christian Institute in central India. Born in Tacoma, Washington, her education included Knapp's Modern Business College, Biola University, Wayne University, and Pacific Lutheran College. In 1948 she was appointed by the Conservative Baptist Foreign Missions Society for service in India, where she was involved with evangelism and Christian education. At the request of the Baptist Association of Churches of central India, she founded the Girls Christian Institute, where village girls could live while getting their education in the city of Warud. As her expertise in Christian education became known, the Evangelical Fellowship of India requested her help in forming the Christian education division of that group. She had many opportunities to speak and participated in conferences and Christian education workshops throughout India.

KNAPP, MRS. JOSEPH FAIRFIELD (PHOEBE PALMER) (1839-1908), philanthropist, hymnist, daughter of evangelist Walter C. Palmer. Her husband was a devoted Christian businessman who founded the Metropolitan Life Insurance Company. He died in 1891 leaving her a considerable sum of money, which she invested in various charitable and religious causes. She published more than 500 hymns and wrote the music for many, but only one remains popular today, "Blessed Assurance," written by Fanny Crosby. She and her husband were members of the John Street Methodist Church in New York City, where Fanny Crosby attended.

KNOX, MARGARET STUART (c. 1547-1612), second wife of John Knox and daughter of Andrew Stuart, and related to Queen Mary Stuart of Scotland. Margaret Stuart and John Knox were married in 1564, four years after the death of his first wife. Margaret was more than forty years younger than Knox. They had three children, all daughters: Elizabeth, Margaret, and Martha. Margaret Stuart Knox was left a widow approximately eight years after their marriage.

KNOX, MARJORY BOWES (1538-1560), daughter of Richard and Elizabeth Bowes and first wife of John Knox, the Scotch Reformer. She and her mother became special friends of Knox and faithfully supported his work. In 1555, when Marjory was about seventeen years old, she and John Knox were married, although she was more than thirty years younger than he. They had two sons, Eleazar and Nathaniel. She was frail in health and died within five years after they were married.

KOMAHI, TETSUKO, Christian evangelist in Japan. She attained the rank of captain in the Salvation Army and became superintendent of the Home of Hope in Osaka.

KREUTTER, RUTH DUNCOMB (1923-1977), an exceptional missionary-nurse who used her expertise in nursing and operated a dispensary, thereby simultaneously reaching the people of Zaire with the gospel while helping to meet their physical needs. She trained many nationals in both nursing and dispensary work, but her ministry among the women was distinctive as she combined evangelism with teaching family care, sewing, and cooking. Born in Minnesota, she went to Northwestern Bible College and took her medical training at Mounds Midway School of Nursing. Her dedication characterized her love for the growing church in Africa. She and her husband, James, were appointed for overseas service in 1949 by the Conservative Baptist Foreign Mission Society.

KRÜDENER BARBARA JULIANA von (1764-1824), born in Russia. She married Baron von Krüdener, a Russian ambassador at Venice in 1782. However, they separated, and she went to Paris, later to Germany, and when she retired, she settled in Switzerland. In 1804 while in Riga, she was converted to Pietism through the influence of a Moravian. Her ideas reflected millenarianism or chiliastic views. She was considered a mystic, and some of her predictions came true, such as the fall of Napoleon. It is evident that she exercised influence over Czar Alexander I, whom she met at Heilbron, which resulted in the Holy Alliance with Austria and Prussia. It was said of her that in spite of opposition, she never grew tired of preaching repentance and proclaiming salvation. She formed prayer groups and urged more vital Christian living and the practice of sharing property with the poor.

KUGLER, ANNA S. (1856-1930), an outstanding medical missionary to India under the General Synod of the Evangelical Lutheran Church, later known as the United Lutheran Church of America. Not only was she the first Lutheran woman medical missionary, but one of the first American women to become a leading physician, receiving special recognition for her work. She completed her M.D. degree in 1879 at the Women's Medical College of Philadelphia and for four years worked as the assistant physician at the mental hospital in Norristown, Pennsylvania, before being sent to India. Soon she had a large and growing practice as the women of India could not under caste strictures allow a male physician to treat them. A hospital fund was soon begun; the church opened a dispensary in Guntur and a hospital for women. Dr. Kugler was decorated by the British government in 1905 with the Kaiser-i-Hind medal in recognition of her medical service; and in 1917 a bar was added to the medal for her continued outstanding work. The door of medicine also opened the way for a spiritual emphasis unique to the situation.

KUHLMAN, KATHRYN (1907-1976), popular radio and television evangelist. Born in Concordia, Missouri, she was ordained by the Evangelical Church Alliance. Later, she joined the American Baptist Convention.

KUHN, ISOBEL MILLER (1901-1957), American author and missionary. Although Isobel Miller grew up in a Christian family, she drifted away from the Lord while attending a secular college. Despondent and weary she sought peace at any cost and called on the Lord of her childhood days. Her prayer was answered during the summer of 1924 while she was attending The Firs Bible Conference in Washington state. There she met J. O. Fraser, a missionary to the Lisu tribe in China. The Lisu people were from the mountain area in the Yunnan province, China, although they were not really Chinese. Isobel's life was never the same after that conference, for it was the Lisu people to whom the Lord called her to reach with the gospel. She prepared for her calling by attending Moody Bible Institute and graduated in December of 1926. Her good friend John Kuhn, whom she met at Moody, also felt led of the Lord to the mission field of China, but not specifically to the Lisu people. She considered this prayerfully as she prepared her reply to John's marriage proposal just before he left for China. Both wanted the Lord's will. She carefully and prayerfully wrote to John that she believed that if the Lord wanted them to work together for Him, He would assign them to the same area, for she was called to work with the Lisu. John was not sure of the location of his assignment until he arrived in China. In the meantime Isobel was serving the Lord in the Vancouver, British Columbia, area where her parents lived. This was a fruitful experience as she waited for clearance of her entrance into China. The letters of John and Isobel crossed in the mail. He wrote to tell her his assignment was in the Yunnan province, exactly where the Lisu lived. That left no question in the mind of either. She proceeded to China. The marriage of Isobel Miller and John Kuhn took place on November 4, 1929, in Kumming, the capital of the Yunnan province. Their first home was in Chengchiang; it was small but open to Bible classes for women, and their work proceeded. Their marriage motto was "God first." Soon, they moved to another location, even closer to the Lisu tribe. In April 1931 their first child was born, Kathryn Ann, whom they dedicated to the Lord. Indeed she did grow up to be a missionary in Thailand. In August 1943 their second child, Danny, was born. Soon war clouds gathered in that area of the world, and their return after a furlough at home was delayed. War broke out between China and Japan. On the last day of August 1937 they started back by way of Hong Kong. Kathryn was to go to the mission school at Chefoo, where the children were to be interned. She later returned to the United States for schooling. Isobel wrote several books that related her experiences: *By Searching, Green Leaf in Drought-Time, Second Mile People, Ascent to the Tribes, In the Arena, Nests Above the Abyss, Stones of Fire,* and *Precious Things of the Lasting Hills.* In 1955 Isobel was flown home, as she was dying of cancer. She died in March of 1957.

KULIANG, YU (c. 1873-c. 1922), a remarkable Chinese relative of Ann and Mary Stone. Her father died when she was a baby, and her mother decided to become a Taoist nun. Although the family was wealthy and aristocratic in Kiukiang, China, they were far from Christianity. Kuliang was tutored and given the best opportunities for education but all the while isolated with her mother and teachers so that she, too, became a Taoist nun; yet she continued to search for truth. When she was thirty-two, she learned that the Stones, Ann and Mary, were her cousins and decided to visit them. She went often to hear about their God and became a Christian herself. She contracted tuberculosis and lived only a brief time afterward. Because of the influence and status of her family, she was used of the Lord as a powerful witness to them.

L

LAMBERT, HELEN CATHERINE (1899-1978), a career home missionary under the Southern Baptist Convention. She served American Indians and other minorities, mainly in southern United States. She attended Southern Illinois University and the Women's Missionary Union Training School in Louisville, Kentucky, receiving a B.R.E. degree. First, she served in several places in Illinois before going to Baltimore, Maryland. She was later assigned to the southern part of the United States for health reasons. Her final years of service were in the Tucson, Arizona, area where she had an effective teaching ministry to five Indian tribes.

LANEY, LUCY CRAFT (1855-1933), a native of Georgia and extraordinary leader who rose from slavery to become an influential teacher. She finished high school and was a member of the first class that enrolled at Atlanta University. After teaching in Macon, Augusta, and elsewhere, in 1886 she established a private school in Augusta bearing the name Haines Normal and Industrial Institute. Although the Institute was affiliated with the Presbyterian Church in the United States of America, it was Mrs. F. E. H. Haines who provided its financial support. Lucy Craft Laney served as a role model, helping black people achieve the advantages of education and vocational training.

LANHAM, EDITH CAMPBELL CRANE (1876-1933), a native of South Carolina; she was a graduate of Bryn Mawr College and served in several leadership capacities of the Women's Missionary Union of the Southern Baptist Convention. She served as editor of *Our Mission Fields* publication and represented the Women's Missionary Union on the planning committee for the first women's meeting associated with the Baptist World Alliance.

LAPP, ESTHER EBERSOLE (1882-1917), missionary nurse who served in India under the Mennonite church. She received her nurses training at Passavant Memorial Hospital in Chicago. She and her husband first went to India in 1905, where she helped with an orphanage and dispensary work. She contracted a fever that took her life at just thirty-five years of age. She was buried in the Himalayas.

LAPP, SARAH HAHN (1869-1943), missionary daughter of Jacob and Anna Eyman Hahn. She studied nursing in Chicago and elsewhere. In 1900 she married Mahlon Lapp, and they served as Mennonite missionaries to India. She remained in India nineteen years after her husband died; she had an outstanding work among Bible women.

LASAULX, AMALIE von (1815-1872), missionary nurse and philanthropist in Germany. She joined the Catholic community Sisters of St. Borromeo and was sent to have charge of the hospital of St. John the Baptist in Bonn. Later she nursed during the Franco-German War of 1870. She was criticized by the Catholic church because she did not approve of some of the decisions of the Vatican Council and was demanded to recant, but she refused to do so, standing true to her convictions by opposing Catholic dogmas. When she died, her habit was removed from her corpse before burial.

LATHBURY, MARY ARTEMISIA (1841-1913), a poet and native of New York state. Her father was a Methodist minister, and she became much involved with the Chautauqua Movement. Her poems first appeared in some of the Methodist Sunday school publications. She originated the "Look-Up Legion" Methodist youth program in 1885. She wrote her first song for the Chautauqua meetings in 1875 but is especially remembered for the hymn "Break Thou the Bread of Life," which she wrote in 1877 for classes during Chautauqua meetings, expressing in it the purpose of their Bible study. Her hymn "Day Is Dying in the West" has also gained some popularity.

LATHROP, ROSE HAWTHORNE (MOTHER ALPHONSA) (1851-1926), remembered for founding homes to help incurable cancer victims. She was also an author and wrote the memoirs of her father, Nathaniel Hawthorne. Her family was wealthy, so she traveled much and was taught at home. She married George Parsons Lathrop, a journalist. They had a child who died at the age of five. She and her husband became Catholic converts in 1891. She was left a widow several years later. When a close friend of hers died of cancer, she decided to relinquish her material possessions, social life, and personal interests to devote herself to aid those who were destitute and suffering from cancer. At the age of forty-five she trained at the New York Cancer Hospital and worked in social relief work directed toward cancer victims. In 1899 she became a Dominican tertiary and founded the Congregation of St. Rose of Lima, known as the Servants of Relief for Incurable Cancer. This work continued for patients of all faiths. In 1957 the St. Rose Home was opened, and five other such homes have been established in St. Paul, Cleveland, Philadelphia, Atlanta, and Fall River, Massachusetts.

LAW, MRS. S. T., Chinese Christian who served for forty years with the True Light Seminary in Canton, China. She was active in organizing the Church of Christ in China. She was an officer in the church and member of the executive board of the synod.

LAWRENCE, UNA ROBERTS (1893-1972), author and leader of the Women's Missionary Union and Home Mission Board of the Southern Baptist Convention. She attended Central College and WMU Training School. From 1926 to 1947 she served as editor for mission study materials and wrote extensively. Several of her books include: *The King's Own* (1920), *The Life of Lottie Moon* (1927), *Pioneer Women* (1929), and *The Word of Their Testimony* (1932).

LEACHMAN, EMMA (1868-1952), a pioneer Christian educator and missionary leader in the home mission program of the Southern Baptist Convention. Born in Kentucky, she attended the Central Teachers College in Evansville, Indiana, and the Women's Missionary Union Training School in Louisville, Kentucky. After teaching for several years, she became an assistant at the Hope Rescue Mission in Louisville, Kentucky, and later was appointed as city missionary there by the Kentucky Baptist mission board. She founded other missions, stimulating local congregations to help. In the meantime she gained permission to audit classes at the seminary there, where only men were admitted. Other women joined her, and this led to the establishment of the Women's Missionary Union Training School, which eventually merged with the Southern Baptist Theological Seminary. Her leadership abilities were recognized, and she became the first woman ever to go before Southern Baptist churches as a representative of the Home Mission Board. She was responsible for the opening of several centers and the supervising of students desiring to serve the Lord in similar mission work.

LEAMAN, BERTHA R. (1893-1975), eminent Mennonite educator. She graduated from Goshen College in 1921; then attended the University of Chicago where she earned an M.A. degree in 1924. She studied at the University of Paris on research for a doctorate and received a Ph.D. degree from the University of Chicago in 1935. She was a professor at the West Liberty State College in West Virginia from 1949 to 1963. She held the distinction of being the first woman graduate of Goshen College to earn a Ph.D. degree.

LECSINSKA, MARY (1703-1768), Christian queen of France, and daughter of Stanislas Lecsinska, who found exile from Poland in the Chateau of Weissemberg, where they settled in 1720. She became queen in 1725 when she married Louis XV in the chapel of the royal residence at Fountainebleau. She reigned for forty-three years and had several children, but lost the affection of her husband. She was a friend of John Calvin and tried to keep her courage and faith in difficult circumstances. Her testimony influenced many.

LEE, ANN (1736-1784), organizer of the Shaker movement and originator of the first American colony of Shakers. Born in Manchester, England, where a series of difficulties in her home life, including a marriage and the death of four infants, caused her to separate from her husband in 1766 and assume leadership of a sect later known as the Shakers. These people had withdrawn from the Quakers because they wished a greater emphasis on the imminent return of Christ and other doctrinal issues. The group was encouraged by her leadership. She pronounced principles for them that included millennialism, pacifism, celibacy, anything associated with the reproductive process (such as eggs), the sharing of material goods, and outward spiritual expressions through dancing and shaking. She implied that Christ spoke directly through her, and thus she became known as "Ann the Word," and acted as a prophetess. She and the group received considerable opposition in England. In 1774 Ann Lee and less than ten followers, now called the United Society of True Believers in Christ's Second Coming emigrated to New York. They settled into a life of communitarian celibacy, pooling their resources, with strict rules and principles that made the Shaker movement appear to be an experiment in socialism. This movement grew in popularity, and during the last four years of her life, public campaigns were made to expand their following in New England. Before she died, eleven such colonies were established, and a total of eighteen was founded before the Civil War. At one time she was put in prison for speaking out against war.

LEE, ANNA MARIA PITTMAN (1803-1838), a brave, pioneer missionary to the Pacific Northwest Territory of the United States. Born in New York state and educated privately, she was converted in her mid-twenties. In 1836 she was selected as a missionary to the Oregon Mission, located in the Willamette Valley of Oregon under the direction of the Jason Lee. Sponsored by the Missionary Board of the Methodist Episcopal Church, she sailed from Boston, and traveled around Cape Horn to Fort Vancouver, arriving in the spring of 1837. On July 16, 1837, she married Jason Lee. Nearly a year later she gave birth to a son who lived but a few hours and within three days she died also. She was buried with the child in her arms at a spot now within the city of Salem, Oregon. In spite of her short term of missionary service, her influence was that of a truly dedicated Christian spirit in difficult situation that was characteristic of pioneer life.

LEESON, JANE ELIZA (1807-1882), a native of London and remembered for her hymn collections for children. One of her hymns is included in *The English Hymnal,* "Loving Shepherd of Thy Sheep." She translated several hymns from Latin including "Christ the Lord Is Risen Today."

LEHMAN, LYDIA LIECHTY (1884-1969), author and missionary to India for twenty-four years. Her many articles on missions published in the *Gospel Herald* kept people informed of the Mennonite work in India.

LEHRER, ELIZABETH (1897-1978), an effective missionary in the important role of homemaker at the Rift Valley Academy, a school for missionary children in Kenya. She and her husband served with the African Inland Mission. Her life touched many with the obvious daily needs as well as valuable spiritual influence.

LELA, CHUNDRA, the daughter of a Brahmin priest. She was born among the Himalaya Mountains and lived a rugged life of idol worship. She saw some Christian literature in the home of a friend, read it and was much influenced. She sought out Christian missionaries and became a Christian. So thrilled was she with her peace and new life in Christ that she went about as an evangelist.

LESLIE, MARY ELIZA (1834-c. 1910), author, hymnist, and missionary teacher. Her father was Andrew Leslie, a Baptist missionary in Calcutta, India, for many years. After college she served eight years as the superintendent of an institution for the education of Hindu women. Later she was involved in several kinds of work with women in Calcutta. Several of her poems and sonnets were published in *School Hymnal* (1880). She wrote several books including *The Dawn of Light; A Story for Hindu Women* (1867); *Heart Echoes from the East* (1861); and *Eastern Blossoms; A Story for Native Christian Women* (1875).

l'HUILLIER, MARIE de VILLENEUVE, founder of the Catholic community for women Daughters of the Cross in France in 1640. Details of her personal life are obscure, but her work was influential and under the supervision of Francis de Sales.

LIEO, I. L. (1879-1927), pioneer leader of missionary efforts in China. A convert of the Chinese Episcopal church, she went to St. Hilda's School in Wauchang. After she witnessed an American woman being dedicated as a deaconess, she expressed the desire to dedicate her life as one also. Later a training school was established for deaconesses, and she was in its first graduating class. Among her ministries were teaching and visiting the ill.

LINCOLN, NANCY HANKS (c. 1787-1818), Christian mother of Abraham Lincoln, sixteenth president of the United States. A native of Virginia, she and Thomas Lincoln had three children, one of whom died in infancy. They lived in Elizabethtown, Kentucky; later they moved near Hodgenville, where Abraham was born, and then to Indiana. Thomas Lincoln did not approve of slavery, and there was no slavery in Indiana. The Bible was a definite part of Nancy's life. She read it to her children and applied its truths in daily living. She was of Baptist persuasion. Nancy Lincoln died when Abe was just nine years old; she contracted an illness associated with milk contamination. Abraham Lincoln visibly reflected and lived the truths of Scripture so clearly taught by his mother. That influence reached out through President Lincoln to the country and the world.

LINCOLN, SARAH BUSH JOHNSTON (1788-1869), second wife of Thomas Lincoln and stepmother of Abraham Lincoln. Sarah or "Sally" was a personal friend of Nancy Hanks and knew the family well. In fact, the sister of Abraham Lincoln was named for her future stepmother. After Sally was widowed with with three children and Tom Lincoln was left with two children, it seemed natural that their families become one. Approximately a year after the death of Nancy Hanks Lincoln, Sally and Tom were married. Although she was not an educated woman, she sensed great potential in Abe and had considerable influence in encouraging him to go to school, read, and study. She, too, carried on the Christian principles taught by Abe's mother. Because Abe was so young, Sally's Christian influence even overshadowed that which he remembered of his own mother. In later years, when he was president, Abraham Lincoln highly praised Sally for her influence and encouragement in his life. He had read the Bible until he knew much of it by heart, and he also knew how to apply it to his life and work.

LIND, JENNY (1821-1887), sometimes referred to as the "Swedish Nightingale." Jenny Lind was a much loved singer on both sides of the Atlantic. Born in deprived circumstances, she had little opportunity for schooling until her unusual singing talent was recognized. It is said that someone heard her singing to her pet cat and was so thrilled with her voice that he reported it to Madamoiselle Lundbery of the Royal Opera. She, too, listened to Jenny and labeled her a "genius." Thus the needed education and training for Jenny was assured. She studied in Paris, and even in her teens her concerts were much praised in Sweden and elsewhere. As she traveled and sang, her popularity grew. She came to the United States and was contracted for 150 concerts. Thousands greeted her arrival in New York City, and Broadway was decorated with arches in her honor. Although she sang opera, classical concerts, and popular songs, she offered her Christian testimony largely through the hymns of Lina Sandell. She gave liberally to worthy causes and voiced her Christian faith. She married a musician, Otto Goldschmidt.

LINDSEY, ANNE (Lady) (c. 1645-c. 1730), Countess of Rothes. Faithful Christian of nobility who aided the Presbyterians. Her mother was a devout Christian, and she was taught the truths of the Bible. She was the oldest daughter of John, first Earl of Lindsay, and his wife, Margaret Hamilton, daughter of the Marquis of Hamilton. She married John, sixth Earl of Rothes, a member of the Privy Council, not a Presbyterian, but for the sake of his wife he willingly helped them. Their palace became a place of refuge where believers could find food and help. Not until his deathbed did the Earl of Rothes realize his own need of the faith he had seen demonstrated so faithfully in his wife. He called for a Presbyterian minister and is believed to have made a profession of faith.

LIOBA (c. 710-799), a relative of Boniface who helped him in establishing Roman Catholicism in Germany. She was only daughter of her parents and apparently not confidential with her brothers but instead sought the counsel of her cousin, Boniface. Educated in a monastery at Wimborne, England, she went to Germany about 748, only a few years before Boniface was martyred. Boniface appointed her administrator of a Catholic community at Bischofsheim and in charge of other such communities in Germany under the Benedictine order. She continued her work long after the martyrdom of Boniface in 754. Boniface went to Frisia the year he died and left orders for his burial at Fulda and that Lioba's remains should be placed in his sepulcher. When she died, some twenty-four years later, the monks were unwilling to open the grave of Boniface and instead buried her near the altar he had built to Christ and the twelve apostles.

LIVINGSTONE, MARY MOFFATT (1820-1862), missionary to Africa, daughter of Robert and Mary Moffatt, and wife of Dr. David Livingstone. She was born at Griquatown, Africa, at the first African home of her parents. She was taught by her mother and later taught at a primary school in Africa. Although the Moffatts knew Dr. Livingstone before, acquaintances were renewed as they returned from a trip to England, stopping briefly some distance from their mission station. A physician, graduate of a medical school in Glasgow, Livingstone heard Robert Moffatt speak in London, which prompted his response to the field of Africa. David Livingstone had been serving in Africa four years as a bachelor, but now he was certain that the Lord had brought Mary Moffatt to be his companion and helper. They were married in 1845 at the mission church where her parents were serving in Kuruman. The years that followed were difficult for Mary, as they moved about often and she was ill much of the time. They had six children, and she was more than once plagued with partial paralysis, so she and the children returned to England for four years that she might recover. Even their time at home was one of near poverty living. David Livingstone was highly praised through the British Isles. On their return to Africa Mary became ill at sea. David was with her on the Zambesi Delta when she was stricken with an illness from which she never recovered.

LOMELINO, VICENTINA (c. 1553-1605), a noble Italian woman of Genoa who founded the Order of the Annonciades and known for her charity. She took special interest in the needy women who were abused because of their plight. She married and had several children, but details of her life are not available.

LOVE, OLIVE DURGIN (1893-1977), a devoted teacher and missionary to the Belgian Congo (Zaire) for many years under the African Inland Mission. A native of Virginia, she attended school there. Some of her education was in law, and she worked for a law firm in Washington, D.C., before going to Africa in 1924. She established an orphanage and a training school for African girls. Her tireless ministry to their spiritual, physical, and intellectual needs resulted in the further establishment of many homes and families devoted to Christ and the teaching of His Word.

LOVEGREN, IDA (1890-1972), a pioneer missionary to China who served in west China from 1917 to 1935. Her husband, Levi, was with the Army Air Corps in China from 1942 to 1946. The Lovegrens returned to west China under the Conservative Baptist Foreign Mission Society until he was taken prisoner by the Communists in 1951. She escaped to Hong Kong, where she remained until he was released in 1955. Although officially retired in 1957, she and her husband served in Taiwan from 1957 to 1963, working with new missionaries to open Conservative Baptist work there. She is especially remembered for the great courage and faith demonstrated during the four years her husband was held in a communist prison.

LUDÄMILIA, ELIZABETH von SCHWARZBURG RUDOLFSTADT (1640-1672), recognized as a German hymnist, credited with 215 hymns, many of which are part of the traditional German sacred music. These were published complete in 1687, fifteen years after her death.

LUEDERS, GILBERTA WALTON (1921-1982), pioneer radio missionary and Bible teacher with the Far East Broadcasting Company and the Sudan Interior Mission. Born in midwestern United States, she graduated cum laude from John Brown University, then took NBC radio script writing classes in Chicago and attended Moody Bible Institute. She was licensed as a first class radio operator, FCC, and gained experience at the WMBI station in Chicago. She became the first program director for the Far East Broadcasting Company in Manila, Philippines, in 1950. During furlough in 1959, she met Arn Lueders, a widower with two small boys, on furlough from the Sudan Interior Mission radio station ELWA in Liberia, West Africa. They married and served the Lord together in radio work in Liberia under SIM. As a Bible teacher she spent her final eight years in a Theological Education Extension context with her husband administering the program to African men and women church leaders.

LUKE, JEMIMA THOMPSON (1813-1906), writer of a favorite hymn of children written in 1841, "I Think When I Read That Sweet Story of Old." She had been teaching in the Normal Infant School, Gray's Inn Road, where marching pieces were used for classroom and exercise singing. While traveling on a stage coach between Taunton and Wellington, she wrote the words of this poem, which were adapted to music. She was born in London; her father directly involved with the ministry of floating chapels for seamen and a founder of the British and Foreign Sailors' Society. As early as age thirteen she contributed poetry anonymously to *The Juvenile Magazine*. As for her poem adapted to music, because her father was superintendent of their Sunday school and this was such a favorite of the children, he sent it to the editor of *The Sunday School Teachers' Magazine*. They published it, so it became a favorite of many more children. She was married to Samuel Luke in 1843. At one time she was accepted as a missionary to the women in India, but her poor health prevented her from going. She served as editor for *The Missionary Repository*, the first missionary magazine for children.

LUMBLEY, CARIE GREEN (1869-1947), pioneer missionary to Nigeria under the Southern Baptist Convention. Born in London, she received a private education and dedicated her life to the Lord in 1890. In 1899 she married W. T. Lumbley and shortly afterward sailed for missionary work in West Africa. She founded a girls school at Abeokuta, and in 1928 the king of England conferred on her the title "Member of the British Empire." Her husband died in 1906, but two years later she was reappointed to Nigeria and went with a British couple. This marked the first time a widow or unmarried woman had been sent as a missionary to West Africa by the Southern Baptist Convention.

LUTHER, KATHERINE von BORA (1499-1552), devout wife of Martin Luther, leader of the German Reformation, and founder of the Lutheran church. She was born in Saxony of a noble family from Meissen, Germany. Her parents were Hans and Katherine (von Haubitz) von Bora. Mrs. von Bora died while Katherine was very young; her father remarried, and she was sent to the Cistercian Cloister Marienthron in Nimbschen, where an aunt was the abbess. Many women there were from noble families. Katherine became a nun in 1515 and soon began hearing of Martin Luther, an Augustinian monk, lecturing on the Bible at the University of Wittenberg. In 1517 he posted his famous Ninety-five Theses against indulgences in the Catholic church. Soon monks and nuns began to seek freedom, including Katherine and eight others from that convent. Just before Easter in 1523, a merchant delivered goods to the convent, and the nuns hid in his wagon and thus were taken into the New Saxony area where the leaders were friendly toward Luther. On to Wittenberg they went, and Luther was able to find them suitable housing or families to take them in for the time. It is believed that Katherine lived in the home of a family of Lucas Cranach, a well-known portrait painter of that day. The other nuns who left with Katherine found husbands. Luther even suggested that she marry Dr. Kasper Glatz, but Katherine was not interested. It is said that Luther had not seriously considered marriage himself because he thought he would likely be burned at the stake. This changed as he became acquainted with Katherine. They were married in 1525; she was twenty-six and he was forty-two. All biographers agree that their marriage was a happy one, and that she was an unusually industrious homemaker, wife, and mother. She had six children of their own, but she mothered several of her husband's nieces and nephews. While her husband was preaching, translating the Bible into German, writing hymns, and performing numerous other ministries, often under the same roof she was faithfully caring for the necessities of the family and teaching the children. Some of the tutors from Wittenberg University stayed in their home as did others traveling through. She took in the homeless and cared for many who were ill other than her own family. She survived her husband by only six years. While fleeing from Wittenberg because of the bubonic plague, she died as the result of an accident. She was fifty-three years of age.

LYON, MARY (1797-1849), a pioneer in higher Christian education for women. Born in Massachusetts, she attended schools there and at the age of seventeen began teaching. She taught for approximately sixteen years in Ipswich and in Londonberry, New Hampshire, at the Adams Female Seminary. Miss Lyon saw the great need of more opportunities in higher education for women, so she left teaching in 1834 and began a campaign to solicit funds for a new school. Her efforts in this venture were succesful, and she established the first school of higher learning for women in the state of Massachusetts. Thus, Mount Holyoke College (then called Seminary) was founded and opened for classes in 1837. Not only was Mary Lyon the founder of Mount Holyoke but the first administrator of the school, a position she held the rest of her life. A dedicated Christian, she planned the curriculum to offer training for various kinds of Christian service, including missions. She also found time to write, some her writing was published in the *Missionary Offering* periodical in 1843. In 1905 Mary Lyon was elected to the American Hall of Fame for this pioneer work in the education of women in America.

M

MANWELL, MARY PAINE (1859-1932), a teacher, school administrator, author. She was active in the Women's Christian Temperance Union and left an impact of leadership and courage. Born in Pennsylvania, she was the daughter of a Wesleyan Methodist minister. She dedicated her life to Christian work with youth. She graduated from Mexico Academy in New York and taught in Wasioja Seminary in Minnesota, later becoming a school administrator there. In 1887 she married S. A. Manwell, a Wesleyan Methodist minister and assisted him. She held several offices in the Women's Christian Temperance Union, but it was through her missionary activities that her influence was felt around the world. For thirty-five years she served as conference treasurer of the Women's Home and Foreign Missionary Society. In 1903 she was elected the first denominational president of the Women's Home and Foreign Missionary Society and served for two quadrenniums. She wrote the first constitution of the Young Missionary Workers Band, a denominational missionary group for children, and contributed many articles to denominational publications.

MARCELLA (325-410), a Christian widow of a Roman family of nobility. She turned her palace into a place of retreat for Bible study, teaching, and Christian activities. She used her wealth and energies for benevolent work, ascetic practices, including prayer and teaching the Scriptures to other women of nobility in Rome. Jerome stayed in her palace three years, taught and translated Hebrew and Greek texts into Latin, for Pope Damasus had commissioned him to do a revision of the Latin gospels in 382. Jerome referred to Marcella's palace as an "Ecclesia Domestica," or church of the household, for not only were Bible classes held there, but it was a house of meditation, prayer, and worship. It was here that Paula and her daughter decided to help Jerome in his translation work and where Fabiola was inspired to establish the first hospital in Rome. Many other projects resulted from the fellowship and seclusion of Marcella's palace. When Rome was besieged by the Goths in 410, Marcella was treated harshly, resulting in her death at age eighty-five.

MARCELLINA (c. 330-c. 398), born into the Christian family of Aurelius Ambrosius in Rome, and the sister of Satyrus and Ambrose of Milan. After her mother was left a widow, Marcellina helped her with Ambrose's education. Pope Liberius consecrated her in 353. In later years she lived with Ambrose at Milan. He dedicated his *De Virginbus* to her, for her influence of prayer was significant.

MARGARET OF ANTIOCH (c. Fourth Century), although little is known about her, various writings concur that she was martyred about 300, during the reign of Diocletian. Reference is made to her actions of self-defense to preserve her virginity. She has been included among patron saints, and in art she is often presented as a shepherdess.

MARGARET OF SCOTLAND (c. 1045-c. 1093), queen consort of Malcolm II and daughter of Edward III. After Edward's death she and her family fled to Scotland from England for safety from the Norman invasion. In 1070 she became the second wife of Malcolm Canmore, king of Scotland, and was influential in promoting the interests of the church of Rome. She became directly involved with helping the sick, poor, orphans, and prisoners. She was left a widow when her husband was killed in Northumberland. The chapel in Edinburgh Castle is named in her honor. Pope Innocent IV canonized Margaret in 1250.

MARGUERITE BOURGEYOS (1620-1700), Catholic missionary who founded the first uncloistered community for women in Canada. Born in Troyes, France, she traveled to Canada in 1653 for pioneer missionary work. Although she founded the Church of Bonsecours in Ville Marie, an outgrowth of her original work is the Congregation of Notre Dame of Montreal, which spread over Canada, Japan, and parts of the United States.

MARGUERITE OF VALOIS (MARGUERITE of NAVARRE) (1492-1549), queen, author, translator, and defender of Protestantism. She was the daughter of Louise of Savoy and Charles de Valois-Orleans Comte de Angouleme, and sister of Francis I of France. She was educated by a governess, Madame Chatillon, who was a learned and devout widow. Marguerite was carefully instructed in Latin, Greek, English, Italian, philosophy, theology, music, and literature. Much of her knowledge of the Scriptures and her faith were attributed to Léfevre, with whom she had a lifelong friendship. She used her influence to protect him at times, as well as Flavel and other prominent Christian men of her time. In 1509 she married Charles, the last Duke of Alencon. She remained in the French court after the crowning of her brother, for he sought her counsel, and they were especially devoted to each other. Francis did not care for the Reformed cause, but she influenced him to aid the Reformers, and what she was able to do in France also affected the Protestant cause in Germany, England, and Holland. No one was put to death for heresy in Paris when Marguerite was in the city. Charles died in 1525, and she married the king of Navarre, Henry d'Albret, leaving her native France and openly doing missionary work in Navarre. She became the mother of Jeanne d'Albret. Marguerite's grandson was Henry IV, who declared the Edict of Nantes in 1598. Clement Marot and other Reformers held worship services in her castle, and she took communion with them. When her husband expressed displeasure with this, she told her brother, Francis, who even threatened war because of her husband's attitude. Her husband soon changed; not only to sympathize with her defense of the Protestants but also to share in their teachings. In addition to being a student, Margaret was ranked as one of the greatest poets of her era, and in 1533 a book of her poems based on psalm 42 was issued, *The Mirror of the Sinful Soul*. In 1548, just before her death, she wrote *A Godly Meditation of the Soul*, and in 1553 her *Heptameron* was published posthumously. She established a home for orphans and with her husband promoted improved agriculture, education, and undertook other endeavors to improve their country. Her dying wish was fulfilled in that her daughter, Jeanne, would carry on the work she had begun. Her palace was a stronghold of Protestantism.

MARIA THERESA (1717-1780), an influential noble woman, daughter of Charles VI, and empress of Austria and Germany. She was born in Vienna and reared as a Roman Catholic; yet she maintained the rights of her crown against the court of Rome. She went to extreme measures to correct some of the worst abuses in the Catholic church. For example, she prohibited the presence of priests at the making of wills and would not permit anyone to take monastic vows before the age of twenty-five. It was her forces that suppressed the Inquisition in Milan and in 1773 the Order of Jesuits.

MARING, MARGARET (c. 1516-1557), a member of a private congregation in London. She was questioned as to her sincerity in the religion she professed, examined, and sent to Newgate and later interrogated a second and third time. In each examination she proved her sincerity and true belief in Christ. She was condemned to death and was fastened to the same stake as John Rough and martyred for her faith.

MARSHALL, CATHERINE LeSOURD (1915-1983), author and widow of U.S. Senate chaplain Peter Marshall. She is especially remembered for writing the biography of her husband, *A Man Called Peter*. It was a New York Times best seller for more than fifty consecutive weeks in 1955. It's popularity grew even more when it was made into a film. She also wrote *Christy*, which has sold more than 8 million copies, and several nonfiction works: *Beyond Ourselves, To Live Again, Something More,*

The Helper, and her autobiography published in 1980, *Meeting God at Every Turn*. It was in 1959 that she married Leonard E. LeSourd, an editor and publisher. Together they founded a group called The Intercessors, which is a prayer fellowship, each member coveting to pray for others. Because of her writing, she continued to use Marshall as her pen name.

MARSHMAN, HANNAH (1767-1847), missionary to India. She and her husband, Joshua, joined William Carey in 1799 to form the famous mission at Serampore, just north of Calcutta. This group was responsible for printing the first editions of the New Testament in more than thirty oriental languages and dialects. Her parents died when she was quite young, so she made her home with her grandfather, John Clark, pastor of the Baptist Church in Wiltshire, England. She was well taught in the Scriptures and committed her life to the Lord while in her teens. When she married Joshua Marshman, he was a weaver but pursuing his studies. In 1794 he became head of a Baptist School at Broadmead, Bristol. Mrs. Marshman and with her husband were challenged by the work of William Carey and the Baptist missionary work in India. Thus, they became a part of the Serampore work, a pioneer mission. In addition to her teaching she had a special ministry with the girls and women of India, helping them with education and teaching them the Scriptures.

MARSTON, ELEANOR AGNES (1860-1904), pioneer missionary to Tibet. Sponsored by the China Inland Mission, she first went to Ganking and then to Hanchung to administer a school. In 1887 she married Cecil Polhill, and they worked among the Tibetans. They survived some extremely difficult situations but tried to live like the nationals to win their respect and confidence. At one time they were attacked and beaten for their witness. Two national Christians offered to be beaten in their stead and apparently were beaten as well.

MARSTON, SARAH H. (c. 1835-c. 1905), The first missionary sponsored by the Women's Union Missionary Society of America for Heathen Lands. This group was organized in Boston in 1860, and the following year the charter was granted. Within that year of charter, Sarah H. Marston went to Toungoo, Burma, as their first missionary.

MARTENS, KATHARINA ZACHARIAS (1867-1929), Russian immigrant to Canada who experienced many difficult times during World WarI, such as the Crimean bloodbath, illness, and poverty. She was not only a faithful wife and mother, but a missionary among women and supportive of her husband in his teaching and preaching. She was influential in organizing the Altonau Evangelical Mennonite Church in Russia and a similar one in Saskatchewan, Canada.

MARTHA, ANNE BRIGET (1749-1824), a nun in France who risked her life to care for many ill and wounded soldiers during the French Revolution and the wars that immediately followed. She cared for prisoners of all nations and ministered to them spiritually. It is for her that the Martha Order is named.

MARTIN, SARAH (1791-1843), an English philanthropist known for her missionary work in improving conditions for women prisoners. She made personal visits to prisons, read Scripture to the women, witnessed, taught them to read, helped them to memorize Scripture, and taught them ways they could work with their hands. Her work was not sponsored by any church or organization; she was simply a dedicated Christian who supported herself in the worthy and needy area of prison reform.

MARVAL, ALICE MARIETTA (1865-1904), a missionary doctor who went to Cawnpore in 1899 and served at St. Catherine's hospital. She was sponsored by the Society for the Propagation of the Gospel. She taught Bible classes, working tirelessly during the plague. In the last month of her life she paid 246 visits to patients in the city. In spite of the shortness of her medical missionary experiences, she was much loved and a memorial for her was established in the hospital.

MARY OF EGYPT (c. 344-c. 421), details of this early convert to Christ are obscure, but she lived in Alexandria, Egypt. Her life was largely devoted to doing penance, but Zosimus, a priest, talked with her in the Jerusalem area and administered communion to her house before her demise. She is mentioned by several historians.

MARY STUART (Queen) (1542-1587), known in literature as "Queen of Scots," she inherited the throne when just six days old. Her father, James V, suffered a mental breakdown and died in December 1542. Her mother was Mary of Guise, known also as Mary of Lorraine, of the de Medici family, and whose grandmother was Mary Tudor, daughter of Henry VIII of England. Mary was born at Linlithgow Palace and crowned queen as an infant; her mother served as regent until her death in 1560. The reign of her father showed favor toward Catholic forces; he, too, had inherited the throne as an infant. But, in 1560 the Estates of Parliament abolished the authority of the pope in Scotland. In the meantime she married Francis II of France, but when he died in 1560, she returned to Scotland to reclaim the throne. In 1565 she married a cousin, Henry Stuart (Lord Darnley), who was killed in 1567 by a strange incident for which some thought she was responsible. After only three months she married again, this time to James Hepburn, Earl of Bothwell. All of these political moves caused her downfall, for the people of Scotland revolted; she was imprisoned; and her son by Henry Stuart, age one, was proclaimed James VI of Scotland, later to become James I of England. In 1568 she sought favor and refuge from her cousin Elizabeth I, monarch of England. Mary Stuart was executed for treason.

MARY TUDOR or **MARY I** (1516-1558), queen of England from 1553 to 1558. She was born of Henry VIII and his first wife, Catherine of Aragon. Mary was educated a Catholic and was much confused by the divorce of her parents as her father declared her illegitimate. Her early betrothal to the heir of France was later promised to Emperor Charles V, and at the age of ten she was declared Princess of Wales to Ludlow. For a while she simply went into retirement. When her father died in 1547, several marriages later, the throne was inherited by her half brother, Edward VI, who lived only six more years. Parliament then annulled the divorce of her parents to establish her as the legitimate heir and queen in 1553. Attempts were without success to have her Protestant cousin Lady Jane Grey become queen. One of Mary's first acts as queen was to have Jane Grey executed. Indeed, Catholic power was emerging. In 1554 she married Philip II of Spain, purposing to restore Catholicism in England. She had nearly 300 Protestant leaders burned at the stake, including Hugh Latimer and Thomas Cranmer. Her five-year reign was a series of tragedies for the Protestant cause. Especially tragic was her own life and failure to win the hearts of her people. She earned the title "Bloody Mary."

MASON, ELLEN B. (c. 1827-c. 1901), organized the Women's Union Missionary Society of America for Heathen Lands in Boston in 1860.

MATHILDA (c. 1046-c. 1115), influential as Countess of Tuscany. She had political connections with Pope Gregory VII. Her father was Boniface, Count of Tuscany. In 1079 she gave all her possessions to the church. She died in a Benedictine monastery of Polirone.

MATILDA (c. 895-968), queen of Germany, wife of Henry I and mother of Bruno, Archbishop of Cologne, Otto I, who became emperor of the Holy Roman Empire, Henry, Duke of Bavaria; a daughter Hedwige who married Hugo, Duke of France, and became mother of Hugh Capet. Her parents were Reinhilda and Count Theodoric, prince of Saxony. Born in Westphalia, she was educated at an abbey school where she was taught the the Bible, Latin, and music. She married Henry I in 909. Even as a queen she lived a devout life and was concerned with helping the poor and oppressed. It was apparent that she was a Bible student and established monasteries devoted to study at Quedlinburg, Nordhausen, Engern, and Poehlden.

MAYO, RUTH (1902-1977), outstanding pioneer missionary in China and Taiwan. A native of Wisconsin, she attended the Baptist Mission Training School of Chicago and the Bethel Institute at St. Paul. She first went to China with the China Bethel Mission and served from 1927 to 1936. Then during the war years she returned for church work in the United States. In 1944 she was appointed by the Conservative Baptist Foreign Mission Society to return to China and was among their first missionaries to go into China in 1946. There her responsibilities were centered in the operation of an orphanage in Kanhsien, southeast China, where she remained until she was forced to leave the country by the Communists in 1951. In October 1952 she was among the first missionaries to enter Taiwan under the Conservative Baptist Foreign Mission Society, continuing there in evangelism, teaching, and church planting ministries until her retirement in 1970.

MEARS, HENRIETTA CORNELIA (1890-1963), Christian educator, author, and leader in Sunday school curriculum work. She was born in North Dakota and went to the University of Nova Scotia. She taught in two towns in Minnesota, where she organized Sunday schools, and in 1928 became director of Christian education at the First Presbyterian Church of Hollywood, California. The Sunday school attendance multiplied, and she began writing the lesson materials, which was the forerunner of what became Gospel Light Press in 1933. She founded several camps and conference centers for Christian education and in 1961 established Gospel Literature in National Tongues for the purpose of sending Sunday school literature throughout the world.

MECHTHILD OF MAGDEBURG (1210-1280), author and spiritual adviser. She was associated with the Beguines, a community of women who devoted their lives to religious activities, including prayer and study, but without taking monastic vows. Early details of her life are obscure, but her family was noble, educated, and probably lived in or near Magdeburg. Some describe her as a mystic, for her writings report visions and parables. She wrote a book titled *The Flowing Light of God*, a collection of essays on her visions, parables, and poems.

MELANCHTHON, KATHERINE KRAPP (c. 1500-1557), devoted wife of Philip Melanchthon, a Reformer and friend of Martin Luther. She and Philip had four children, two boys and two girls. Her father was a magistrate of Wittenburg, Germany, where it is believed she married Philip in 1520. Details of her early life are vague.

MILLER, DOROTHY RUTH (1873-1944), teacher, author, dean of women and registrar at Prairie Bible Institute. A native of Pennsylvania, she attended Columbia University, New York University, and Nyack Bible College. She became a faculty member at Nyack and later with Simpson Bible Institute at Seattle. Her specialized teaching areas were English and history, but realizing that there were no adequate textbooks for history written from a biblical viewpoint, she wrote *Ancient History in Bible Light*. From Simpson Bible Institute she was invited to Prairie Bible Institute in Alberta, Canada. In the fall of 1928, she began teaching at Prairie and remained there until poor health forced her to retire in 1944.

MILLER, MARY M. (1897-1963), author and professor of English at Hesston College and for whom the college library is named. She wrote the book *A Pillar of Cloud*, published in 1959. She served in France during World War II with the Mennonites.

MILLER, RUTH BLOSSER (1893-1977), a pioneer missionary in India. She was a leader of women's work in the Mennonite church both at home and in India. She had considerable influence among young people considering missionary work.

MILLS, MINNIE (1872-1965), missionary educator and college president under the American Board of Commissioners for Foreign Missions. A native of Iowa, she received a degree from Olivet College in 1893 and in 1930 was honored with an L.H.D degree from her alma mater. She taught several science subjects at the American Collegiate Institute in Symrna (now Izmir), Turkey, then worked with refugee students in the school for girls named Pierce College at Athens, Greece. She served this college as president from 1928 to 1941 and was honored by the Greek government for her work there.

MINER, LUELLA (1861-1935), missionary, school administrator, founder and for many years president of the North China Union College in Peking, later called Yenching University, and now Beijing University. A native of Ohio, she graduated from Oberlin College in 1914 and received her doctorate. She spent nearly forty-seven years as a missionary to China under the Women's Board of Missions of the Interior and the American Board of Commissioners for Foreign Missions.

MINN, NELLIE YABA, pioneer missionary in her native Burma, she became the first Burmese Young Women's Christian Association secretary. She studied at the University of Michigan and returned to Burma planning to establish a much needed home for Christian nurses working and studying in Rangoon. Several Christian projects resulted from the YWCA work, including a hostel for nurses.

MIRAMION, MARIE BONNEAU (1629-1696), whose life showed an unusual commitment to charitable service and munificence. Born in France of a wealthy family. She married Jean Jacques de Beauharnais, Lord of Miramion, who died the same year. As a widow she became involved with many charitable projects such as founding a house of refuge at Paris, another at Sainte-Pelagie for needy women. In 1660 she helped twenty-eight poor monks who had been driven from Picardy by the war and cared for them for several months. She contributed large amounts for establishing a seminary of foreign missions. In 1661 she organized a society of twelve girls to go out and teach country children first aid that they might care for wounded soldiers. She established a hospital for infants, and much of her work was formed into a community named Sainte-Famille, later incorporated into Sainte-Genevieve.

M'NAUGHT, MARION (1585-1643), a special correspondent of Samuel Rutherford, the Scottish Covenanter who was once exiled but later helped in the preparation of the Westminster Confession. During his exile he wrote many letters of importance. Among his published letters, forty-five were to Marion M'Naught. They seemed to be means of mutual spiritual encouragement. Her father was Laird of Kilquhanatie of Kirkpatric Durham at Kirkcudbright, Scotland. Her mother was associated with the House of Kenmure. Marion M'Naught became the wife of William Fullarton, provost of Kirkcudbright.

MOE, PETRA MALENA MALLA (1863-1953), an evangelist who ministered in Africa. She was born in Hafslo, Norway, and accepted Christ under the preaching of Hans Wielsen Hauge in 1884. After her parents were gone, she and a sister came to America to be with another sister. She attended Moody Memorial Church and was especially edified by the preaching of R. A. Torrey and Dwight L. Moody. After being counseled by Scandinavian evangelist Fredrick Franson, and through personal study, she prepared for the Lord's direction. In April 1892, she was commissioned with others at Bethesda Church and went to Mashonaland on the east coast of South Africa. She also served at the Bethel Mission in Swaziland, where a school was established. Her missionary activity was primarily one of evangelism; she was sponsored by The Scandinavian (later Evangelical) Alliance Mission and continued her work after she retired. In fact, she had a "gospel wagon" built and spent ten winters in Tongaland with a group of faithful African helpers, visiting areas that were still untouched by the gospel. At one time she spent twenty-eight years on the mission field without a furlough.

Her final days were spent in Africa. She won the hearts of every rank, and even government leaders in Swaziland spoke highly of her.

MOFFATT, MARY SMITH (1795-1870), pioneer missionary to Africa, wife of Robert Moffatt, and mother of Mary, the wife of Dr. David Livingstone. Born in New Windsor, England, she was the daughter of James Smith and Mary Gray Smith. She received her early education at a Moravian school, and she grew up in Dukinfield, England. In 1819 she traveled from London to Africa to marry missionary Robert Moffatt. They were married two days after Christmas in 1819 at Cape Town, South Africa. After some traveling, they settled at Kuruman in Bechuanaland (now Botswana) and established a mission there, which was one of the largest stations in the area and included a church. Difficulties were many: problems with the nationals, the translation of the Word, numerous times of illnesses and deaths in the family; but Mary Moffatt was true to the Lord in the mission to which He had called her. She taught in the primary school and had ten children of their own, several of which died in infancy. She took in three homeless native children who otherwise would have been buried alive with their dead mothers, as was the custom. She spent forty years in Africa. They returned to England from 1839 to 1843 to gain support and workers for the mission. Dr. David Livingstone was one of those answering the call to Africa. They returned to Kuruman and continued their work, retiring in 1870. They had been back in England only a brief time when Mary Moffatt died; her husband lived twelve years longer.

MONICA (c. 331-387), the devout Christian mother of Augustine. She was born in a Christian family at Tagaste, North Africa. Her faith, prayers, and Christlike life influenced her entire family to become Christians. She married Patricius, a man of limited means and known for his difficult temperament before he became a Christian, shortly before his death. Although she had other children, Augustine was the best known because he became Bishop of Hippo and was considered the greatest of the Latin Fathers. He was converted in Milan in 384 at age thirty, only three years before Monica died. They were moving to Rome when Monica died on the way, at Ostia. Her life has inspired many works of literature and art; a painting of her and Augustine hangs in the National Gallery of Art in London.

MONTGOMERY, CARRIE FRANCES JUDD (1858-c. 1931), an author, home missionary, and native of Buffalo, New York. She published a book of poems and had work published in a number of periodicals. She established a Faith and Rest Home, which was a faith project to provide accommodations for those in need of living quarters. She married George Simpson Montgomery of San Francisco, and in 1891 they both entered the Salvation Army.

MONTGOMERY, HELEN BARRETT (1861-1934), an author, translator, mission promoter, and first American woman to lead a major denomination. Born in Kingsville, Ohio, she was reared in New York state. Her father was a school administrator and Baptist minister. She graduated from Wellesley College with honors in 1884 and in 1877 married William A. Montgomery, a manufacturer. She was active in the Women's Central Committee of the Baptist Church; successful in working with others to raise funds for missionary endeavors; traveled to mission fields to evaluate needs, especially related to women missionaries; was the first president of the combined Women's American Baptist Foreign Mission Society, a position she held for ten years. In 1921-22 she served as the first woman president of the Northern Baptist Convention. In 1924 she completed the translation of the Greek New Testament into modern English known as the *Centenary Translation*. She also wrote: *The King's Highway; Following the Sunrise: A Century of Baptist Missions, 1813-1913; The Bible and Missions; From Campus to World Citizenship*; and *Western Women in Eastern Lands*, which sold 50,000 copies in its first six weeks. She was co-founder of the World

Wide Guild in 1915 and co-sponsor of the World Day of prayer in 1919. She was awarded honorary degrees from Brown University, Denison University, and Franklin College, and an LL.D. from her alma mater, Wellesley College. In addition to her many honors and leadership positions, she taught a Sunday school class for forty-four years.

MOODY, BETSEY HOLTON (1805-1896), faithful homemaker and mother of Dwight L. Moody. She was born near Northfield, Massachusetts. In 1828 she married Edwin Moody, a bricklayer. They made their home not far from her family. One of her husband's first gifts to her was a family Bible in which she recorded the birthdates of their children. Dwight Lyman was sixth of their nine children. Edwin was working when suddenly stricken with severe pain and died in May 1841, when Dwight was only four years old. Just one month later Betsey bore twins, Elizabeth and Samuel. The family had a difficult time financially, but she was able to carry on with routine matters and faithfully each Sunday she had the children in the Lord's house. The religion of her family was nominally Unitarian, but there was a simple trust in God and a deep loyalty for Puritan ethics. When it came to one of her own becoming a minister, she disapproved. Not until Dwight Moody became well known did she consent to hear him preach. She heard him for first time in the Northfield Congregational Church in 1876. He was surprised to see his mother in the congregation, but when those who wished prayer were asked to stand, she did. She continued to grow closer to the Lord as she aged, and Moody's love for her deepened. Her Christian character was felt by the children of the Northfield Schools as was her influence for the Lord.

MOODY, EMMA CHARLOTTE REVELL (1842-1903), wife of evangelist Dwight L. Moody. Born in London, she was the daughter of Emma Manning and Fleming Revell, whose roots were French Huguenot. Her family emigrated to Chicago in 1849, when she was only seven. She graduated from high school in 1860, taught briefly, and in 1862 married Dwight L. Moody. She was twenty, he was twenty-five; she was a Baptist, he was a Congregationalist. Because of her education and his lack of formal education, she helped and actually taught him, although he was well read. He became an outstanding evangelist of his day, and his work lives on primarily through the Moody Bible Institute and its outreach ministries. The Lord blessed them with several children. She worked with him in Sunday school work and evangelistic campaigns, doing much of his correspondence.

MOODY, MAY WHITTLE (1876-1963), composer of the music for the two hymns "Moment by Moment" and "The Story of Jesus Can Never Grow Old." Details of her life are not available.

MOON, CHARLOTTE (LOTTIE) (1840-1912), a dedicated missionary martyr who served in Tenchow and Pingtu, China, for nearly forty years under the Southern Baptist Convention. Born in an aristocratic family in Virginia, she was taught at home, then sent to Albermarle Female Institute and Hollins College. She was an honor student, and in 1861 was one of the first Southern women to receive a master's degree. She taught briefly and established a school in Georgia, then answered a call to the mission field of China in 1873. Her sister, Edmonia, had gone to China the previous year, and they worked together until her sister became ill and had to return home. Lottie learned Chinese quickly, taught, and did evangelistic work, giving herself without reserve. Often her letters urged her denomination leaders to send more missionaries and help supply missionary needs in China. The Lottie Moon Christmas Offering was established in 1888 and provided three additional missionaries the first year. She survived the Boxer Rebellion and was evacuated to Japan only briefly. Back in China, her letters continued to plea for money and food to relieve the famine conditions. She spent her own savings and did what she could until her health began to fail. Fellow missionaries sent for a doctor for her. The doctor concluded that Lottie was starving to death. A nurse accompanied her, and they started for the United States, but in Kobe, Japan, the Lord took Lottie home. Memorials stand in her memory in China and in her native state, but her greatest memorial is the many young Christians who have been challenged by her life and by the Lottie Moon Christmas Offering taken by thousands of Southern Baptist Churches each year for the cause of missions.

MOON, EDMONIA HARRIS (1851-1908), missionary to China and sister of Lottie Moon. They worked together at Tenchow in northern Shantung province. Born in Virginia, her family was aristocratic, her education private, as she was tutored by her sister and attended the Richmond Female Institute. She went to China before Lottie, having been appointed by the Southern Baptist Foreign Mission Board in the spring of 1872. Soon after appointment, budget limitations made her going uncertain, so she determined to go at her own expense. The women of five missionary societies of Richmond pooled their efforts to raise support for Edmonia. They formed the Richmond Female Missionary Society to provide her support. Later, their efforts were expanded to include a similar state organization. Their support provided building a home in China for the Moon sisters. She was an effective missionary for several years but limited by ill health, and in 1876 her sister, Lottie, accompanied her home, thus terminating her appointment in 1878.

MOORE, MARY PRIMM (1894-1980), one of the first Southern Baptist missionaries to Chile and a founder of the Chilean Woman's Missionary Union. A native of Florida, she completed her early education in 1917 and went to the Woman's Training School of Southwestern Theological Seminary in Fort Worth, Texas. She graduated with honors in 1919, receiving two degrees: a bachelor and master's of missionary training. She married Cecil Moore in 1918, and they worked among the Mexicans in Fort Worth. Later she and her husband were appointed to Chile, where they worked for forty-four years.

MORATA, OLYMPIA (1526-1555), an Italian Christian of influence. She was the daughter of Fulvio Pellegrino Morata, a teacher. She was taught well during her early years and especially enjoyed writing poetry, although much of her work was lost in the seige of Schweinfurt. She dropped her studies briefly to care for her aged father but was encouraged to study for herself the great doctrinal truths of the Bible. She wrote to Curione and urged him to translate Luther's catechism into Italian. After her death, Curione collected some of her letters to publish. She was interred in the St. Peter's Church at Heidelberg.

MORE, HANNAH (1745-1833), author, teacher, philanthropist born near Bristol, England. She was the youngest child of Mary Grace and Jacob More; her father was a teacher. She attended a school founded by her four sisters. She wrote a number of plays, the first of which was *A Search for Happiness*. She went to London and found popularity among well-known literary and intellectual leaders of the day, including Dr. Samuel Johnson, Sir Joshua Reynolds, Edmund Burke, and others who encouraged her to do more writing. Later she gathered a different circle of friends who encouraged her more in spiritual matters. She knew hymnwriter John Newton, who became a strong influence in her life, as did William Wilberforce. She accompanied Wilberforce and visited the Mendips mining district and was much impressed with the needs. She and her sisters established Sunday schools in that area. She not only gave out Bibles and prayer books, but clothing and necessities as well. She offered classes to help girls in domestic responsibilities and classes instructing mothers how to take better care of their families. Because of the influence of the Clapham group, she published the two-volume work *Coelebs in Search of a Wife*, the most widely read of her books. She also wrote many gospel tracts, some of which were translated into other languages. Other books by her include:*Slavery, On Female Education, Practical Piety, Christian Morals, Character and Writings of St. Paul,* and *Spirit of Prayer*. Her writings gained considerable funds, and at her death that money was distributed among seventy religious societies and charitable projects.

MOROZOWA, EFROSINIA (c.1800-c. 1850), a devout Russian Christian whose life influenced the origin of the Mennonite Brethren church. She is believed to have been born in the Ostrikow area and orphaned when about ten years old. She lived with a Catholic aunt and uncle who arranged for a Mennonite family to take her so she could work for a living. She became a Christian and learned to read the Bible. The teachings of that home and the meetings of the brethren there influenced her life, and when she desired baptism there was concern because of Russian authorities. However, she was baptized by Abram Dyck, who was brought to trial for having done so. Their testimonies were a witness to the authorities. However, after that little was written concerning her life. The Wirt Huebert family where she lived and the congregation that met in their home were vital in beginning the Mennonite Brethren church.

MORRIS, LELIA NAYLOR (1862-1929), author and hymnist born in Ohio. In 1881 married Charles H. Morris and was active in the Methodist Episcopal church. Not until the 1890s did she begin writing poems and setting them to music as hymns. Unlike many hymnists, she composed the music to go with her poems. She wrote both words and music to the following more familiar hymns: "Nearer, Still Nearer," "The Everlasting Arms," "Let Jesus Come into Your Heart," "What If It Were Today?" "Bring Your Vessels, Not a Few," and "Sweeter as the Years Go By." Another hymn, lesser known, is "I Cannot Tell It All," and was written following her return from Mountain Lake Park Camp Meeting, shortly after her conversion. Her eyesight began to fail about fifteen years before her death, and she became completely blind. Yet she continued to write and compose music. Her son provided her with a large blackboard on which were lines of the staff for her to use as long as she could see.

MOTT, LUCRETIA COFFIN (1793-1880), a Quaker minister, teacher, and leader in the American anti-slavery movement. In 1818 she was ordained in the Society of Friends and preached with an emphasis on justice. Details of her early life are unavailable.

MÜLLER, MARY GROVES (1797-1870), remembered as the faithful wife and co-worker of evangelist George Müller. They were married in 1830. Their lives together were characterized by mutual self-denial, selling what they had except necessities and accepting voluntary poverty for the sake of Christ. Their primary interest for the poor children of England led them to establish orphanage houses in Bristol, England. Through prayer and faith they not only evangelized, but helped needy children with material provisions.

MÜLLER, SUSANNAH GRACE SANGAR (1817-1895), second wife of George Müller. They were married in 1871, the year following the death of his first wife. She was able to continue with the ongoing work of the orphanage and assist with making the work known elsewhere. As others were trained to carry on the work in Bristol, the Müllers began a series of tours in 1875 that took them throughout the British Isles; on the European Continent; to America; later to Europe again, the Holy Land, Australia, several times back to the United States, and elsewhere. These evangelistic tours lasted about seventeen years and took place in forty-two countries. In addition to the evangelistic thrust, money was freely given for the work of the orphanages, caring for thousands of children. She preceded her husband in death by approximately three years.

MUSSELMAN, ROSE LAMBERT (1878-1974), author and pioneer missionary nurse in Turkey. Born in Pennsylvania, her parents were George and Amanda Lehman Lambert. Most of her childhood was spent in northern Indiana. She received her nurses training in Cleveland, Ohio, before going to Turkey in 1899 to become head of an Armenian Orphan School. During her time in Turkey there was great famine and disease. Because of ill health, she returned to the United States in 1910. The following year her book *Hadjin and the Armenian Massacres,* was published. She married D. G. Musselman, a Chicago businessman, and they later they moved to Texas. He preceded her in death by some forty-one years.

Mc

McAULEY, CATHERINE (1787-1841), founder of the Catholic community Sisters of Mercy. It began in Ireland in 1831 and spread to the United States in 1843. Born in Dublin, Ireland. Catherine's influence there during the cholera epidemic in 1832 was praised for organizing the distribution of food, clothing, and other necessities, She administered a house of refuge for women, teaching them useful arts and employment skills. Ten such Catholic communities were established in Ireland and two in London. Within a few years more than 200 Sisters of Mercy communities were established in Great Britain, United States, Newfoundland, South America, Australia, and New Zealand.

McCALLUM, EMILY (1858-1956), a missionary, educator, and school administrator serving with the American Board of Commissioners for World Missions. A native of Canada; her father was David McCallum, a well-known Methodist Episcopal minister. She taught and served as a school administrator in Constantinople and in Smyrna, now Izmir, Turkey. She was principal of the American Collegiate Institute, and later she founded the American Junior College in Athens for refugee students. This school was named Pierce College, and she remained there after her retirement. She attended Queen's College and McGill University and in 1921 was awarded an honorary master's degree from Olivet College. She was given special recognition by the Greek government for her missionary efforts.

McCORMICK, NETTIE FOWLER (1835-1923), a dedicated Christian philanthropist who made it possible for many to study for the ministry, prepare for missionary work, and perform a wide variety of services for the Lord. Born in New York state, Nettie Fowler attended the Genesee Wesleyan Seminary. While visiting in Chicago she met Cyrus H. McCormick, inventor of the grain reaper. They were married in 1859. Both were active in the Presbyterian church through teaching and in music, but the ministry of their wealth reached far beyond their local church and denomination. When her husband died in 1884, his large estate was left to her and their several children. She prayerfully administered this as a trust from the Lord. She designated more than $4,000,000 for the McCormick Theological Seminary in Chicago and to help many train for the ministry. The library there was her special gift, as was the gymnasium, built later. She provided the needed funds for John R. Mott and others to organize the World's Student Christian Federation. Mr. McCormick had given generously to Tusculum College, and she gave to other such southern mountain schools, Sunday schools, and churches. Numerous foreign missionary efforts were also helped by the McCormick estate. Such projects included a hospital in Siam, theological education in Korea, a women's hospital and a college in Tehran (capital of Persia), a language school and the provision of agricultural machinery at Nanking, and a school in Egypt. She visited some of the missions she helped support and served thirty-four years as vice president of the Women's Board of the Presbyterian Mission of the Northwest.

McDONALD, JESSIE (c. 1887-1980), the first woman missionary-surgeon to China under the China Inland Mission. A Canadian by birth, she received her medical training at Toronto University and completed her internship in Boston. She went to Scotland for Bible training and to London for a special course on the treating of tropical diseases. She sailed to China in 1913 and served in the Kaifeng area. Kaifeng was taken by the Japanese eventually, and she went to Yunnan province with access to Burma, where supplies could more easily come through. Here she worked with John and Isobel Kuhn. In 1941 the China Inland Mission Hospital in Tali was officially opened, but more problems led to the withdrawal of CIM missionaries from China. The Tali hospital was taken over by the communist government. She retired in 1952 to California and became an American citizen.

McDOUGALL, HARRIETT BUNYAN (c. 1811-1886), a pioneer missionary to Borneo. From a missionary-minded upper class family of Britain; she was married to Francis McDougall in 1843. He was the first bishop of Labuan and Sarawak, but studied medicine at Oxford, qualifying as a surgeon at King's College, London, in 1839. She encouraged him to offer himself as a missionary to Borneo, and in 1845 he was ordained. She taught Dyak women, and together she and her husband founded a school and established a church in the Sarawak area. Her health problems were complicated by the climate of Borneo, and the McDougalls lost three of their children in less than three years; two more died before they returned to England. Yet, through the Chinese insurrection, massacres, and other extreme difficulties she was a devoted wife and helper. They returned to England in 1867.

McFARLAND, AMANDA (c. 1837-c. 1898), believed to have been the first woman missionary to Alaska. A native of West Virginia, she served with her husband, D. F. McFarland, among the Indians of New Mexico and the Nez Perces in Idaho. He died in 1875, and in 1877 she was sent by the Presbyterian Board to Fort Wrangel, Alaska. There she established a home for girls trying to escape from white traders who had purchased them in exchange for goods the Indians desired. She had Bible classes and also taught the girls to sew and learn new ways. Soon she had over 100 girls. A larger house was secured but later destroyed by fire. Finally, a more convenient place was found at Sitka. Funds were scarce, and she used much of her own money. This venture grew into a boarding school that later became the Sitka Training School and today is known today as Sheldon Jackson Junior College.

McKEBBIN, ALMA E. BAKER (1871-1974), pioneer educator and author of Bible study textbooks. She was the first church school teacher in California under the Seventh Day Adventist church. In 1972 she was awarded the Adventist education Medallion of Merit, and the administration building of the Pacific Union College Preparatory Academy is named in her honor.

MACKENZIE, ANNE ALEXANDER (Lady) (c. 1619-1706), a faithful Christian of nobility and influence, she was the oldest daughter of Colin, first Earl of Seaforth and his wife, Lady Margaret Seton. Her father was considered a devout and benevolent man but died when she was a child. As a youth she heard Richard Baxter and apparently was converted under his preaching. She married Alexander, a staunch Covenanter and son of Lord Balcarres. Alexander was in the Covenanter's army at the battle of Alford, then was commissioned by the parliament of Scotland to King Charles I with proposals for agreement. Their family was forced to take refuge in France, where Alexander died, leaving her with five children. After his burial in Scotland she moved to London. Her family complicated her situation as not all of them agreed with her faith. She became friends with Richard Baxter and corresponded with him for some time. Later she married Archibald, ninth Earl of Argyll, also a Christian. Because of his Protestant stand he was put in prison in 1681 and later martyred. In spite of her problems, she was faithful. She died more than twenty years after the execution of her last husband.

McKERNAN, AGNES H. (1883-1982), a compassionate counselor, outstanding administrator, and director of the Women's Prison Bureau of the Salvation Army. A native of Northern Ireland, she served in Scotland, England, and the United States from 1907 to 1945, achieving the rank of lieutenant colonel. She won the respect of attorneys and officials in the U.S. Department of Justice for her work with women prisoners, especially for helping the women to find work after their release from prison. Twice she was elected president of the National Prisoners Aid Society and was the first woman to hold that office. One of the high spots in her career was her appointment as a delegate and speaker at the International Prison Congress at Berlin in 1935. Prison superintendents considered her their friend and respected her discernment in decisions concerning women inmates. She took time to go over the records of women prisoners to evaluate their improvement and conduct. Her spiritual counsel was highly honored as was her personal concern for the welfare of prisoners long after their release.

McPHERSON, AIMEE SEMPLE KENNEDY (1890-1944), a native of Canada, a missionary, author, evangelist, and founder of the International Church of the Four Square Gospel organized in 1927. Although she had a Methodist background, she was converted in her teens through the preaching of a Baptist evangelist who became her husband. They were missionaries to Hong Kong only briefly before he died, and she returned to the United States with her infant daughter. Later she married Harold S. McPherson, a businessman from New England. Miraculously healed during a serious illness, she launched out on an evangelistic ministry that carried her to many places at home and abroad. As she began to have an increased following, she settled in Los Angeles and built the Angelus Temple dedicated on New Years Day, 1923. During a revival service in San Francisco in April 1922, she became the first woman to broadcast a sermon. A Bible college was opened in connection with Angelus Temple, and radio station KFSG became the first station in the United States to be owned and operated by a church. The church also maintained a rescue mission ministry and a bookstore. She wrote a number of books and booklets and composed more than 175 songs and hymns and thirteen drama-oratorios.

MACRINA (327-379), founder of one of the earliest religious communities of women in the East. Macrina was born in Neocaesarea, Cappadocia, and reared in Pontus, the area to which Paul addressed his first letter. Her family was Christian; her grandmother was Macrina, the elder; her father a distinguished attorney and professor; her mother, Emmelia, a godly woman; and her brothers were Basil the Great, Gregory (Bishop of Nyssa), a younger brother, Peter, who became Bishop of Sebaste; and an older brother who became a jurist. Her family traveled to Pontus to escape the persecutions of Christians by Galerius and Maximianus. It was on their family estate that she founded two religious communities; one for women and one for men. She taught the Scriptures and devoted much time to prayer and meditation. She established a large hospital where healings and miracles were recorded. These communities, were at Tabennisi, on the bank of the Nile River. Basil especially praised his sister for the progress of her religious communities, which she founded and administered. He and Macrina decided to establish monasteries using a similar plan to the brother-sister community.

MAKANYA, VIOLET SIBUSISSIWE, a missionary, teacher, and social worker of South Africa. She graduated from the teachers college at Amanzimototti in Natal, South Africa, then became associated with the Purity League and witnessed and presented the gospel primarily to youth. Emphasis was put on the results of the gospel as she spoke in both government and mission schools. In 1928 she was sent to the United States for training, with her expenses paid by the government because of her influence in strengthening the morale of her people. Her work was with her own Zulu people; as she was a "pure" Zulu.

MALLENCKRODT, PAULINE von. *See* **von MALLENCKRODT**

MALLORY, KATHLEEN MORE (1879-1954), a promoter of missions, an editor, and executive in the Women's Missionary Union of the Southern Baptist Convention for thirty-six years. Born in Alabama, she graduated from Goucher College, taught several years, and was active in her local church before becoming a national officer. Twice she visited foreign mission fields in connection with her position and was editor of the *Royal*

Service publication. She wrote the manual for the Women's Missionary Union methods along with other materials. She was awarded an honorary doctorate by Louisiana College and Selma University in recognition of her work in promoting better racial relationships through mission institutes. Named in her honor were a hospital in Laichowfu, China, a building in Birmingham, and a chapel in Japan.

N

NAGLE, NANO (1728-c. 1790), pioneer educator and social worker born in Ireland. She established schools and a nursing home for women as part of founding the Order of Presentation Nuns. Originating in Ireland in 1775, it was first established in the United States in 1854. She studied in France and was a relative of the statesman Edmund Burke.

NATION, CARY AMELIA MOORE (1846-1911), activist in the drive for prohibition who fostered an opportunity for the church in America to respond in curbing alcoholism. Born in Kentucky, her first marriage to Dr. Charles Gloyd was unhappy largely because of alcoholism. After he died she taught and in 1877 married David Nation, a minister. In 1908 she joined the Prohibition Party and went about the United States and England lecturing against alcoholism. Several times she put her ideas and words into action by literally going into taverns with a hatchet and wrecking the places. She took the initiative for legislation to curb the sale and use of alcohol, exercising the democratic process with responses from Christians individually and the church in general to improve and to some extent correct this social blight.

NELLI, SUORA PLATELLA (1523-1588), a Italian painter remembered especially for three of her paintings: *The Crucifixion, The Descent from the Cross,* and *Adoration of the Magi*. She became a nun, entering the Dominican Convent of St. Catherine at Florence.

NELSON, EFFIE VICTORIA (1901-1977), influential American educator. As a teacher and dean of women she influenced many students to enter full-time Christian ministries. Received her B.A. degree in 1925 from Des Moines University; an M.A. degree from the University of Minnesota in 1940; began teaching at Bethel Academy, later appointed dean of women at Bethel College, also in St. Paul, Minnesota. She served in that position for forty years.

NEWELL, HARRIETT ATWOOD (1793-1812), missionary to India and wife of Samuel Newell and daughter of Moses Atwood. They sailed for Calcutta in 1812 with Adoniram Judson and others of the General Association at Bradford. After arriving in Calcutta restrictions required them to go elsewhere. They served only a few months before she died. She is remembered for her faithfulness and humble dedication as a missionary wife in spite of her brief life.

NEWMAN, ANGELA F. (1837-c. 1905), author, teacher, and pioneer missionary working to aid Mormon women who wished to escape from polygamy. She was born in Montpelier, Vermont. In 1856 she married Frank Kilgour, who died within a year after they were married. Later she married D. Newman, a merchant of Beaverdam, Wisconsin. She served for a time as the western secretary of the Women's Foreign Missionary Society, and it was at the request of leaders of the Methodist Episcopal church that she sought help for the Mormon Women and to minister to them herself. She appealed to Congress about this situation and received appropriations for a home to be built in Salt Lake City for her work. She contributed articles to religious journals about the need and exercised considerable influence to relieve the situation. As a home missionary she was able to travel and speak for reform. Results were fruitful in the presentation of the gospel and the practice of biblical living.

NIGHTINGALE, FLORENCE (1820-1910), an English Christian nurse who originated scientific nursing and elevated it to a ministry. Born in Florence, Italy, for which she was named; her father was a wealthy British banker, whose name was originally William Edward Shore, but he took the name *Nightingale* when he fell heir to the estates of Peter

Nightingale. Her mother was from a wealthy London family; the grandfather a member of the House of Commons. Her early childhood was spent on the family estate in Derbyshire, where she received a private education. Her father taught her several languages including Greek, by which she could read the Bible. She became very fond of an aunt, her father's sister, who understood and shared her spiritual life. Florence became interested in nursing and as she traveled in Europe was much distressed by the care given to those who were ill and the poor hygienic conditions of hospitals in England. She entered nurses training, studying at the Theodore Fliedner Deaconess Institution of Kaiserswerth and in the Institute of St. Vincent de Paul in Paris. She reorganized the Governesses Sanitarium in London in 1853. The following year, when the war in Crimea broke out she volunteered her services. She organized a group of thirty-eight nurses to go to Scutari with her and there originated a barrack hospital, a revolutionary concept. She was willing to scrub floors along with her nursing staff and care for the wounded day and night. The soldiers never before had received such respect and care. The death rate was reduced from forty percent to less than three percent. Some of the soldiers compared their hospital to a church with Florence Nightingale as their minister. Her spiritual life and compassion were reflected in her daily ministry. After the war, money was raised in recognition of her heroic service and used to establish schools for training nurses in the scientific methods she had developed. Schools for training nurses were established at St. Thomas and King's College hospitals. She wrote a classic guide to nursing called *Notes on Nursing*. In her later years she served as a valuable consultant for nurses, especially those working in military hospitals, and she was influential in founding the Red Cross. She helped establish other schools for training nurses, was honored by Queen Victoria, and in 1907 received the Order of Merit.

NITSCHMANN, ANNA (1715-1760), missionary, hymnist, and effective deaconess of the Moravian church. She was born at Moravia in Saxony, and was the daughter of David Nitschmann. She had a broad ministry with the expected deaconess duties among women in Germany, France, England, and America. She was known for her hymns and composed many of them for the Moravian church.

NOEL, CAROLINA MARIA (1817-1877), author and hymnwriter, and daughter of an Anglican minister. She wrote a number of poems included in a volume titled *The Name of Jesus and Other Verses for the Sick and Lonely*. She wrote a children's prayer, which was made into a hymn and was included in *The English Hymnal*. Perhaps she is best remembered today for "At the Name of Jesus."

NONNA (c. 329-374), devout Christian teacher and mother of Gregory of Nazianzus. Reared in a Christian home, she was largely responsible for the conversion of her husband, Gregory the Elder. He had been in a sect but was converted and consecrated as the bishop of Nazianzus, a position he held for many years. Details of her early life are not available. She had two grandsons who became bishops, and she is remembered largely for her testimony and Christian influence.

O

ODILIA (OTHILIA) (c. 690-720), an abbess of Alsace believed to have been blind and later healed. The daughter of Adalric, a Frank nobleman, she is credited with founding the nunnery in his castle of Hohenburg. It was located in the Vosges Mountains, where she recovered her sight. It has become a place for special pilgrimage for those blind or with eye diseases.

OKKEN, NELLIE (1915-1983), a pioneer missionary nurse who had a medical and dispensary ministry in addition to her evangelistic efforts in Zaire and Rwanda. She received her nurses training at the Marietta Phelps School of Nursing in Illinois and took postgraduate work in Chicago at the Cook County Hospital. She also attended the Moody Bible Institute. In the spring of 1944 she and her husband Paul were among the first missionaries appointed by the Conservative Baptist Foreign Mission Society going to go to Zaire (Congo). The combination of her medical expertise and unique evangelistic thrust touched the lives of many.

OLGA (c. 902-969), a Russian queen who promoted Christianity. When her husband Igor, ruler of Kiev, died suddenly in 957, she became the ruling monarch and served about ten years, until her son was old enough to rule. She was baptized by Theophilaktes at Constantinople in 957, the year her husband died, and worked hard to advance the cause of Christianity.

OLYMPIAS (368-408), a remarkable woman of great faith remembered for her sincerity as a deaconess in the church at Constantinople, her benevolence, and as a friend of John Chrysostom, bishop of Constantinople. She was the daughter of Seleucus, a wealthy count. When he died she inherited his fortune but used it for good causes. In 384 she married Nebridius, a man of good character who died less than two years after they were married. She bought hundreds of slaves to set them free, gave much to the poor, and helped relieve suffering in many ways.

OUCHTERLONY, HANNA (1838-1924), a pioneer evangelist largely responsible for establishing the Salvation Army in Sweden. She was a leader of women and encouraged them in spiritual matters. She served in Norway and England and in her native Sweden for twenty-two years.

P

PAK, ESTHER KIM (CHYOM TONG) (c. 1857-1910), the first Korean Christian woman to become a physician and minister to Korean women. She became a Christian in her teen years. After her marriage, she and her husband worked together in founding the first Christian work among women and children in a Korean city. They came to America, where she took her medical training at the Women's Medical College in Baltimore. After she was widowed, she continued her medical practice and ministry among her own people. The Korean government honored her with a medal of achievement for her outstanding work.

PALMER, PHOEBE WORRAL (1807-1884), an author influential in founding the holiness movement in the United States and Great Britain. She was a native of New York state. Her parents, Dorothea and Henry Worral, were converted under the ministry of John Wesley. In 1827 she married Walter Palmer, a doctor. She was active in visiting prisoners and distributing tracts in the slums of New York City. As part of her work in the Methodist Ladies' Home Missionary Society, she established the Five Points Mission in 1850, which was the beginning of settlement houses. She also founded the Hedding Church in a New York slum area. The Holiness movement grew through her influence and resulted in such groups as the Church of God (Anderson, Indiana), the Church of the Nazarene, the Assemblies of God, the Pentecostal-Holiness church, the Church of God (Cleveland, Tennessee), and others. Her writings include such books as *The Way to Holiness* and *Promise of the Father*, and she edited the *Guide to Holiness* periodical for some time. She was outspoken about women's rights in the church and through that influence many in the Pentecostal-Holiness movement began to ordain women.

PARMELEE, RUTH AZNIV (1885-1973), one of the early women physicians in the Near East, serving with the American Board of Commissioners for Foreign Missions. She was born in Pennsylvania of missionary parents and graduated from Oberlin College in 1907, later receiving an honorary degree from her alma mater. She also did graduate work at the University of Illinois and receiving her M.D. in 1912 and much later an MPH at Harvard in 1943. Between 1914 and 1922 she served as medical relief worker in Harpoot, Turkey, and American women's hospitals in Greece from 1923 to 1941 for refugee relief and public health projects. She organized a nurses training program including a model hospital and dispensary system in the Athens area from 1923 to 1933. During World War II she was a senior medical officer for Greek refugees near Gaza in Palestine; then for British and Americans in the Cyclades islands. Twice she was decorated by the Greek government for her work as a medical officer and help with the United Nations Relief Administration. Her service as a missionary penetrated into "high places" because of her medical expertise.

PARR, CATHERINE (1512-1548), exercised Christian influence as the sixth and last wife of Henry VIII. Before her marriage to him she had been a widow, a Christian who spent much time studying the Scriptures and having chapel in her castle with the Reformers. She influenced the king to sanction the free distribution of the Bible, and within little more than four years 24,000 copies of the entire Bible were printed in London and distributed. She married Henry VIII in 1543 and had considerable influence with his successor, Edward VI. She taught Edward scriptural truths, and her care and Christian influence greatly affected the reign of Edward and Elizabeth. Henry VIII died in 1547, and Catherine later remarried. Of her several marriages, she had only one child, Mary Seymour, by her last husband. During the last year of her life she wrote *A Lamentacion or Complaynt of a Sinner*.

PARSONS, EDITH F. (1878-1959), an outstanding missionary educator who taught at a school for girls in Brouse, Turkey and the American Collegiate Institute for Girls in Smyrna (Izmir), Turkey. She served as the school's administrator 1926 to 1945. She was a native of New York, a graduate of Stanford University, and took graduate work at Teachers College, Columbia University. She served with the American Board of Commissioners for Foreign Missions.

PARU, Dr. P. an eminent physician-evangelist in India. She was from Cannanore, South India, along the Malabar coast. Her father was an attorney, and her mother died when Paru was only two. Her father read the Bible to her and taught her from it, although he did not profess Christianity. After high school she enrolled in the Medical College in Madras, where she lived in a hostel of the YWCA. There she formed close ties with Christian students and accepted Christ as her Savior. After medical school she became an assistant to Dr. Anna S. Kugler of the Guntur Hospital and worked there for twelve years. She taught student nurses and wrote *Manual on Midwifery* in the Telugu language. She visited the United States and studied at Johns Hopkins and other great medical centers and then returned to India to initiate a medical practice of her own.

PATRICK, MARY MILLS (1850-1940), a Christian educator, author, college founder, and pioneer missionary in Turkey for fifty-three years. She was sponsored by the American Board of Commissioners for Foreign Missions, now the United Church Board for World Ministries. A native of New Hampshire, she studied at the Lyons Collegiate Institute in Iowa and received her M.A. degree from the University of Iowa. She pursued further graduate work at the University of Heidelberg in Germany; and in Zurich, Switzerland, and in Leipzig. She received a Ph.D. degree from the University of Berne in 1895; an LL.D. degree from Smith College in 1914; and an Litt.D. from Columbia University, New York, in 1922. As a missionary she first went to teach in Erzurum at what became the American Academy for Girls and became the administrator there in 1883. In 1890 she founded the American College for Girls in Constantinople. She served as president of the college from 1890 to 1924. She was decorated by Sultan Mehmed V with the Order of Shephet and decorated by King Boris of Bulgaria. One significant tribute to her work was the intercession of Bulgarian and Turkish governments in 1914 to enable her to cross war-torn Europe to Constantinople to continue her work. In addition to her many articles and contributions to *Hastings Dictionary of Religion,* she wrote an autobiography titled *Under Five Sultans* (1929) and *Prosperous Adventure: Story of the College* in 1934.

PATTISON, DOROTHY WYNDLOW (1832-1878), sometimes referred to as Sister Dora. She was a teacher, nurse, philanthropist, and worker in an Anglican church sisterhood. Born in Yorkshire, she was the daughter of a rector, Mark James Pattison, and youngest of a large family. She was much impressed with the work of Florence Nightingale in Scutari and even considered nurses training, but her father objected. She taught in Woolston but became ill, and in 1864 joined the Sisterhood of Good Samaritans in spite of the disapproval of her family. She found this more like a secular community and was not quite satisfied. Her heart was inclined more to a Christian missionary kind of service, but she was sought out as a caring nurse who prayed for guidance and healing. In 1874 she broke all connections with the community of Good Samaritans, became a nurse in College Hospital at Walsade, and was able to be a Christian testimony by performing many charitable activities.

PAUL, ELIZABETH RIEMANN (1894-1966), faithful missionary teacher for more than forty years in Africa with the African Inland Mission. She worked with her husband in teaching the Word of God and caring for their own family of six children, who served on the mission field as well.

PAULA (347-404), a wealthy Roman widow and friend of Jerome. A descendant of Gracchi and Scipio, she married Toxotius when just seventeen years old. She was widowed in her early thirties with five children; four daughters (Blaesilla, Paulina, Eustochium, and Ruffina) and a son (Toxotius). It is likely that she owned a large part of the city of Nicopolis. It is recorded that before she was converted Paula dressed and lived royally but after her conversion lived in an austere manner, protesting against materialism, giving much of her wealth to help the poor and to build hospitals, churches, and monasteries. In 380 she dedicated herself to an ascetic life and with her daughter, Eustochium, followed Jerome to Palestine. After visiting various holy places, they settled at Bethlehem and founded three nunneries and a monastery. She was in charge of the nunneries, while Jerome presided over the monastery. These served as places of refuge for sick, orphans, and needy and as places of study, prayer, and devotion. Jerome dedicated some of his work to Paula and to both Paula and Eustochium his versions of Job, Isaiah, Samuel, Kings, Esther, Galatians, Philemon, Titus, and the twelve minor prophets. Paula helped Jerome in his translations and obtained for him at her own expense books and rare manuscripts essential to his translation task. At her memorial service six bishops carried her body to the burial place.

PAVLOVA, RADA EVANOVA, a Bulgarian Christian educator who had to escape from her country when the Turks attacked. She went to a German school in Constantinople and later elsewhere. After graduation, she accepted a teaching position with the American Missionary School at Monastir. After some teaching experience she came to the United States and took three years of Bible and some medical training. She returned to Monastir to teach the gospel.

PAXSON, RUTH (c. 1889-1949), Bible teacher, missionary, and author, whose writings are classic. Born in Manchester, Iowa, she dedicated her life to Christ while young. After graduating from the State University of Iowa she went to Moody Bible Institute. Several years later she served as YWCA secretary and college secretary in her home state and later traveled as secretary for the Student Volunteer Movement. She sailed for the mission field of China in February 1911, sponsored by the YWCA. Before long she left that work to devote herself entirely to Bible teaching for conferences among missionaries in China. She left China for health reasons and went to Switzerland. During the fifteen years prior to World War II she taught the Bible in various parts of Europe and at Keswick Bible Conference in England. She taught in the United States after the war and in 1947 returned to Europe to continue teaching the Word of God.

PEABODY, LUCY McGILL (1861-1949), teacher, missionary, and missionary leader. Lucy McGill was born in Kansas but reared in Rochester, New York, where she became a teacher of deaf children. Within a few weeks after she married Norman Waterbury in 1881, they left for Madras, India, as missionaries under the American Baptist Missionary Union. There she taught Indian women. The Waterburys had two small children when Mr. Waterbury died, so she returned to the United States with them. She taught deaf children in the United States and was asked to speak of her mission work in various churches. It was at one of these meetings that she met Helen Montgomery, with whom she had a long working relationship in missions. In 1890 she was influential in setting the date for a World Day of Prayer that was not only international but interdenominational as well. She became head of the Women's Baptist Foreign Missionary Society and in 1900 formed the Central Committee for the United Study of Foreign Missions. The purpose of this committee was to keep the churches informed about missions and encourage prayer and material support. She served in this capacity for twenty-four years. She married Henry Wayland Peabody, a businessman from Boston in charge of the Board of Managers of the Baptist Missionary Union. He died just two years after they were married. Lucy and Helen Montgomery visited mission fields around the world, raised funds, recruited missionaries, and kept their denomination informed of missionary needs. Lucy was especially concerned with the promotion and financing of women's colleges abroad. Seven colleges benefited from her fund-raising efforts. She founded and edited the magazine *Everland* for children.

PECK, SARA ELIZABETH (1868-1968), educator, writer, and missionary. A native of Wisconsin, she was educated at Battle Creek College and became one of the first women missionaries to serve in Africa under the Seventh Day Adventist church. She is especially remembered for her series of textbooks *True Education Readers.*

PELAGIA (c. 296-311), Christian martyr. Little is known about her, but it is recorded in church history that when she was a girl of fifteen, soldiers approached her home and she jumped into the ocean to preserve her chastity. It is likely that this was during the persecution by Diocletian.

PELLETIER, MARY (OF ST. EUPHRASIA) (1796-1868), founder of the Catholic community of women called Our Lady of Charity of the Good Shepherd. It originated in France in 1835 for the purpose of social service work, especially among young girls. It was established in the United States in 1843.

PEMBROKE, ANNE (Countess of Pembroke) (1589-1674), a devout Christian and noted English philanthropist. She was the daughter of George Clifford, Earl of Cumberland. She married Richard, Earl of Dorset; after she was widowed she married Philip, Earl of Pembroke, whom she survived forty-five years. She is said to have been exemplary in her own religious observances and Christian attitude. She used her wealth for helping many, especially in building hospital and relieving needy.

PENN, GULIELMA (1644-1694), wife of William Penn, founder of the Commonwealth of Pennsylvania. Born in London, she was the only child of Mary Proude and Sir William Springett. Her father died as an officer on the Puritan side of the Battle of Edgehill a few weeks before she was born. Several years later her mother married Isaac Pennington, distinguished among early Quakers. Gulielma became a Quaker at the age of fifteen. In 1672 she married William Penn and lived in Hertfordshire, England. They had five children, three of whom survived infancy. They spent some time in Northern England at the home of Margaret Fell Fox, and although William Penn was imprisoned several times for his Quaker faith, she was steadfast in her support and care of the family. In 1682, leaving his family behind to join him later, William Penn decided to journey to American for religious freedom. Gulielma feared making the trip with the children, so Penn returned to England. She died soon after his return, having been a faithful wife who had spent much energy with her children and in the cause of religious freedom for the Quakers.

PENN-LEWIS, JESSIE JONES (1861-1927), a British writer and conference speaker born in Neath, South Wales. Samuel Jones, a Calvinist-Methodist minister, was her grandfather. She had a private education and became a leader in the British YWCA. She later represented that organization, speaking in Norway, Finland, Russia, and India. She spoke at English Keswick conferences and influenced the Great Awakening in Wales and many parts of the world. When Evan Roberts had a breakdown from the many services during the Awakening, she assisted those carrying on for him and advised many who were caught up in "false fire." She founded the Overcomer Literature Trust and edited the *Overcomer Magazine. War on the Saints* and *The Cross of Calvary* are considered most outstanding among her many books, although one of her booklets, *Word of the Cross,* was issued in many languages with millions of copies sold.

PERKINS, EVA (1858-1942), an educator and missionary. She graduated in 1880 from Battle Creek College and worked preparing grammar books. She was one of the first officers of the General

Sabbath School Association of the Seventh Day Adventist church.

PERPETUA, VIBIA (181-203), a well-educated Christian of high rank martyred at Carthage under the persecution of Septimius Severus. She lived in North Africa at Carthage, where Roman Christians spread the gospel. Perpetua and the others martyred at the same time had been imprisoned and much of the information about her is from her writings there in prison. She, along with several others, including her maid, Felicitas, her teacher, deacon Saturus, and three others, were put into the arena together. Because the wild beasts did not at first devour her, she was beheaded.

PETRIE, IRENE ELEANORA VERITA (1809-1896), an unusual Bible teacher and missionary to India. Born into a wealthy, aristocratic family in England, she had considerable talent and was refined. She taught a Sunday school class and did much local Christian work with the Latymer Road Mission. In 1891, she answered a call to the mission field of India at Lahore. She learned both the Urdu and Kashmir languages and was appointed to Kashmir under the Church Missionary Society. She offered her services as a volunteer. She became affectionately known as "Irene petrie of Kashmir." She not only taught Bible classes and did the usual missionary work but also set hymns to native airs and helped the Indian children sense the true gospel and its power. In 1896 she went to Tibet on vacation and there became ill with typhoid.

PETTER, BERTHA KISINGER (1872-1967), author and missionary to the Cheyenne Indians for more than sixty-one years. She graduated from Wittenberg College in 1896 and became the wife of Rodolph Petter, Swiss linguist and missionary. Together they served the Cheyenne Indians under the General Conference Mennonites. In 1911 she wrote a book about their work simply called *Cheyenne Mission Souvenir*.

PHILIP, SARAH, Indian Christian astronomer who studied at the University of Madras and was the first woman of Guntur to earn a degree from that university. After graduation she taught in the high school of the mission in which she was educated.

PICCARD, JEANNETTE RIDLON (1895-1981), one of the first women to be ordained to the priesthood in the Episcopal church. Born in Chicago and educated at Bryn Mawr College, she held advanced degrees from the University of Chicago, the University of Minnesota, and General Theological Seminary. She assisted her husband and at one time had a pilot's license. Later she served as a consultant to the National Aeronautic and Space Administration's Manned Spacecraft Center in Houston. She had a ministry among the elderly at St. Philip's Church at St. Paul, Minnesota.

PLAYFAIR, JOYCE NETHERCOTT (1886-1978), a native of Canada. She and her husband were the first missionaries to the Igbomina-Yoruba people in the Lafiagi District of Nigeria, an extremely primitive area. She worked many years under the Sudan Interior Mission, and when her husband was appointed its general director, she served as his secretary. She attended a business college in Ontario and Moody Bible Institute at Chicago. In spring 1935 both she and her husband were given special recognition by King George V as "Officers of the Order of the British Empire" for their work in opening up the tribe at Oro Agor, the base of their work in the Lafiagi District.

PLUMMER, HILDA (1899-1980), a British missionary nurse who helped hundreds of leprosy patients in India. She served for thirty-four years with the Salvation Army, joining it in Nottingham, England, where she was born. She came to the United States briefly before going to India in autumn 1926. She worked in Kerala until 1949 as an evangelist and nurse and in 1955 at the Northern Travancore Leper Colony, the Cochin Leper Colony, and a leprosy hospital at Futhencruz. In 1950, she was transferred to the Evangeline Booth Leprosy Hospital at Bapatla where she served until retirement in 1960, though she stayed on nursing the leprosy patients of

Bethany Colony. She was awarded the Royal Investiture of the Most Excellent Order of the British Empire and was a much loved leader in medical centers for the treatment of leprosy patients. Her highest rank in the Salvation Army was major. Many of her patients became Christians, and she was a unique witness to those of other religions who came for treatment.

PLUMMER, LORENA FLORENCE FAIT (1862-1945), educator and author. In addition to teaching and writing several books, she is be remembered for her long-time editorship (1904-1936) of *Sabbath School Worker* of the Seventh Day Adventist church.

POCAHONTAS (1595-1617), considered the first American Indian woman to become a Christian at the English settlement of Jamestown. She was baptized and given the name Rebekah. Her father was Chief Powhatan. She married John Rolfe in 1613 in a Christian ceremony in Jamestown. Governor Thomas Dale took interest in her and assisted in teaching her English. Later she went to England and was presented to James I and Queen Anne. While there she contracted smallpox and died at the age of twenty-two, leaving a small son, Thomas, who was educated in England before returning to Virginia. Some of her descendants were John Randolph, William Henry Harrison, and Edith Bolling Wilson.

POLALLION, MARIE de LUMAGUE (1599-1657), a French teacher and founder of the Institute des Filles de la Providence in 1630. Born in Paris of a wealthy family, she dedicated her life to the ascetic practices of the monastery of the Capuchins. However her health would not allow her to continue more than a brief stay. In 1617, she married Francois de Polallion, who died about a year after they married. She lived in retirement and for a while tutored a daughter of the Duchess of Orleans. Then she founded the Institute for the purpose of teaching children of the poor. She used up her own wealth for this work, and Anne of Austria provided a place for them to live.

PONIATOWA, CHRISTINE (1610-1644), a German visionary born in Prussia. Her father was Julian Poniatowa, a Polish gentleman who escaped from a monastery to become a Protestant and ministered as a librarian at Duchnick in Bohemia. Christine reported having visions about the future of the Reformed church. She married a Moravian minister in 1632. Some of her visions were recorded and later published.

POTKINS, ALICE (c. 1501-1556), the only woman among five Christian martyrs who were allowed to starve to death at Canterbury Castle in 1556. One of the group wrote a letter describing the treatment they were receiving during their confinement and threw the letter out the prison window. The letter is quoted in John Foxe's *Book of Martyrs*.

POUNDS, JESSIE BROWN (1861-1921), an American writer and hymnist. She was born in Ohio, and for more than thirty years wrote regularly for religious periodicals. In 1897 she married John Pounds. Her published work includes nine books, some fifty cantata librettos, and more than 400 gospel song texts. Perhaps her most familiar hymns used in American hymnals today include: "'I Know That My Redeemer Liveth," "Anywhere with Jesus," "The Touch of His Hand on Mine," and "Beautiful Isle of Somewhere."

PRENTISS, ELIZABETH PAYSON (1819-1878), an American poet, author, and hymnist. A native of Portland, Maine, she became a teacher. At the age of sixteen she contributed an article to *Youth's Companion* magazine. She was married to George Lewis Prentiss in 1845. He was a Congregational minister and seminary professor. She had several books published including *Religious Poems* in 1873, but perhaps she is best remembered for the hymn "More Love to Thee, O Christ," included in many American hymnals today.

PRESTON, ANN (1810-1906), a dedicated servant of the Lord experiencing ethereal-type answers to prayer. Born in Armagh County, Ireland, of a humble family, she tried going to school but was unable to learn to read. She became a Christian and had a great desire to read the Bible. She would look at a Bible and prayerfully ask God to help her read it, and that is exactly what happened. She could read and comprehend portions of the Bible but no other writing. She tried to read other things but could not. She was employed by a doctor, caring for the home and family. When the doctor's wife died, Ann took charge of the household. The story of her life has been written as a series of miracles Ann reflected the secret of abiding in Christ. The miracles of her life became a witness for Christ, and many marveled thereby. The Lord answered her prayers regarding daily responsibilities and decisions, but perhaps most amazing was His answer concerning her reading ability.

PRISCILLA or **PRISCA** (First Century), one of two Phrygian women believed to have left their families to accompany Montanus and promote his teachings, which taught the near approach of the millennial reign. She was likely of high noble character with a great desire to restore discipline in the early church. She tended to be charismatic.

PROCTER, ADELAIDE ANN (1825-1864), born in London, the daughter of Bryan Waller Procter, a poet and an attorney. She was a brilliant scholar of mathematics and spoke several languages. Some of her first poems were published by Charles Dickens in his magazine. Her first book of poems, *Legends and Lyrics*, was published in 1858. Some of her better-known poems that have been set to music as hymns are "I Do Not Ask, O Lord, That Life May Be" "The Shadows of the Evening Hours," and "The Lost Chord"; and for children, "My God, I Thank Thee, Who Has Made the Earth So Bright."

PULCHERIA, AUGUSTA (399-453), a Greek empress and daughter of Emperor Arcadius and sister of Theodosius, whom she succeeded. She showed wisdom and piety, and the empire flourished during her influence. She defended the purity of the Christian faith against the doctrines of Nestorius and Eutyches and sponsored the Council of Chalcedon. She provided for the building of many churches and helped to open the University of Constantinople.

Q

QUATREMERE, ANNE BOURJET (1732-1790), a wealthy and noble Christian born in Paris and known for her benevolence. She took in poor and abandoned girls and others from the poor sections of Paris and cared for them.

R

RADEGONDE (518-587), Christian queen of the Franks and daughter of the royal family of Thuringia. She was taken captive when twelve years old by the invading Franks. Clotaire, king of Neustria in Gaul, insisted Radegonde marry him. He was not a Christian even though the son of Christian queen Clotilda. Radegonde fled, but the king had her returned and forced their marriage. King Clotaire presented Radegonde with a beautiful palace, which she turned into a refuge for the poor and sick, including those with leprosy. The king became so angry that she left and became a deaconess. She later founded the first double monastery, the Monastery of the Holy Cross. Venantius Fortunatus was inspired by her life and in 569 wrote the majestic hymn of the early church "Vexilla Regis Prodeunt," which was translated into English by John Mason Neale in 1851. Clotaire finally begged her forgiveness for his having members of her family killed, the destruction of Thuringia, and his treatment of her, but she did not return to him. She spent her remaining years in prayer, studying the Scriptures, and doing mission work.

RADER, ALMA (1885-1966), missionary and influential professor of Bible who encouraged many young people to enter Christian service. Born in Columbus, Ohio, she first went to a business college there, then to Moody Bible Institute as a student, and later served on the faculty from 1919 to 1926. She was general secretary of the YWCA in Atlantic City for seven years and held the same position in Butler, Pennsylvania, for nineteen years. She served as a missionary to India under the Presbyterian Board of Foreign Missions, and in 1941 accepted a position in the Bible department at Bryan College in Dayton, Tennessee, where she remained for twenty-one years. She was awarded an honorary doctorate by Bryan College for her scholarly and dedicated service. She specialized in Old Testament studies.

RAINER, CAROLINE ELIZABETH FARABEE (1927-1983), missionary with a unique and far-reaching ministry of radio with the Far East Broadcasting Company. Born in Florida, attended schools in Pasadena, California, Bob Jones University, and John Brown University. She joined the FEBC with her husband, Hiley, in 1958 and served in Manila, Philippines. Her work was vital in beaming the gospel to unknown numbers of people who might not have heard it otherwise, for she served in the tape editing department of the station as well as the tape library, where there were messages in ninety-two languages and dialects. Her role as a devoted wife and mother of three children further extended her ministry as a quiet and faithful servant.

RAMABAI, PANDITA SARASVATI (1858-1922), an educator, missionary, Bible translator, and founder of the Mukti Mission in Kedgaon, Poona District of India. Before she became a Christian she memorized thousands of verses from the sacred Hindu writings, and knew the Marathi, Kanarese, Hindustani, and Bengali languages. Some of her family died during the famine of 1874; she had a special burden for the plight of women in India; in her own situation she had not found desired peace through faith in idols, as she had been taught. Her brother had been a comfort to her, but he died at the age of twenty-one, likely of malnutrition. She married Bipin Bihari Medhavi, an attorney and graduate of Calcutta University. Less than two years after they were married she was widowed and left with a baby daughter, Manorama. Seeds of the gospel were planted when she found a Sanskrit Bible and a copy of the gospel of Luke in the library of her husband, and later she met a Baptist missionary. She founded an organization, Areja Mahita Samaj, for the purpose of promoting the education of women, thus discouraging child marriages. In 1883, she and her daughter went to England and were taken in by the Church of England Sisterhood at Wantage. There she saw first hand the differences between Christianity and what she had been taught. Indicating her decision to accept Christianity, she was baptized in the Church of England and stayed a year at Wantage before being appointed professor of Sanskrit in Cheltenham Ladies College. She was invited to America where she stayed for some time studying kindergarten methods. In the meantime, she wrote *The High Caste Hindu Woman*, which opened the hearts and purses of many in the United States when published. She returned to India as a committed Christian with faith and administrative ability to establish the mission work needed there. She opened a school at Bombay bought land at Kedgaon, where a larger mission was established. She helped hundreds of girls and women after the 1896 famine. The Mukti mission became a revival center where Christ was preached and many converted. One of her last contributions to her ongoing work for Christ was translating the Bible into the Marathi language. She influenced such men as George Müller, J. Hudson Taylor, and others.

RANDALL, SALLY PARSONS (1775-c. 1850), one of the first woman evangelists in New England. She became a Christian during a revival in Westport, New Hampshire in 1792. She was enthusiastic about her faith, but her father was opposed to it and turned her away, so she lived with a neighbor. She studied the Scriptures and went about holding evangelistic meetings. Her work was commended by the Freewill Baptists at their annual conference in 1797. Members of her family, including her father became Christians. She married Benjamin Walton Randall, a Freewill Baptist minister.

RANELAGH, Lady (KATHERINE BOYLE JONES) (1614-1691), author, evangelist, and influential wife of Arthur Jones, Viscount Ranelagh. Born in Ireland, she was part of a large family. Details of her childhood are obscure. Even the date of her marriage is uncertain, but was it was sometime before 1641. Katherine's father-in-law was a member of parliament. After he died, Arthur, a member of the House of Commons, was ousted because of his father's stand against Charles I. Katherine wrote to Edward Hyde and to other important officials and expressed the doctrines of Puritanism and urged a peaceful settlement of the civil war. Her writing influenced Oliver Cromwell and other leading officials, especially when common people were mistreated and in danger of civil disobedience. Mistreated by her own husband, she was drawn closer to the Lord, and in London just prior to the 1664 plague, which took nearly 100,000 lives, she went about doing evangelistic work, turning people to the Bible and God. She was buried at St. Martins-in-the-Fields, London.

RANFAING, MARIE ELIZABETH (1592-1649), a distinctive French woman who founded a religious community to shelter women in need. Her parents arranged for her marriage, but she refused their wishes and chose to enter a monastery. Later, she was forced to return to her parents and marry a gentleman by the name of Dubois; they had three daughters. After she was widowed she established the religious community Our Lady of Refuge for others who had had a similar experience to hers. Her three daughters were also a part of that community in France.

REED, MARY (1854-1943), an American pioneer missionary to India for fifty-two years. Born in Ohio, she attended college and taught for several years. Answering a call to the foreign mission field, she was appointed to work with the zenana women of India by the Women's Missionary Society of the Methodist Episcopal Church. She arrived in India in 1885 and first served at Cawnpore but was soon forced to leave for health reasons. Advised to go to the Himalayas to recover, she visited a leper colony in Chandag and was deeply concerned about their plight and treatment. She continued her work for four years, but again had to return home because of her health. While she was home it was discovered that she had contracted leprosy. This made her all the more anxious to improve and return to India to work directly with the lepers, for now she could freely share the fact that she was "one of them" and knew first-hand of the trauma and separation they experienced. Accepted by the Mission to Lepers in India and the East, she became superintendent of the Leper Homes at Chandag. The years following were extremely fruitful as many lepers were saved and a church, chapels, and improved living quarters were built so that it became a self-supporting colony. Much of this work she did without assistance from other missionaries. But in 1933 J. Singh was appointed to help her in the in 1938 a Miss K. Ogilvie was appointed to take over administration of the Leper Homes. At age eighty-four Mary Reed retired after fifty-two years of faithful work for the Lord among a needy group in India.

REHWINKEL, ANGELA (1882-1973), pioneer missionary nurse who began a Lutheran medical work in South India. She served thirty-seven years with the Lutherans (Missouri Synod) Board for Mission Services. In addition to her nurses training at St. John's Hospital Training School in Minnesota and St. John's Winfield in Kansas, she went to Concordia Seminary in St. Louis, Missouri. She first arrived in Bombay the day after Christmas in 1921 and later went to Ambur Hospital, where she became superintendent of nurses. After her service at the hospital she served in India and did missionary work along with her professional nursing.

RENEE OF FRANCE (1510-1575), a distinguished Christian of noble birth, friend of John Calvin, and influential during the Reformation. Born in Blois, she was the youngest daughter of Louis XII and Anne of Brittany. Her mother was wealthy and discreet in caring for the education of her children by securing a refined Christian governess, Madame de Souboise, from England. With a copy of Wycliffe's Bible hidden in a safe place by her family, Madame de Souboise was able to teach Renee the truths of the Scriptures. When Renee's mother, Anne, died, the governess was given charge of Renee. Even when Renee's father remarried, she remained in the palace under the care and teaching of Madame de Souboise. In 1528 Renee married Hercules of Estes, Duke of Ferrara, of a noble Italian family. Five children were born to them. Renee kept true to her religious teachings in opposition by her husband. She encouraged Bruccioli to prepare an Italian version of the Bible, and she gave shelter and help to Protestant refugees. After his exile John Calvin resided at her court under the assumed name of Charles d'Esperville. It is believed that while there he completed writing *Institutes of the Christian Religion.* At one time, Renee's husband had Calvin arrested for heresy, but Renee found out about it and secretly sent help to Calvin. When the Duke died in 1559 he bequeathed his fortune to her on the condition that she be loyal to his Roman Catholic faith. She no longer concealed her true Christian faith but publicly spoke out in favor of the Calvinists. She moved to her original castle, and it became known as Hotel Dieu or the "Hotel of the Lord," for there she protected many Reformers, built a chapel for them, and employed two Reformed pastors. She aided the Reformers both during and after St. Bartholomew's Massacre in 1572, when thousands of Protestants were killed throughout France. In spite of much opposition from those of authority, Renee kept her queenly dignity and was steadfast in her Christian faith and witness.

RESSLER, LINA ZOOK (1869-1948), a remarkable missionary, teacher, author, and editor with the Mennonite church. When she was in her early twenties the *Herald of Truth* magazine published at least eleven articles by her. She kept valuable descriptions and accounts of the history of the Mennonite church, which are now kept in the archives of that denomination in Goshen, Indiana. She served for a while in a gospel mission in Chicago, taught Bible in the Elkhart Institute, and wrote a regular column in a denominational publication for children, *Words of Cheer,* and later became its editor. She edited *Beams of Light* and compiled four volumes of poems and stories for children and youth, *Poems for Our Boys and Girls.* In 1903 she married Bishop Jacob

A. Ressler, superintendent of the American Mennonite Mission in India. After working in India for a time, they returned in 1908 because of her health. She and her husband wrote *Lights and Shades from Hindu Land.*

REUSS, BENIGNA von (1695-1751), a German hymnist from a royal family and the sister of Count Henry of Reuss-Ebersdorf and Countess Erdmuth Dorothea, wife of Count von Zinzendorf. She is described as a godly woman, although information about her early life is obscure. Of the number of hymns she wrote, perhaps the best known of those translated into English is "Attend, O Lord, My Daily Toil."

RHODES, MARY, American founder of the Roman Catholic community Sisters of Loretto at the Foot of the Cross, commonly referred to as the Lorettines. This order was founded in 1812 in Kentucky and was the first such religious order originating in America without foreign affiliation. The purpose of this group was largely educational.

RIDLEY, MRS. WILLIAM (c. 1810-1896), missionary with her husband to the Indians of British Columbia under the Church of England. She had a home for Indian girls, taught Bible classes, and assisted as needed to establish permanent mission work there. They served as missionaries in Peshawar and Afghanistan between 1866 and 1870 as well.

ROBERTS, ELLEN LOIS STOWE (1825-1908), writer, speaker, wife of the founder of the Free Methodist church. A native of New York state, she became the first president of the Women's Foreign Missionary Society of her denomination. She was a strong influence and actively participated in the founding of Robert Wesleyan College in New York state. Often she was asked to speak about their pioneer work as Free Methodists. She assisted her husband in editing and publishing *The Earnest Christian* magazine.

ROBINSON, JANE MARIE BANCROFT (1847-1932), a Methodist of considerable distinction and influence beyond her own denomination. Born in Massachusetts, she attended Emma Willard's Seminary at Troy, New York, and graduated in 1871. She also attended the New York State Normal School at Albany and later studied at Syracuse University where she received both a master's and Ph.D. degrees. Served as a professor of French and literature and as dean at Northwestern University in Evanston, Illinois, between 1877 and 1885. It was there that she founded the Western Association of Collegiate Alumnae, a forerunner of the American Association of University Women. In 1885 she was awarded the first history fellowship of Bryn Mawr. She studied at the University of Zurich in Switzerland and was often asked to speak at Methodist church conferences. She was influential in organizing deaconesses to minister specific functions within the church.

ROGERS, HESTER ANN ROE (1756-1794), author. She was born in England and at the age of twenty converted under the preaching of John Wesley. Her husband was a minister. She is mentioned here because her journal is considered part of the Methodist literature. It is not certain whether she had other writing published.

ROLDAN, LUISA (1654-1704), a distinguished Spanish artist whose principal productions are the statues of Mater Dolorosa, John the Evangelist, and St. Thomas. Details of her life are obscure. She died in Madrid.

ROSE OF LIMA (1586-1617), known for her mystical gifts, especially in her native Peru. Her father was a Spaniard, Gaspar de Flores, and her mother was an Inca Indian, Maria d' Olivia. She was baptized Isabel de Flores but later took the name Rose de Santa Maria in honor of the Virgin Mary. She tried to model her life after Catherine of Siena. Lima, Peru, was her home. She became a Dominican tertiary in 1606 and known as Rose of Lima. Her work among the needy was especially noted including the care of destitute children. She was credited with extraordinary spiritual powers, was proclaimed a patron saint of Peru, America, the Indies, and the Philippines. She was buried in the Dominican Convent at Lima, but later her body was disinterred and taken to the Church of San Domingo in Lima. She was canonized by Clement X in 1671.

ROSE OF VITERBO (1235-1252), an Italian Catholic lay sister who urged people to support the papacy in response to a vision she had. She was ousted from the town of Viterbo in 1250 by order of Emperor Frederick II. Later she returned to live in seclusion and spent much time in prayer and doing penitence, as she was too poor to afford entering a convent. In 1457 she was declared a saint.

ROSENBLATT. *See* **WILBRANDIS**

ROSS, DOROTHY BLATTER (1901-1977), missionary artist and author born in Nebraska. She graduated from Doane College in 1925. She also took courses from the University of Colorado and Columbia University. In 1958 received an L.H.D. degree from Doane. Most of her ministry was in Turkey as a teacher and author. She was sponsored by the American Board of Commissioners for Foreign Missions, United Church Board for World Ministries. She taught art and English in Merzifon, Turkey, between 1931 and 1937, and at Uskudar between 1939 and 1967. She specialized in writing for children and had more than fifteen books published, some relating to Turkish culture. She became assistant director for a publisher in Istanbul and promoted reading. In 1968 she received a citation from the Committee on World Literacy and Children's Literature for her pioneer work in children's literature in Turkey. She married after retirement, and a Dorothy Blatter Scholarship was established for training writers.

ROSSETTI, CHRISTINA GEORGINA (1830-1894), author and hymnist born in London. Her mother was English and wrote poetry; her father was an Italian and professor of Italian at King's College. Her brother, Dante Gabriel Rossetti, was a highly recognized painter. When she was just twelve years old, her grandfather published some of her first poems. Two of her poems were included in *The English Hymnal*; perhaps the most familiar is "In the Bleak of Mid-Winter." Other hymns for which she is remembered are "None Other Lamb, None Other Name" and "Love Came Down at Christmas." Some consider her finest work to be found in *Goblin Market, The Prince's Progress,* and *Sing-Song*.

ROWE, ELIZABETH SINGER (1674-1737), British author and philanthropist, daughter of Walter Singer. Although details of her early life are vague, perhaps her best known published work includes *Friendship in Death* and *Devout Exercises of the Heart*.

ROWELL, MABLE G. (1889-1969), a remarkable missionary nurse who established a new mission station and a school, which had widespread influence in Central America. A native of Canada, she attended Toronto Bible College, took nurses training in New York, and obstetrics studies in Costa Rica. After serving eleven years as a missionary nurse in Costa Rica, she became affiliated with the Central American Mission in 1938. She established a mission station in the northeastern corner of Honduras in Minas de Oro, having been allowed entrance privileges because of her medical expertise. She trained national workers for the mission station and was accountable for sixteen villages and twenty-two hamlets. People came from twenty towns and villages seeking medical help, which she gave along with the gospel witness. Because of her concern for children of believers in the villages where there were no schools, she brought them to live with her and hired a teacher. As the word of this spread, more and more Christian parents wanted to send their children, both for the excellent education and to escape the persecution they faced in the public schools. Bible study and Scripture memorization were required, so the school became a special ministry. At one time she bought land and kept a herd of cattle to raise money for the school. The student body grew to several hundred and the campus expanded, adding a classroom building and chapel. Over the years the influence of Instituto Evangelico graduates has been felt through that area and many students became Christians while attending.

ROYER, CHRISTINA NEWHOUSER (1875-1967), eminent Christian educator in the Mennonite church. She attended high school in Knoxville, Tennessee, and graduated from Friendsville Academy, a school sponsored by the Philadelphia area Quakers. She also attended the Holbrook Normal School and the University of Texas. She taught briefly, and in 1906 married I. W. Royer, a Mennonite minister in Goshen, Indiana, and they later moved to Chicago. Both she and her husband studied at Bethel Biblical Seminary. Her influence on Christian education was recognized in the Mennonite church.

RUPP, GRACE KENNEDY (1883-1967), pioneer missionary to Africa first under the Christian church, and then under the Missionary Alliance church, and later under the Missionary Church Association. Attended Slippery Rock Teachers College in Pennsylvania and the Missionary Training Institute in Nyack, New York. In 1908 she and her husband, David, arrived in Sierra Leone, where she administered a school for girls. Later when they went to French Guinea, where she was instrumental in founding a school for the children of missionaries. In 1944 they returned from French Guinea and the following year opened a work for the Missionary Church Association in Sierra Leone. While in Mayoso she began a literacy class for villagers, for she knew several native languages. Her life influenced others to become missionaries, including both of their own sons, Kenneth and David.

RUSSELL, FRANCES CROMWELL (1638-1720), influential Christian and youngest daughter of Oliver Cromwell and his wife, Elizabeth. She married Robert Rich but was widowed within a few months. She later married John Russell, and they had several children. Her sphere of Christian influence was largely among other women of her immediate area and family.

RUTHERFORD, EUPHAM HAMILTON (c. 1567-1630), first wife of Scottish theologian Samuel Rutherford. Details of her early life are vague, but there is considerable evidence of her influence in his life. It is believed that she was largely responsible for his resignation from the faculty of Edinburgh University, where he was a professor of Latin. At the time of her death he was facing charges for refusing to obey the Articles of Perth.

RUTHERFORD, JEAN McMATH (c. 1618- ?), second wife of Scottish Covenanter Samuel Rutherford. They were married in 1638, the year he was appointed professor of divinity at St. Mary's College, St. Andrews, by the Glasgow Assembly. Details of her life are obscure, but she and a daughter, Agnes, survived him. She was influential in his life and work at the college and in the lives of some of the students.

S

SA, Dr. MA SAW, the first Christian Burmese woman physician and surgeon. She served as superintendent of the Dufferin Maternity Hospital in Rangoon. Born in Prome, Burma, her mother taught in a Baptist mission school. Her family was converted to Christianity from Buddhism. She graduated from Judson College and the medical school of the University of Calcutta. For her outstanding work the Burmese government awarded her a scholarship to study at the University of Dublin in Ireland. There she received their highest honor, a Fellowship in the Royal College of Surgery. She also had the distinction of being the first accredited woman to represent Burma, India, and Ceylon at the international conference of the Women's American Baptist Foreign Mission Society. That experience gave her opportunities to visit hospitals in Cleveland, Ohio, and attend the summer school at Johns Hopkins University. Later, she opened a clinic in Rangoon and supervised the work of many others.

SALES, JANE MAGORIAN (1931-1974), a missionary educator and author who worked under the United Church Board for World Ministries in South Africa. A native of Ohio, she graduated from the College of Wooster, and her graduate work was at the University of Chicago Divinity School, where she received B.D., M.A., and Ph.D degrees. She went to the South Africa Mission in 1956 for evangelical work, teaching at Ifofo and Inanda Seminaries from 1958 to 1968, and at Adams College until 1970. As a author she wrote *The Planting of the Churches in South Africa*. In spite of her fight with cancer, she returned to Africa in 1972. She died in 1974 at Botswana.

SAMBINE (c. 99-125), a notable widow in Umbria who was converted to Christianity by the witness of her slave girl, Seraphia. Both were martyred for their faith.

SANDELL, LINA (1832-1903), a devout Swedish musician and hymnist, sometimes called the "Fanny Crosby of Sweden." Born in Frödervd, she was a child of frail health, and she spent much time at home and with her father, who was a parish pastor. A turning point in her life came after the tragic death of her father. As a young woman she was accompanying him to Gothenburg, when the ship on which they were sailing suddenly rolled and tipped in such a way that her father was accidently thrown overboard and drowned. She witnessed the tragedy and long suffered from the shock. She found comfort in writing hymns. Altogether she wrote more than 650 hymns and lyrics. Fourteen of her lyrics were published anonymously in a Christian periodical, *Budbareren*. The music for many of her hymns was written by Oskar Ahnfelt, who also went about the Scandinavian countries singing them. She married a Stockholm businessman, C. O. Berg, in 1867, but continued to sign her hymns with her maiden name or initials. She is best remembered for these hymns: "Saviour, O Hide Not Thy Loving Face from Me," "Children of the Heavenly Father," and "Day by Day Thy Mercies, Lord, Attend Me."

SATHER, MYRTLE (1905-1971), an influential American missionary and nurse-administrator. She studied at St. Helena Sanitarium and graduated in 1942. She went to Africa in 1945 and served as administrator at Kanye Hospital in Botswana. Later, her responsibilities of administration widened to over eleven hospitals, forty-eight clinics, and six schools for medical trainees, all sponsored by the Seventh Day Adventist church.

SAYER, MARY GENEVA (1895-1980), a missionary and author serving under the General Missionary Board of the Free Methodist Church of North America. She was a native of Kansas and attended college in Oregon. She went to China in 1921 and established Bible schools and churches. She had an unusual command of both written and spoken Chinese. During the war in China she was forced to move and attempted to do evangelistic and hospital work. But the Japanese imprisoned her and then released her to return to America. In 1946 she again tried to get into China and again was imprisoned, but later released and did relief work in Hong Kong. Later, she went to Taiwan and in 1952 acquired property and founded a Bible school, which became the indigenous Free Methodist Church in Taiwan. In 1947 she was one of the first women to be granted full ordination by the Free Methodist church. She wrote two books: *Triumphs,* the story of her missionary work in China, and *On the Brink,* an account of her later years under Japanese and Communist influences.

SAYERS, DOROTHY LEIGH (1893-1957), a British author and translator born in Essex. She graduated from Oxford University and taught briefly before she became known for her writings. Her first work that brought attention was a series of novels that became very popular in England. Later she lived at Oxford and was a member of a group of authors that included C. S. Lewis and J. R. Tolkien. Her translation of the *Divine Comedy* is considered one of the best and includes study notes. She wrote a series of radio plays on the life of Christ called "The Man Born to be King." Another of her best works is considered to be *The Mind of the Maker,* which expresses Christian doctrine and biblical truths in an unusual way. Her writings have influenced many people.

SCHELLENBERG, KATHARINA (1870-1945), the first woman medical missionary of the Mennonite Brethren church; she served thirty-eight years in India. She was born in the village of Tiegerweide, South Russia. As freedom of religion in Russia became more threatened, her family came to America in 1879. When she was fourteen her mother died, and the care of her brothers and sisters became her responsibility. Some of her formal education had to be postponed. She accepted Christ when she was nineteen years of age and expressed a desire to go to the mission field. After nurses training, medical school, and some practical medical experience, she sailed for India in the autumn of 1906. The long and fruitful ministry of Dr. Schellenberg in India touched many lives.

SCHOLASTICA (480-543), twin sister of Benedict of Nursia, born at Nursia in Umbria. Her parents were of the upper class. She founded the Benedictine Sisters Catholic community for women in Italy, and her twin brother founded the Benedictine order for men. The purpose for which the Benedictine sisters was formed was threefold: education, medical or hospital work, and charity. The Benedictine Sisters did not begin in the United States until 1852.

SCHROLL, ELEANOR ALLEN, a hymnist remembered especially for the familiar words of "The Beautiful Garden of Prayer." A native of Newport, Kentucky, Mrs. Schroll was at one time a teacher. She wrote many hymns, poems, and program materials for children's services. "The Beautiful Garden of Prayer" was written while she and her husband lived in a small apartment with a view quite unlike a garden setting. It was her most popular writing and continues to be a blessing to many.

SCHULTZ, ELIZABETH UNRUH (1866-1943), a faithful Mennonite missionary during a difficult time. She was born of Cornelius and Eva Unruh in South Russia, an area between Poland and Odessa. They lived in Gnadenheim in the Molotschna in the Ukraine, moving to Asia and later to America and Canada. After settling in midwestern United States in 1887, she married Abram H. Schultz, and in 1902 both were baptized and joined the Krimmer Mennonite Brethren Church. They were farmers, had several children, and actively served the Lord. Later they moved to the Saskatchewan area to be near her parents. She was left a widow at age thirty-eight with her oldest son, Henry, only seventeen, and her youngest child, Phillip, just ten months old.

SCHÜRMANN, von ANNA MARIA (1607-1678), author and French intellectual, follower of Jean de la Badie, who accepted Protestantism in 1650. Her book *Eucleria* proclaimed the principles of simple living, holding property in common, the continuance of prophecy, and the continuous Sabbath. Although by 1730 the movement began by Jean de la Badie and promoted by Schurmann ceased to exist; common communities had been established in the states of Maryland and New York. She had a love for the Word of God, knew Latin, Greek, Hebrew, Italian, Spanish, Arabic, Syriac, and Coptic and was able to read and write in all of those languages. She was proficient in mathematics, history, music, and art. Her writings influenced many.

SCOTT, CLARA H. (1841-1897), an American musician and hymnist; native of Illinois. She attended the first musical institute in Chicago, conducted by C. M. Cady in 1856. Three years later she began teaching music in the Ladies Seminary at Lyons, Iowa. She contributed a large number of songs to the collections of Horatio R. Palmer and had much piano music published in sheet form. In 1882 she was the first woman to publish a collection of anthems, *The Royal Anthem Book*. Another collection, *Short Anthems*, was published in 1897; and yet another volume called *Happy Songs: Truth in Song for Lovers of Truth*. She was killed in a horse and buggy accident in Dubuque, Iowa, and is especially remembered today as the writer of the familiar hymn, "Open Mine Eyes That I May See."

SCOTT, HELEN MAY (1882-1963), a Bible teacher and school administrator in Korea. She went to Korea from the United States in 1908, taught, and then was in charge of the mission school at Chinnampo. She served with the Seventh Day Adventist church.

SCUDDER, CATHERINE HASTINGS (1825-1849), Presbyterian missionary to India. She was the daughter of professor Thomas Hastings, known for his influence in improving the standards of church music in America. She was a native of New York. Even when young she organized a missionary group to prepare needed items for missionaries. She married William W. Scudder in 1846, and they went as missionaries to India. First they worked in Ceylon, learning the language, teaching, and doing some evangelistic work. She contributed much to the ministry of her husband. After only two years she became ill with cholera and died. She was faithful in the work the Lord had given her.

SCUDDER, IDA SOPHIA (1870-1960), an outstanding missionary physician in India and founder of the Christian Medical College and Hospital at Vellore. From a family of four generations of missionaries. Born in India, she came to the United States for her education and attended Northfield, founded by D. L. Moody. In 1890 she was called back to India to be with her mother, who was ill. Previously undecided as to a vocation, a series of three cases in just one evening influenced her decision to become a missionary doctor. Those situations involved three Brahmin men who came to their home individually for help because their wives were dying in childbirth. They wanted Ida to help, but she did not know how, and she insisted that they allow her father to help, but the men would not accept a male doctor. Thus, all three mothers died that night. Ida Scudder came back to the United States determined to become a missionary doctor. She went to the Women's Medical School in Philadelphia, and then to Cornell University, and received her M.D. degree in 1899. She returned to India, arriving on the first day of the twentieth century, January 1, 1900. With her specialization in obstetrics and gynecology, she began with a one-bed dispensary. The vision of Ida Scudder grew to put this facility on the medical map of the world. It now has a staff of about 3,000, including 400 general personnel and 200 engineers. Ida Scudder was sponsored by the Reformed Church in America, and now sixty Protestant churches and church-related organizations sponsor this facility. Medical students and nurses are trained there also. Some of the "firsts" of this center include: the first in Southern Asia to set up a Department of Neurological Sciences, the first neurobiochemistry lab in India, and the first kidney transplant was performed there. It has the largest cardiology department in India, the largest number of successful operations on blue babies and children with congenital heart defects. It is recognized as among the top four in the world in research on diarrhoeal diseases and the first in treatment of cancer. Their former orthopedic surgeon, Dr. Paul Brand, pioneered here in leprosy surgery. It is considered the largest non-governmental research group in the country, and behind all the services and honors is a Christian ministry and personalized patient care.

SEARS, MINNIE SANDBERG (1894-1968), a missionary teacher and school administrator. A native of Kansas, she graduated from the University of Kansas and later completed an M.A. degree at Columbia University in New York City. She first served as a teaching principal at the Mary L. Colby School in Yokohama, Japan, later in Washington, D.C., with the Young Women's Christian Association, and as Foreign Vice President with the Women's American Baptist Foreign Mission Society, working as their secretary for Japan, Philippines, Hong Kong, and China. She returned to America to serve as a professor of missions at the Central Baptist Seminary in Kansas City from 1959-1966. She also served as YWCA secretary and General Secretary of Women's Division of the New York Protestant Council.

SELZER, GERTRUDE (1892-1979), a faithful missionary nurse who served in Shanghai, China, from 1923 to 1952 and later in the Philippines with the Episcopal church.

SERAPHIA (?-125), a slave girl of Antioch and servant in the household of Sambine, to whom she witnessed. Later Sambine was converted to Christianity. Both she and Sambine were martyred for their faith.

SETON, ELIZABETH ANN BAYLEY (1774-1821), an educator and founder of the Sisters of Charity in the United States. Her father was Dr. Richard Bayley, professor of anatomy at Kings College, and her mother, Catherine Charlton Bayley, was the daughter of the rector of St. Andrews Episcopal Church in New York. Her mother died when she was a small child, and Elizabeth was reared by her stepmother, Charlotte Barclay, the pioneer American family of Andrew Barclay. She was educated at home, largely by her father and private tutoring. She married and lived in Pisa, Italy, for a number of years. She was widowed with five children and returned to the United States. In 1805 she joined the Roman Catholic church. She and two relatives of her husband founded a community of women for the care of orphans and poor widows with small children, following the plan of the Sisters of Charity of St. Vincent de Paul in France. This group was approved by the archbishop and became a recognized sisterhood. She became the first superior and served until 1821. Because of her ideas about education, she is credited with laying the foundation of Catholic parochial schools in the United States. In 1809 she founded the first free parochial school, which was followed by many other schools, orphanages, and hospitals in several states.

SEXTON, LYDIA CASAD (1799-1873), the first licensed woman minister of the United Methodist church and a prison chaplain. Daughter of a Baptist minister, Lydia was born in Rockport, New Jersey. Her father died when she was young, and her mother distributed the children with relatives and then remarried. In 1819 Lydia married Isaac Cox; they had one child, a boy. But in 1822 Isaac died from a fall. When her boy was three, she gave him to a Dutch family who had no children but much money. In 1824 Lydia married Moses Moore, a school administrator. They had a son, but within a year Moses Moore died. She took back her first son to rear with her younger one. Then in 1829 she married again, this time to Joseph Sexton, a blacksmith, and she was his wife for the next fifty years. They had three sons. Through all of her experiences she was reminded of her early training in a Christian home and longed to know God. After visiting several congregations and becoming involved with Bible study, she eventually became the first woman licensed to preach by the United Methodist church. Later, this practice was changed, but she renewed her license regularly. Her preaching was effective, and the Lord used her in many churches. In 1869 she moved to Kansas and started a ministry in the state prison there. She was asked to be the first woman prison chaplain at the Kansas state prison.

SHANK, CLARA BRUBAKER (1869-1958), author, teacher, and exceptional rural missionary of the Mennonite church. She took teacher preparation courses at Elkhart Institute in Indiana. She worked among the people isolated from urban centers and churches. She taught, set up Sunday schools, and had a definite evangelistic outreach.

SHANK, CRISSIE YODER (1888-1929), a remarkable leader among Mennonite women and an author and missionary; she was born near Holden, Missouri. She received her B.A. degree from Goshen College in 1913 and the following year accepted the position of dean of women and instructor at Bethel College in Kansas. She married Charles L. Shank, and they served in India as missionaries. Later, they had to return because of family health problems. She wrote *Letters from Mary,* a book about the missionary work in India, and became editor of the monthly newsletter for the Mennonite Woman's Missionary Society. She served in other ways and was an encouragement to many.

SHANK, EMMA HERSHEY (1881-1939), a Christian educator and missionary to Argentina. She received her education and taught eleven years before she married Josephus Wenger Shank in 1910. They went to Argentina in 1917 under the Mennonite church board. Her particular contribution was in organizing Sunday school work in Trenque Lauquen, home visitation, and a prayer ministry, in addition to helping her husband.

SHATTUCK, CORINNA (1848-1910), an exceptional missionary teacher and social worker for thirty-seven years in Turkey in the communities of Aintab, Adana, and Marash from 1895 to 1910, and in Oorfu, ancient Edessa. She was especially effective in helping the Armenians after the Oorfu massacre. She was described as a "missionary heroine." Her work was sponsored by the American Board of Commissioners for Foreign Missions.

SHAW, ANNA HOWARD (1847-1919), in 1880 became the first woman ordained by the Methodist Protestant church. Born in England, she came to the United States when young and settled in the Cape Cod, Massachusetts, area. Only three years after she was ordained, she enrolled in a medical school at Boston University and in 1886 received a degree. Although she did some preaching, she turned her attention to the suffrage movement. She became a personal friend of Frances Willard and in 1891 was appointed a national lecturer of the newly formed National American Woman Suffrage Assocation and its vice-president when Susan B. Anthony became the association's president in 1892. With her religious education background, she was highly recognized for distinguished leadership.

SHAW, FRANCES JERVIS (c. 1857-1903), missionary nurse in Japan and Zanzibar. She was a Britisher educated in Birmingham and London and also studied French and German in Europe. She had two years of nurses training at the St. Thomas Hospital. She went to Japan for seven years, sponsored by the Church Missionary Society. While home on furlough, she heard of the great need in Zanzibar and felt called there. She transferred to the Universities Mission and sailed for Africa in 1886. This mission operated on a faith plan, offering no specific salary, but paid travel expenses and small sums for necessary personal expenses. All of their missionaries were unmarried and had to be completely committed to serve the Lord as faith servants, believing that their needs would be supplied. She served in Zanzibar for some time, not only as a nurse but also as a teacher of the Bible. In addition to those responsibilities, she performed many other general missionary duties.

SHENK, ALTA BARGE (1912-1969), an outstanding missionary to Africa. Her parents were Witner and Elnora Ebenshade Barge. After attending both Elizabethtown and the Eastern Mennonite Colleges, she spent thirty-three years doing pioneer evangelistic work in Tanganyika. She and her husband opened Mennonite work among the Zanaki people, the Ngoreme people, and in southwest Kenya.

SHEPHERD, ANNE HOULDITCH (1809-1957), a British hymnist born at Cowes, Isle of Wight. In 1843 she married S. S. Shepherd. She is remembered for her volume of sixty-four hymns and other books. Perhaps her best known hymn was "Around the Throne of God in Heaven."

SHERWOOD, MARY MARTHA (1775-1848), a distinguished British author born in Worcestershire. In 1803 she married a military officer. They lived in India, where she taught children of his regiment. In 1818 they returned to England. She is especially remembered for writing some ninety volumes, including *Dictionary of Scriptures Types.*

SHUCK, HENRIETTA HALL (1817-1844), the first American evangelical woman missionary to go to China and the second woman missionary to open a school in Macao for Chinese children. She was married in 1835, and she and her husband became missionaries of the Triennial Baptist Convention. They served in Hong Kong, where she died in childbirth at the age of twenty-seven.

SIBLEY, GEORGIANA H. (1887-1980), an Episcopalian church leader who served on numerous committees for her own denomination and for interdenominational agencies. She served on the national board of the YWCA, as president of the United Council of Church Women, and in several other positions of leadership. She was chosen to represent all American Protestant churches at the United Nations Conference in 1945. She held thirteen honorary doctorates in the humanities.

SIDNEY, MARY (c. 1530-1601) a British Christian author and translator. She was the Countess of Pembroke and wife of Henry Sidney, Earl of Pembroke. Details of her childhood are obscure, but she is included here for her writing and translation work. She translated from Hebrew many of the psalms and wrote *Elegy, A Discourse of Life and Death* and the poem "Our Saviour's Passion."

SIEDLISKA, FRANCES (1842-1902), founder of the Roman Catholic order Sisters of The Holy Family of Nazareth in Italy in 1875. She was from a wealthy Polish family, and the purpose of her order was primarily education.

SIEVEKING, AMALIA (1794-1859), a German deaconess and founder of a society for the care of needy and ill in Hamburg, Germany. It was apparent that her humanitarian efforts were biblically based and that her testimony reflected compassion. Branches of her society spread to other parts of Europe and were especially effective during the cholera epidemic of 1831. The society provided an opportunity for middle and higher class women to actively participate in helping the needy. One of her rules was that no one visit the schools or homes of the society without taking a useful gift that was not money.

SINGH, LILAVATI, distinguished Christian educator born in Lucknow, India, of Christian parents. Lilavati was only ten years old when her mother died. Her father sent her to a mission school and then to Isabella Thoburn's boarding school. After graduation she taught and eventually became an administrator and teacher there for seventeen years. In 1899 she visited the United States with Miss Thoburn. In 1901 when Miss Thoburn died, Lilavati became president of the school. Because of the addition of post-secondary courses, it became the Lucknow Women's College and affiliated with Calcutta University. Later the name was changed to the Isabella Thoburn College.

It was the first Christian college for women in Asia.

SLESSOR, MARY (1848-1915), a missionary to Nigeria. She was a native of Aberdeen, Scotland, but was reared in Dundee. Her father, Robert Slessor, died when she was young, so at age eleven she began working in a factory to help support the family. She had to work long, hard hours for fourteen years. Her education was limited to personal reading and study. Her mother was a devout Christian, and Mary became a believer in her teens. Although she became involved in the local church work, it was not until 1876 that she responded to the needs expressed earlier by David Livingstone and went to the United Presbyterian church's Calabar Mission in Nigeria. Her first three years were at Okoyong and extremely difficult, so she returned to Scotland for a much needed rest. Her faith was steadfast, and in 1880 she returned to Nigeria. She acquired much skill in languages and was able to communicate well with the Africans in her area. She taught the women many things besides the Bible, and she was used in a unique way to communicate with the savage chiefs and teach them about business and trade. They respected her, and she was able to reach them with the gospel. She was largely responsible for the Hope Waddell Institution for the training of Africans in useful trades. So impressed was the British government with her work, it appointed her the first woman vice-consul in the British Empire when British rule was in Okoyong. She founded a home for girls and trained several of those girls to carry on the work when she was no longer able to do so. They were with her when she died of a fever that had plagued her for years.

SMET, EUGENIE MARIE (MARY OF PROVIDENCE) (1825-1871), born in Lille, France, she was founder of the Catholic community for women called Helpers of Holy Souls. Originating in France in 1856, this order was largely for education and charitable purposes. In time it had branches in several countries including China.

SMITH, AMANDA (1837-1915), internationally known evangelist born of slave parents in Maryland. She became a Christian at the age of thirteen while attending services in a Methodist Episcopal church near York, Pennsylvania. She endured many difficulties including hard work, caring for her brothers and sister, the death of her first husband, and much disappointment with her second one. She dedicated her life to the Lord's service in 1855 at the Green Street Methodist Episcopal Church in New York. Although she had little formal schooling, she studied her Bible and via the Holy Spirit was used of the Lord in a special way to reach others for Him. She had speaking and singing talents and used them to express her faith and devotion. She was asked to speak in many places in the United States, and in 1876 she was invited to England to speak at a Keswick conference. She later she went to Scotland, Liberia, and India. She organized women's prayer bands in Liberia and temperance groups and children's groups elsewhere. She did not have a regular salary and served by faith. In her retirement years she served as administrator of the Amanda Smith Orphans Home for black children in a suburb of Chicago.

SMITH, ELIZABETH LEE (1817-c. 1888), a writer and hymnist and daughter of Dr. W. Allen, one-time president of Dartmouth University. In 1843 she married H. B. Smith, a professor in New York. At least two of her hymns are included in Schaff's *Christ in Song*, first published in 1869.

SMITH, HANNAH WHITALL (1832-1911), a Bible teacher and author born into the Quaker family of John M. Whitall and Mary Tatum of Philadelphia. Her father was a wealthy glass manufacturer. She married Robert Pearsall Smith, a Quaker, in 1851. He became involved with her father's business; they lived in Germantown, Pennsylvania. Both of them preached and did some writing, but she is remembered largely for her book *The Christian's Secret of a Happy Life*, published in 1875. It has been translated into several languages. She wrote a number of other things including her autobiography, *The Unselfishness of God and How I Discovered It,* published in 1903. She also conducted Bible classes for women in her home. Hannah and her husband conducted a series of religious meetings in England in 1873-1874 and in 1888 moved to England.

SMITH, HELEN HUNTINGTON (1902-1971), a pioneer missionary and teacher in China under the United Church of Christ. She served first as a teacher at the Orlinda Childs Pierce Memorial School in Foochow form 1930 to 1941 and from 1945-1950. She also taught and had a student ministry in Chengtu, China, between her terms of service in Foochow (1944-45). Born at Intai, China, She was the daughter of missionaries. Her early schooling was at the Shanghai American School, and she later she attended Mount Holyoke College, where she received her B.A. degree. She continued her education at Union Theological Seminary and Teachers College and at Columbia University, after which she received her master's degree. In 1963 she received an honorary doctorate from Defiance College. Following her work in China she served as director of Women's Work, Ohio Conference of United Church of Christ, and later on the executive council for the Lay Life and Work program of that church. She was the first woman chosen to serve in the national work of that denomination.

SMITH, SARAH L. HUNTINGDON (1802-c. 1871), an American pioneer missionary. Married Eli Smith in 1833, and they went as missionaries to Palestine. Later she worked as a home missionary with Mohegan Indians of the United States. She exerted considerable influence by her correspondence with Lewis Cass, U.S. Secretary of War, in securing aid for improvement of schooling and work with the Indians. Through her efforts a chapel and school were built for an Indian ministry.

SOKEY, KOSHUM, an eminent Christian educator born in India to a family in the area of Chota Nagpur. After her mother died, Koshum was sent to a school for girls supported by Anglican missionaries. She prepared for teaching, and when there was a need of a headmistress in the girls school she was selected. Not only was she a capable school administrator but apt at soliciting funds for further building.

SOMERSET, ISOBEL (Lady Henry) (c. 1854-c. 1924), a Christian heiress of England and leader in the Women's Christian Temperance Union. She married Lord Henry Somerset in 1873. She was a student of the Scriptures and a woman of prayer. She held her first temperance meeting and gave her first address in a classroom she had established near her castle gate. She went about teaching bible classes, building mission rooms and employing evangelists, and was involved in a number of temperance endeavors. She spoke in various parts of England, giving her testimony as a Christian and promoting the temperance crusade. In 1890 she became president of the British Women's Temperance Association. She visited the United States by the invitation of the American WCTU, accompanied by Hannah Whitall Smith. She became a close friend of Frances Willard, founder of the World WCTU. Lady Henry returned to England in 1892 and traveled widely speaking for the cause of the WCTU. She assisted Frances Willard, editor of the *Union Signal* publication, and later started the *Women's Signal* publication.

SOMMERVILLE, MARY (1780-1872), a learned botanist and mathematician who is credited with contributing to the advancement of Christian scholarship. Born in Scotland, her father was Admiral William Fairfax. Not only did she have a great love for learning, but she was an author, artist, and musician. Details of her early education are not clear, but it is believed her education was self-perpetuated or private. In 1804 she married Samuel Greg, and they lived in London. In just three years she was widowed with two children; yet she continued to study. In 1812 she married Dr. William Sommerville. She was elected to learned societies and was highly respected for her knowledge and application of it.

SOMNER, MARYANNE AMSTUTZ (1858-1930), a Christian music educator. She was born and reared in Switzerland. She was sent to a school in Bendorf, France, for her early education. When twelve years old she emigrated to the United States with her Mennonite family. They settled in Wayne County, Ohio, where she attended school and her gift of music was developed. She taught music later and conducted seminars on church music, a rather new addition to traditional churches at that time.

SOONG, MRS. CHARLES JONES (c. 1869-1931), a dedicated Christian teacher and mother. She was a direct descendant of Wen Ting-kung, prime minister of the Ming dynasty, who was converted to Christianity in 1601 by a Jesuit missionary. Her mother left the Roman Catholic church and became a Protestant, like her husband, Yuin San, who was converted by a British missionary in Shanghai. Mrs. Soong's maiden name was Ni Kwei-tseng. She was well educated, and at the age of seventeen married Charles Jones Soong, a Chinese-born Methodist minister educated in America. He preached, was an agent for a Bible society, and later published Bibles in Chinese, and distributed them. The Soongs had six children. One of the best-known, Meiling, became China's first lady, Madame Chiang Kai-shek. Mrs. Soong was described as a devoted mother and a person of prayer. Her family had regular Bible study, prayer, and personal worship. She was a hostess to many travelers. Chiang Kai-shek attributed his own conversion to the example and efforts of Mrs. Soong. Her oldest daughter became the wife of the government minister of finance; the middle daughter, Ching-ling, married Sun Yat-sen, considered "father" of the Republic of China; her son, T. V. Soong, became a foreign minister and statesman. Her daughters were went to McTyeire School in Shanghai, a Methodist school, and later to Wesleyan College in America. Not long after Mrs. Soong was widowed, she became ill with cancer.

SOUTHCOTT, JOANNA (1750-1814), in spite of being described as a self-styled prophet, she had a number of followers and at one time a chapel in London. Born in Devon, she had an unusual personality and claimed to have special spiritual insight. She was an Anglican but in 1791 became a Methodist. She wrote a number of books that included prophecies she claimed to have received. Her spiritual insight may have influenced some for the better, but there was no evidence that such insight was based on the Scriptures.

SPALDING, CATHERINE (1793-1858), an American Catholic nun who became one of the original group in the order Sisters of Charity of Nazareth established in 1813. Later she became head of that order and was instrumental in the establishing of a number of hospitals and orphanages in Kentucky and schools in the southern United States.

SPURGEON, SUSANNAH THOMPSON (1832-1903), an author, book supplier, and devoted wife of Charles Haddon Spurgeon. She grew up in London and attended the New Park Street Chapel. Susannah and Charles were married there in January 1856 by Dr. Alexander Fletcher of Finsbury Chapel. They had only two children, twins, Charles and Thomas. The same year they were married, her husband founded the Pastors' College, which she took special interest. She saw many ministers anxious to own theological books for personal study and sermon preparation, but many of them could not afford to buy books. She started a fund to enable these men to buy the books they needed. When her husband's monthly magazine *The Sword and The Trowel* announced her intention of doing this by inviting Baptist ministers to apply for the use of this fund, many people sent in gifts. This special ministry spread to missionaries as well, and thousands of books were distributed to many who otherwise could not have afforded them. By 1902 more than 10,000 volumes had been distributed. Mrs. Spurgeon wrote three books, including *A Basket of Summer Fruit.*

STATLER, ANNA (1874-1933), a missionary to India for twenty-two years.

She worked among the women and taught them the Bible and how to read and write. She was born in Lima, Ohio.

STAM, ELIZABETH ALDEN SCOTT (1906-1934), a missionary martyr. Betty Stam was born in the United States but reared in China as her parents were missionaries there under the Presbyterian Board, U.S.A. She was a direct descendant of John and Priscilla Alden, who came over on the Mayflower. Her father, Dr. Charles Ernest Scott, was a professor, author, and missionary. They had an unusually beautiful home life with several family members later serving the Lord's work in important positions. It was at Moody Bible Institute that Betty met John Stam. She dedicated her life to missionary work in China and was accepted by the China Inland Mission. John was not finished at Moody nor was he sure where the Lord wanted him when Betty sailed for China. Her first assignment was changed because of uncertain conditions. Her parents met her in Shanghai, where she went for medical attention. In the meantime, John finished school, was accepted by CIM, and was on his way to China. By the Lord's planning his ship docked in Shanghai while Betty was still there. Both worked for a year in their assigned places before they went to Tsinan at the home of her parents. They worked as a team in Tsingtao. She had one child, Helen, on September 11, 1934, in the hospital at Wuhu. They returned to their assigned work area, and before that year ended the Communists captured Tsingteh, and Betty and John were martyred.

STANLEY, AGNES (c. 1501-1557), a British Christian martyr who lived in the county of Essex. She was arrested and questioned for her belief in Christ and the Bible. She was sentenced to Newgate where she spent about three months. After further questioning, she was sentenced to death. She is quoted as saying that she would rather die than renounce her faith in Christ and the gospel. She was burned at Smithfield in 1557.

STEAD, LOUISA, M. R. (c. 1850-1917), a dedicated missionary and hymnist, born in England. She was converted when nine years of age. She came to the United States in 1871, and it was during a camp meeting at Urbana that she dedicated her life for missionary work in China. However, she was unable to receive such an appointment for physical reasons. About 1875 she married Mr. Stead. They had a daughter, but only four years after they were married Mr. Stead drowned. She and her daughter went to South Africa in 1880 and served for fifteen years at Cape Colony. While in South Africa, Mrs. Stead married Robert Wodehouse, but by 1895 her health required that she return to the United States. Mr. Wodehouse ministered in a local Methodist church until her health improved. They were then appointed to a Methodist mission at Umtali, southern Rhodesia. She died in Penkridge, near the Mutambara Mission, Umtali. One of her hymns continues to be a favorite today, "'Tis So Sweet to Trust in Jesus."

STEELE, ANNIE (1716-1778), considered England's first woman hymn writer to have her work published in many hymnals. Her father, William Steele, was a merchant in Broughton, where he served as a Baptist minister as well. Her mother died when she was but three years old. She wrote poetry even as a child, but she was not published until about 1760, when two volumes of her poetry appeared under the title *Poems on Subjects Chiefly Devotional*. Her health was delicate and she suffered even more when the man she was to marry tragically drowned on their wedding day. Many of her early poems were published under the name Theodosia. The hymns for which she is best remembered are "He Lives, the Great Redeemer Lives" and "Almighty Maker of My Frame."

STEINER, CLARA EBY (1873-1929), author and pioneer leader of the Mennonite Women's organizations. Not only did she assist her husband as a church leader, but she initiated the movement of Mennonite Women's Missionary Society and later wrote the history of this work. Vitally interested in missions, she started a Newsletter to help Mennonite women know of the needs and prayer requests of the missionaries they supported. She was widowed quite young but had given much time and effort to the work of Mennonite missions.

STEINER, MARTHA WHITMER (1878-1928), memorable pioneer educator from Ohio. She had a successful teaching career and in 1903 married Albert Steiner. They had several children; all served in Mennonite church and were active in Christian education.

STEPHENSON, ISABELLA (1843-1890), a British hymnist and daughter of an army officer. She spent all her life in Cheltenham, and many of those years as an invalid. She is remembered especially for her hymn "Holy Father in Thy Mercy," which was published in *The English Hymnal*. It was considered a prayer for travelers, as it was written under stress when her brother sailed for South Africa.

STERLING, MARY MALINDA (1859-1933), a native of Masontown, Pennsylvania, with B.A. and M.A. degrees from Monongahela College. She became the first woman ordained in the Brethren church. Her ordination took place in 1890 in her home church. She had taught previously at Ashland College, did some evangelistic work, and wrote for denominational periodicals. She was known as the "State Evangelist of Pennsylvania," at one time.

STETSON, AUGUSTA EMMA (1842-1928), the founder of the Christian Science Institute to spread Christian Science ideas and train practitioners. She was a minister in the First Church of Christ, Scientist in New York from 1888 to 1902. Later, because of some of her teachings, she was expelled and began another group.

STUART, MARY. *See* **MARY STUART**

STEVENSON, LILIAN (1870-1960), an Irish hymnist. One of our most-loved hymns, "Fairest Lord Jesus," was written by Lilian Stevenson. She was the daughter of Fleming Stevenson, pastor of the Rathgar Presbyterian Church in Dublin, Ireland. Miss Stevenson was especially active as a leader in the Art Students' Christian Union, forerunner of the Student Christian Movement. She served as editor for the journal of this organization and was also involved with the Fellowship of Reconciliation.

STILLMAN, MILDRED WHITNEY (1890-c. 1969), an author and hymnist; born in San Francisco. Her education included Barnard College. She is remembered for her children's books, especially *A Boy from Galilee*. She wrote one hymn, "Now Once Again for Help That Never Faileth."

STONE, ANNA (c. 1880-c. 1906), Bible teacher and sister of Mary Stone (M.D.). Much of her basic education was learned from her mother. She went to the boarding school for girls at Kiukiang, China. She admired her sister and desired to come to America for schooling. When the Methodist Bishop Joyce and his wife visited the Kiukiang area in 1898, they offered to bring her back with them for school. Anna and a friend, Illien Tang, came to the United States. Anna studied at Hamline University, but because of illness she had to take less than a full load of studies. She went to the Folts Mission Institute for a three-year Bible course in the hope that her health would improve and that she possibly could follow in the path of her sister and become a medical doctor. While she was at the Institute it was discovered that she had a good singing voice. She sang to many, determined to sing only pieces that would be pleasing to the Lord. She was not physically able to endure much, and it was discovered that she had tuberculosis. Gradually she improved and returned to China to do evangelistic work among women. She was a witness to many who came to the hospital, and she assisted her sister in many ways.

STONE, ELLEN MARIA (1846-1927), an American missionary to Turkey who gained considerable attention when she was kidnapped by bandits in 1901. Various church groups in the United States raised $65,000 ransom money, and she was released safely. After that she spent some time lecturing and writing about this experience and raised interest and money for missions.

STONE, Dr. MARY (Shih Maiyü) (1873-1954), a Chinese medical missionary born in Kiukiang, Kiangsi, China. Her father was a national Methodist minister, the first Chinese minister ordained in central China; her mother was the first Chinese Christian woman of central China. She had two sisters, Anna and Phoebe. Her early education was in a Methodist Mission school in Kiukiang. In 1892 she and her friend Ida Kahn came to the United States with an American missionary, Miss Gertrude Howe. Mary Stone and Ida Kahn attended the University of Michigan medical school, and graduated with honors. They were the first Chinese women to become medical doctors. While in the United States, Mary Stone and Ida Kahn met with Dr. I. N. Danforth in Chicago concerning the need for a hospital in their home area. Thus, funds were made available for the Danforth Hospital in Kiukiang. Dr. Stone returned to China with Dr. Kahn in the fall of 1896. When the Elizabeth Skelton Danforth Hospital was complete, Dr. Stone became the first superintendent and served in that position from 1902 to 1920. Part of her efforts were devoted to the training of nurses. Hundreds of Chinese nurses received their initial training at this hospital under the administration of Dr. Stone. Mary Stone returned to the United States in 1917 for graduate study at Johns Hopkins University. After her return to China, she worked along with Miss Jennie V. Hughes in founding the Bethel Mission in Shanghai in 1920. Part of this mission was the division for nurses training, the largest such school of its kind in China, which trained more than twenty-five thousand nurses. The mission also included orphanages, elementary and secondary schools, an evangelistic band, Bible schools for both men and women, and a hospital. In 1938 Bethel mission was moved to Hong Kong. Dr. Stone left a rich heritage of mission work and medical service for the Lord in reaching out with the message of salvation to the people of China.

STOWE, HARRIET ELIZABETH BEECHER (1811-1896), an American author and hymnist. Her name immediately reminds many Americans of her famous novel, *Uncle Tom's Cabin*. Born in Litchfield, Connecticut; her father was the distinguished clergyman Dr. Lyman Beecher. Her mother was a devout Christian but died when Harriet was less than four years old. Harriet Beecher attended school in Hartford, Connecticut, and was taught by her sister, Catherine, who had started the Female Seminary there. In 1824 Harriet became a Christian. The family moved to Cincinnati, Ohio, in 1832 when her father became president of Lane Theological Seminary there. In 1836 she married one of the faculty members of Lane Seminary, Calvin E. Stowe, a professor of Hebrew. Mr. Stowe was outspoken against slavery, and as Harriet traveled with him and observed the condition of many slaves, she was inspired to write her powerful book, *Uncle Tom's Cabin*. It was published first as a serial in the Washington *National Era* in 1851 and 1852. It was released in book form in 1852, and ten thousand copies of it sold in just one week. It would sell five hundred thousand copies in this country in the following five years. Many were also sold in Great Britain, and it was translated into many languages. The influence of this book did much to promote antislavery and issues related to the Civil War. Her other writings include *Footsteps of the Master*, and she also wrote hymns, three of which were included in the 1865 edition of the *Plymouth Collection*, edited by her brother, Henry Ward Beecher. One hymn, "The Secret," was written during an especially dark time her life, which was sprinkled with a number of personal difficulties. She had seven children, two of which she lost because of tragic circumstances. Her infant son born in 1849 died of cholera; another son drowned while a student at Dartmouth College; a third son was wounded during the war and left with a permanent impairment. Her husband became ill, their income was low, and she began writing more to support the family. Through it all she is said to have remained a firm and steadfast Christian.

STRACHAN, SUSAN BEAMISH (1874-1950), a notable missionary leader and administrator in Latin America. Born in Ireland to an Irish Protestant family, she completed her missionary training studies at Harley College in London and became interested in career missionary work in the Congo. She was rejected for a slight physical difficulty but sought guidance to serve elsewhere. Accepted by the Regions Beyond Missionary Union, she sailed for Argentina in 1901. Before long her friend and college classmate Harry Strachan also came as a missionary. They were married in 1903 and for the following eighteen years served in Argentina. She founded the Argentina League of Evangelical Women, which became the Evangelical Union of South America. After much evangelistic progress and three children later, the Strachans were led to establish the Latin American Evangelization Campaign in 1921, now the Latin American Mission. Her spiritual qualities and administrative gifts contributed to her success in originating several different kinds of ministries, which are still fruitful. Those include: the Women's Bible Training School (1922), later called the Latin American Biblical Seminary; a hospital, the Clinico Biblico, dedicated in 1929; a home for neglected or abandoned children in 1932; opening of a field in coastal Colombia in 1937; evangelism by means of a river launch instituted on the Magdalena River in Colombia in 1939; the opening of a Bible Institute at Sincelejo, Colombia, in 1942; and the inauguration of radio station TIFC in Costa Rica in 1948.

SUMNERS, GERTRUDE (1900-1978), a missionary educator in Japan with the Episcopal church. She taught at the St. Agnes School, Kyoto; returned during World War II, then back to teach until she retired in 1969. She was honored by the emperor of Japan for her contribution to the education of women.

SUNDAY, HELEN THOMPSON (1868-1957), wife of Billy Sunday; an evangelist and unofficial general manager of her husband's revival meetings. Her father was a prosperous owner of a dairy products company. In 1888 she and Billy Sunday were married, and she became adviser and director of the planning for his evangelistic campaigns. In 1917 she wrote a newspaper advice column that appeared in several papers. After the death of her husband, some twenty-two years before hers, she was active in the work of several Christian groups, including Bob Jones University, the Winona Christian Assembly, Youth For Christ, and the Voice of the Andes radio station.

SWAIN, CLARA (1834-1910), first woman missionary physician to India and the non-Christian world, working for thirty years training nurses and midwives, building hospitals, treating hundreds of patients, in addition to spreading the gospel. She was born in Castile, New York, the youngest of the ten children of John and Clarissa Swain. Her education was in Castile, followed by the Woman's Medical College of Philadelphia, where she graduated in 1869. She was accepted as a missionary by the Women's Foreign Missionary Society of the Methodist Church and sailed for India in 1869 along with Miss Isabella Thoburn. Her work for the next fourteen years (except to return home in 1876-1879 for health reasons) centered in Bareilly, where she treated women and children in the area. In 1873 established the first women's hospital in India, the property of which was donated by a Moslem prince. In 1885, at the request of the Moslem Rajah of Khetri, Rajputana, Clara became physician to his wife, Rani, and other women of the palace. Rani improved quickly under her care, and the Rajah asked that Dr. Swain open a dispensary for women of the area. She was free to teach Christianity to Rani and distribute copies of the Bible to women there. In 1896 Dr. Swain retired from active service and returned to the area of her birthplace in New York. She visited India briefly in 1907-08 when she attended the golden jubilee of the Methodist Mission.

SWENSON, BLENDA CHARLOTTE (1870-1907), born in Sweden, the oldest daughter of a Swedish immigrant family to the United States, she became the first

Augustana Lutheran churchwoman missionary and the first to minister specifically to women. She graduated from Bethany College in Lindsborg, Kansas, in 1894, and pursued a year of graduate studies in education. She went to Rajahmundry, India, serving as a "Bible woman" or "Zenana Sister," which allowed her to have access to the homes of high caste Hindu women where male missionaries were not allowed. Her faithful weekly visits opened the door for her to read the Bible to them and instruct converts in the Christian faith. She returned home for health reasons in 1900, but went back to Rajahmundry in 1905, where she died. Her life inspired Swedish Lutheran women to be more concerned for the support of world missions, as well as the many women of India converted under her teachings and testimony.

SZOLD, HENRIETTA (1860-1945), an author, editor, school founder, teacher, and leader in helping Jewish people. She was the founder and first president of Hadassah, organized an evening school for immigrants, and helped American Jewish women concerned for the future of Israel. She contributed articles for the *Jewish Encyclopedia* and edited the *American Jewish Year Book*. She also directed the Youth Aliyah group rescue of some 30,000 young Jews from Germany and Poland between 1933 and 1948, and in many ways directed public attention to the needs of Jews. Her father, a rabbi, was from Hungary, so much attention was given to education. She began writing for Anglo-Jewish publications while yet in her teens.

T

TAKAMORI, MAJU (c. 1897-c. 1968), a Christian educator of Japan. She earned four college diplomas; she studied in America at Chicago, then completed her master's degree at Columbia University in New York City. She spent thirty-six years in Christian education, primarily training teachers in Osaka.

TAYLOR, EMILY (1795-1872), a British author, editor, and hymnist; She was the daughter of Samuel Taylor of Buckenham, Norfolk. She wrote natural history stories for children including *Flowers and Fruit in Old English Gardens* (1836); *Letters of a Child in Maritime Discovery* (1820); *Tales of the English* (1833); *Rainbow Stories* (1870); and others. She edited a publication called *Sabbath Recreations* and had several hymns published in the Unitarian *Collection of Psalms and Hymns* printed for the Renshaw Street Chapel in Liverpool in 1818. She was associated with the Unitarian church but later joined the Church of England. Some of her hymns were Scripture illustrative poems, as her *Poetical Illustrations of Passages of Scripture* published in 1826. A number of her hymns appeared in various collections, including American hymnbooks. A few are: "Who Shall Behold the King of Kings?," "The Gospel Is the Light," "Come to the House of Prayer," and "Here, Lord, When at Thy Table Meet."

TAYLOR, IRENE BLYDEN (1885-1958), a missionary evangelist in her native West Indies. She came to America for Bible school in Cincinnati, Ohio, but returned to serve her own people. The impact of her ministry will long be effective, as many souls were saved, and four main churches and more than twenty-two Sunday schools established there. She was married to Richard Alfred Taylor, a minister, also of the West Indies. After his death she served as dean of women in a Bible training school in Jamaica.

TAYLOR, JANE (1783-1824), author, hymnist, and daughter of Isaac Taylor. She was born in London and composed music at an early age. Her first piece was published in the 1804 edition of *Minor's Pocket Book*. She wrote *The Beggar's Boy, Original Poems for Infant Minds, Rhymes for the Nursery,* and other works for children. Many of her songs were prepared for use in Sunday schools; some were reprinted in America and later translated into German. A few of her hymns are: "A Sinner, Lord, Behold I Stand" (1809); "Almighty God Who Dwellest High" (1809); "When Daily I Kneel Down to Pray" (1809); "How Dreadful to Be Turned Away" (1812), and "Love and Kindness We May Measure."

TAYLOR, JENNIE FAULDING (1843-1903), missionary to China and second wife of J. Hudson Taylor. She was a Britisher who sailed to India in 1866 with the same group that included the first Mrs. Taylor and her husband. Maria Dyer Taylor died in 1870, and less than two years later J. Hudson Taylor married Miss Jennie Faulding. Her primary responsibilities as a missionary were not only to care for her husband, who had been injured and was sometimes ill, but also to edit the periodical *China's Millions* for the China Inland Mission. She also had a special ministry among the women. In her later years she traveled with Dr. Taylor, speaking, writing, and organizing the work of the mission. She preceded him in death by approximately two years.

TAYLOR, MARIA DYER (c.1840-1870), missionary to China who became the wife of J. Hudson Taylor, founder of the China Inland Mission. They had several children, most of whom died in infancy or very young. After her death, a sister of J. Hudson Taylor, Amelia Broomhall, reared the three remaining children, two of which became associated with the China Inland Mission. The rigors of missionary life were difficult for Mrs. Taylor, but she was a great help and comfort to her husband.

TEKAKWITHA, CATHERINE (c. 1657-1680), an unusual Christian witness among her own people. She was born in Gandahouhague, Mohawk Territory, in what later became the Fonda, New York, area. She was half Iroquoian, the child of a Mohawk man and Algonquian woman. She had smallpox when only four years old and was left disfigured and with very poor eyesight. She was not wanted by her family and was raised by an uncle. She met some Jesuit missionaries about 1667, but her uncle was opposed to anything related to Christianity. She was drawn to the religion of missionaries and on Easter day in 1676 she was baptized. For this she was much criticized, as baptism did not coincide with tribal ways. In 1677, helped by a Christian visitor, she fled to an Indian mission near Sault St. Louis in Canada. The mission, St. Francis Xavier du Sault, became her home. She helped with the work as best she could and practiced austere measures such as fasting, praying, and honoring her personal vow of chastity. In 1679 she established a convent similar to the Hospital Sisters of Ville-Marie in Montreal. She was much loved and had a unique missionary impact among those of her community. She was revered as a prayer warrior and one concerned for the spiritual life of her own people.

ten BOOM, CORNELIA (CORRIE) (1893-1983), devout survivor of the Ravensbruck concentration camp during World War II. Corrie became a Christian as a young child in her native Haarlem, Holland. Her father had a watch shop, which had been part of the ten Boon family for more than one hundred years. She became the first licensed woman watchmaker in Holland. When World War II came to Haarlem, she and her family became part of an underground movement to protect Jews in Holland from Nazi persecution. Corrie, a sister, a brother, and their aged father were imprisoned at the Ravensbruck camp. Just ten days later, her father died at the age of eighty-four. Betsie, her sister, became one of the 96,000 women who perished at Ravensbruck. Only by the Lord's plan was a clerical error made that resulted in the release of Corrie just before thousands more were put to death. Soon after the war she helped turn what was once a concentration camp in Darmstadt, Germany, into a home for war refugees and victims. Corrie was a popular speaker, for her testimony of the Lord's grace was firm and challenging. She wrote eighteen books. Her best-known book, *The Hiding Place,* which relates her experiences, was made into a film. More than a million copies of the book have been sold. She came to the United States to make her home and lived here until the Lord took her on her ninety-first birthday.

TENNEY, HELEN MARGARET JADERQUIST (1904-1978), a leader of the Women's Union Missionary Society, an officer of the National Association of Evangelicals, and wife of Dr. Merrill C. Tenney. She was born in Buffalo, New York; received her B.A. degree from Wheaton College in 1925; a master's degree in history from Northwestern University in 1926; and taught at Northfield Seminary until her marriage in 1930. She served on the board of the Women's Union Missionary Society and was an officer of the Women's Fellowship of the National Association of Evangelicals. She wrote a number of articles and other materials especially related to Sunday school and teaching.

TERESA OF AVILA (1515-1582), author, mystic, and Reformer within the Roman Catholic order of Carmelites. She was born in Avila of Old Castle, Spain, to Alonso Sanchez de Cepeda and his second wife, Beatrice Ahumada. Her mother died when Teresa was twelve, and shortly afterward her father sent her to school in the local convent. Soon Teresa became quite ill and returned home to recuperate. In the meantime she read the work of Jerome and others and decided to commit her life to the work of the church. Again, illness plagued her, but it was especially during such times that she communicated with God and had visions. Her journal entries record a number of mystical experiences. She withdrew to a life of prayer, dedication, and communion with God. When she was middle-aged, a new revelation came to her of the needs for nuns to take more austere measures of dedication and service. She became a leader of a counterreformation within the Carmelites and formed the order of Discalced Carmelites. She first established a house in Avila, then traveled to other places in Spain establishing seventeen such houses for nuns. Fifteen others were originated for men. She was an example of austerity and encouraged others to put God first and depend on Him for all their needs. She wrote five major books and several shorter works. Her autobiography has been likened to Augustine's *Confessions*. Her *Book of Foundations* describes the founding of the Carmelite convents and monasteries; and her books *The Way of Perfection* and *The Interior Castle* describe the progress of the soul toward perfect union with God. She was canonized by Pope Gregory XV and was the only woman on whom the Roman Catholic church conferred the title Doctor of the Church.

TERESA OF LISIEUX (1873-1897), a noted Carmelite nun and author. She was born in Alencon, France, and was the youngest daughter of Azelia Marie Guerin and Louis Martin. Her mother died when Teresa was four years old, and a few months later the family moved to Lisieux in Normandy. She was not a healthy child and was plagued by tuberculosis until her death at age twenty-four. She was converted in 1888, expressed rebirth, and surrendered her life to Christ. In turn, that led her to commit her life to the work of a Carmelite convent at the age of fifteen. Her personal commitment and life of prayer as expressed in her autobiography, *The Story of a Soul*, was first published in 1897 and became almost required reading for those in the Carmelite convents. Pope Pius X praised her, and her work contributed to the personal Christian life of many, especially her spiritual sisters.

THECLA (First Century), visited by Paul and Barnabas on their first missionary journey. She was a native of Iconium in Asia Minor and became a Christian. Details of her life are obscure, but she is mentioned in the writings of Augustine and other church Fathers. Two churches were dedicated to her, and some believe she may have founded a convent near Seleucia. There is some indication that she was the first martyr in Greece. It is known that she taught the teachings of Paul and was a devout Christian of her day.

THEODELINDA (568-628), Christian queen of Lombardy responsible for the building of many churches and monasteries in northern Italy. She encouraged many to turn back to orthodoxy from Arianism, which denied the divinity of Christ. Pope Gregory the Great dedicated his *Dialogues* to Theodelinda. Before she married King Autarie, she was a part of Bavarian royalty. After he died, she married Flavius Agiluphus of the province of Pavia. He also died, and she became full regent of Lombardy. She encouraged agriculture, supported charitable endeavors, and built up the church. It is believed that she sponsored the Irish saint Columba, who became a missionary to northern Scotland.

THEODORA (508-548), eminent wife of Justinian I, emperor of the East. She was born in Constantinople, and apparently her parents' beliefs were far from being Christian. She married Justinian in 525. In 527, when Justinian was elected emperor, she was included, and they reigned together. Their long reign was described as the most brilliant of the Byzantine Empire. They tried to restore the Roman Empire to its former state of distinction. Wars were common but apparently necessary to eradicate paganism.

THEVENET, MARIE CLAUDINE, founder of the religious order of Jesus and Mary at Lyons, France, in 1818. Education was the purpose of this community.

THIESSEN, ANNA J. (1892-1977), author and beloved missionary to immigrants to the United States. Born in Wassieljewka, Russia, to Jacob W. and Helena Siemens Thiessen, she emigrated with her parents to Manitoba in 1903 and later settled in Saskatchewan, Canada. She served in a local Mennonite church and went to the Los Angeles Bible Institute (later named Biola University) for Bible and English training. She was assigned to do city missionary work in Winnipeg. Aware of the great need for a Christian mission especially planned for women immigrants, she organized a mission of her own. For thirty-four years she administered the Mary-Martha Home she had founded and began other related missions. Mennonite immigrants were streaming into Canada from Russia and needed assistance. She helped them spiritually but also helped them to find jobs. Her missionary efforts were a great blessing to many.

THOBURN, ISABELLE (1840-1901), pioneer American missionary educator to India. A native of St. Clairsville, Ohio, she was educated at the Wheeling Female Seminary and the Cincinnati Academy of Design. After her brother, Bishop James Thoburn, returned home after ten years in India, he made her much aware of the need for women missionaries to reach the women of India. In 1869 she became the first missionary to be appointed by the Women's Foreign Missionary Society of the Methodist Episcopal Church. She went to India in 1869 and was on the same ship as Clara Swain. She opened a school for girls in Lucknow and in 1871 established a Christian boarding school for girls in addition to evangelism, teaching the Bible, and zenana work. In time, her Christian boarding school increased with the addition of high school courses, and by 1887 a post-secondary division was established. Thus, it became the first Christian college for women in Asia. In 1895 the British government granted a charter for this college to become the Lucknow Women's College and to be affiliated with Calcutta University. The college name was changed to the Isabelle Thoburn College. Isabelle was the college's first president, but she trained Lilavati Singh, one of its students, to take over the position after she retired. However, Isabelle never really retired before she died of cholera in 1901.

THOMAS, SALLY (1769-1813), a missionary-minded domestic worker who gave the first gift to the American Board of Commissioners for Foreign Missions. Little information has been recorded about this faithful Christian, but long after her death her pastor's son, Joseph Rowell, wrote of her life in the *Missionary Herald* magazine. She is an example to others concerned with sharing in missions, not by the amount she gave in comparison with anyone else, but by the amount she gave in comparison to the wages she received. She lived in Cornish, New York, and apparently became a Christian as a young woman, while working for a family by the name of Chase. She worked in their home over twenty years but received little wages. She was a member of the Congregational Church in Cornish and vitally interested in missions. Perhaps in considering her station in life she felt this was her way to the mission field, and surely many lives were brought to the Lord through her prayers and gifts. In her will, whatever was left after expenses was designated for missions.

THOMPSON, ELIZABETH MARION (1794-1869), significant British missionary educator with a special gift of organization and administration. She was a missionary to Syria with her husband, Dr. James Bowen Thompson, who was in charge of the British Syrian Hospital at Damascus. She began her work with women at Antioch by founding several schools. When the Crimean War erupted, Dr. Thompson offered his medical expertise to the government and was sent, but he became one of the early victims of malignant fever. As a widow she became much involved with organizing relief work, especially for widows. She founded the Association for the Wives of Soldiers Under the Patronage of Queen Victoria. In 1860, during a massacre of Christians in Lebanon, she issued a plea for help, going herself for an intended stay of six months but instead staying the rest of her life. She taught Bible classes and literacy classes for women. In 1861 she established three schools in addition to a house where thirty Hasbeyan widows lived. Money came in, and the work grew rapidly. In 1862 the Prince of Wales visited the schools. By 1864 eighteen schools had been started, and requests came for more. One school was established at Zachlen with the full accreditation of the Turkish governor of Lebanon and with the authority of an Imperial Firman from Constantinople. These schools became centers of gospel teaching and secular knowledge.

THOMSON, MARY ANN (1834-1923), a British poet and hymnist who came to America. Born in London, she lived most of her life in England. She came to America where she married John Thomson, the first librarian of the Free Library in Philadelphia. A number of her poems and hymns were published in *The Churchman* and in *The Living Church*. She is remembered most for her beautiful hymn included in many hymnals today "O Zion Haste, Thy Mission High Fulfilling."

THRUPP, DOROTHY ANN (1779-1847), British writer, editor, and hymnist. Born in London, she served as editor of *Hymns for the Young*, in which she did not sign her name to her own hymns. She also contributed hymns to two publications by W. Carus Wilson, *Friendly Visitor* and *Children's Friend*. She is best remembered today for the popular hymn "Saviour, Like a Shepherd Lead Us," included in many American hymnals.

THRUTGEBA, LEOBA (c. 703-779), from a family of English nobility; daughter of Aebba and Dynno Thrutgeba. She was well educated while in the care of the abbess of Wimborne. It was said that she loved her Bible, had it with her constantly, and even had other nuns read it to her as she slept. Her devotion came to the attention of Boniface, whom some believe was a relative. He asked that she and others go to Germany to found monasteries; she was selected to be the abbess at Bischofsheim. She trained other women to become superiors of other convents. She was consulted by bishops and many scholars largely because of her knowledge of the Bible, she and was highly respected by Carolingian nobility. Boniface respected her and provided for her care in old age. In fact, he requested that she be buried beside him. She went to Germany about 748 and later founded and ruled the double monastery at Tauberbischofsheim.

THURSTON, LUCY GOODALE (1795-1876), an author and pioneer American missionary to Hawaii. Her father was Abner Goodale, a deacon in a Presbyterian church in Marlboro, Massachusetts. She graduated from Bradford Academy. She and her husband, Asa G. Thurston, were sent to the Kona district in Hawaii in 1820, shortly after they were married. Her husband was a graduate of Yale College and Andover Theological School. She assisted her husband and taught Bible classes for women, in addition to teaching them sewing and home economics. She wrote an autobiography primarily to help her family realize the work they were doing and how the Lord was directing.

THURSTON, MATILDA S. CALDER (1875-1958), missionary, author, teacher, and distinguished first president of Ginling College in China. A native of Connecticut, she graduated from Mt. Holyoke College in 1896 and later received a doctorate from there. She first went as a missionary teacher to the Central Turkey College in Morash; then was married and with her husband went to Yale-in-China Mission in 1902. She was widowed in 1904. She worked with the Student Volunteer Movement and from 1906 to 1911 taught in Yale Mission, Changsha. In 1913 she was appointed by the Presbyterian Board for service in Nanking, China, and with representatives of five denominations planned the establishment of Ginling College in 1915. She served as its first president until 1928 and as an adviser until 1936. She wrote a book with Ruth Chester, *A History of Ginling College.*

TINGLEY, KATHERINE AUGUSTA WESCOTT (1852-1929), leader in the Theosophical Movement worldwide. She was a native of Massachusetts. She considered herself a professional spiritualist medium and was interested in humanitarian work, including missions and the

Emergency Relief Organization. In 1896 she became head of the Theosophists and in 1897 founded the International Brotherhood League. She established a theosophical colony at Point Loma, California and went worldwide promoting the beliefs of the Theosophical Society. In California she founded the Raja Yoga Academy, an orphans home, and another school. She acquired property in Cuba, Sweden, and England and organized seven theosophical centers in Europe. Some of her writings were published. She edited the *Theosophical Journal*.

TITCOMBE, ETHEL McINTOSH (1881-1970), a significant missionary to Nigeria with an unusual ministry to mothers in the Yagba tribe. A Canadian and converted when young, she worked in her local church in Toronto and met Thomas Titcombe while he was home on furlough from Nigeria. In 1915 she went to Nigeria, where they were married. Sponsored by the Sudan Interior Mission, she was used to reaching many women with the gospel and worked to break the taboo against twin births in the Yagba tribe. She was responsible for saving the first pair of twins and taught the women about sanitation, child care, and many other improvements. She also taught them the love of the gospel, and many became Christians. Before the ministry of Mrs. Titcombe, the tribeswomen were taught that not only were twins evil, the mother was less than human. It was commonly expected that twins were killed right after birth and the mother was no longer accepted in the village. Mrs. Titcombe was able to show them firsthand that such teachings were false and that Christianity was the vital element needed. How gracious of the Lord to allow Mrs. Titcombe herself to give birth to twins in 1919. A forty-bed maternity hospital was built, with her husband doing the bricklaying. In 1935 she unexpectedly was awarded a medal and citation from King George V of England in recognition of her work at Egbe and the contribution she had made to the welfare of the women and children of that area.

TOKE, EMMA LESLIE (1812-1872), Irish hymnist; daughter of John Leslie, Bishop of Kilmore. In 1837 she married Nicholas Toke of Kent. She first began writing hymns at the request of a friend who was collecting material for *Hymns for Public Worship*, published in 1852. Her most popular works, which have been included in collections in both Great Britain and America are: "Glory to Thee, O Lord," "O Lord, Thou Knowest All the Snares," and "Thou Art Gone Up on High." She wrote a series of hymns for the volumes in 1870: *Sunday School Liturgy and Hymn Book*.

TOURJEE, LIZZIE SHROVEL (1858-1913) a New Englander, daughter of Dr. Eben Tourjee, who was founder of the New England Conservatory of Music. She was educated at Wellesley College and in 1833 married Franklin Estabrook. She is remembered especially for her hymn "There's a Wideness in God's Mercy," which is included in many hymnals today.

TRASHER, LILLIAN (1887-c. 1965), a dedicated missionary of great faith and compassion, founder of the Assiout Orphanage in Egypt. The orphanage began as a faith mission greatly blessed and has expanded and improved facilities to care for thousands of homeless Egyptian children. Lillian was born in Jacksonville, Florida; her father was a businessman, and her mother was college-educated with Quaker ancestry but became a Roman Catholic. Lillian did not remember seeing a Bible until sixteen years of age. She requested one for her birthday and eventually led her mother back to the Lord. Lillian was a talented artist and had two books of pen drawings published in Egypt. Her sister, Jennie, accompanied Lillian to Egypt, first going with her in 1910. The people of Assiout grew to love her, and after she had been there fifty years, many sent words of congratulations, including Egypt's President Nasser. The story of Assiout Orphanage continues as an ongoing expression of God's love.

TROTTER, ISABEL LILIAS (1853-1928), a missionary to North Africa. The daughter of a London businessman, her education was private. She became a

Christian through the ministry of Mr. and Mrs. Pearsall Smith. Recognized as a capable artist, she specialized in painting miniatures. Called into missionary work, she began in Algeria in 1888. She went about preaching the gospel and establishing preaching stations. She organized teams for evangelistic work, and her helpers grew from three to thirty full-time workers. One of her major accomplishments was to translate the New Testament into the Algerian dialect. Then, using her artistic talents, she prepared attractively illustrated tracts for Moslems. Her mission organization was incorporated into the North African Mission.

TROYER, ESTHER FREED (1913-1961), a Mennonite missionary in Tanzania and pioneer educator in the Franconia Mennonite school in the United States.

TROYER, KATHRYN SOMMERS (1893-1973), a missionary to India and later in Puerto Rico under the Mennonite church board. Her parents were Daniel and Elizabeth Zook Troyer.

TRUTH, SOJOURNER ISABELLA (c. 1797-1883), an outspoken preacher against slavery and for the rights of women. Born in Ulster County, New York, she began to preach in 1843. Later she spoke for the rights of women in relation to the Scripture. She traveled, speaking and preaching in several states, including Indiana, Illinois, Connecticut, Massachusetts, Ohio, and Kansas.

TSENG, MISS (c. 1874-c. 1938), founder of a Christian school in China. The granddaughter of Teng Kuofan and largely responsible for saving Changsha from the T'ai Ping rebels. She went to a mission school sponsored by the Church Missionary Society. She continued her schooling in London. She returned to Changsha and established a school that was closed down by the Communists in 1927.

TUBMAN, EMILY H. (1794-1885), a Christian of early America whose compassion touched many for the Lord. Born in Ashland, Virginia, during the presidency of George Washington, she was the daughter of Ann Chiles and Edmund Pendelton Thomas. She lived under twenty-two American presidents; her father died when she was nine, and her legal guardian was Henry Clay. In 1818 while visiting relatives in Augusta, Georgia, she met Richard C. Tubman, a British merchant and exporter who owned much property in the southern United States. They were married and lived in Augusta. They attended the St. Paul's Episcopal Church, and she became a true student of the Bible. Later she became acquainted with Alexander Campbell and shared his teachings. A group met regularly in her home to read Scripture, sing hymns, and observe Communion. This group organized the First Christian Church in Augusta, Georgia. Emily felt a great responsibility before the Lord for her stewardship of the family wealth. Her husband died in 1836, leaving in his will a provision that she apply to the Georgia legislature to pass a law enabling her to free their slaves. However, she would need to provide a place for these people to go after their freedom was granted. Thus, she looked to Liberia because of the work that was being done there by the United States government. She called all her slaves together, explained the situation, and gave them a choice of staying with her in America, or accepting freedom, which most likely meant going to Liberia. Nearly seventy of them chose freedom and Liberia, whereas seventy-five chose freedom but preferred to stay in the United States. For those going to Liberia, she chartered a ship and provided supplies and a home for them there. For those freed but remaining in America, she gave clothing, land, and the necessary provisions for becoming self-supporting. Truly she enacted the Emancipation Proclamation more than twenty-five years before it was officially declared. The eighteenth president of the Republic of Liberia, William Vaccanarat Shadrach Tubman, was a grandson of two of the couples Emily Tubman helped to send there in 1844. Here and there over the southern United States, Emily Tubman quietly gave funds for numerous needs, whether they were in her own denomination or other churches, schools, and libraries. When a church in Atlanta and another in Athens needed building improvements or additions, she helped; she gave to Butler University and other schools. In 1882 she provided for a church and the minister's salary in Augusta; she helped to provide for the transportation of soldiers home after the Civil War; and she made numerous provisions for Christian education, for Bibles, and other means of spreading the gospel of salvation. She was a wise steward and much loved by many.

TUCKER, CHARLOTTE (1821-1893), a British missionary, author, and teacher in India. She began writing when young, had approximately eighty books published in England, and more than forty of them issued in India, where they were translated into various dialects. Her books and plays sold so well that she designated much of the royalty income for charity. Her father served in India, opening a school at Futteypore, and her brother founded the Christian Literary Society for India, whereby he distributed some of her writings along with others. She did not go to India as a missionary until she was middle-aged, but by that time she had sixty-eight books in circulation. In India she taught Bible and was associated with the Indian Female Normal School and Instruction Society. Some of her work was in zenanas. She was described as not only having a special gift of writing but also of being a good steward in giving of her royalty money to Christian work.

TUDOR, MARY. *See* **MARY TUDOR**

TURKINGTON, FLORENCE A. (1896-1982), a nurse and hospital administrator who served with the Salvation Army for forty-two years. Born in Connecticut, she entered the Salvation Army Training College in New York in 1917. Soon after, she was sent to France and served there until after the Armistice. After that she returned to the United States, took nursing at the Covington Kentucky Hospital, and in 1937 was appointed superintendent. In 1943 she was appointed to the important position of Women's Social Service Secretary at the Territorial Headquarters in New York, a position she held for more than fifteen years. She supervised ten hospitals, general and maternity; nine maternity homes for unmarried mothers; four day nurseries; a children's home; a foster home service for children; two lodging houses for women; and a girls training school for first offenders referred to the Salvation Army by New York City and country courts. She was especially influential in promoting the education of women officers in her department, insisting that they were completely qualified and competent in their fields of service. She was the first woman officer of the Salvation Army to receive a degree in nursing. She was awarded an honorary fellowship in the American College of Hospital Administrators.

U

UCHIDA, HAMA (c. 1847-1920), Bible teacher for twenty-five years in Tokyo and another twenty-five years in Sendai, Japan. She became a Christian while living in the home of a missionary. Her influence with other Japanese women was great as she taught the Bible. Some have referred to her as the "mother" of the First Baptist Church of Japan.

UNDERHILL, EVELYN (Mrs. HUBERT STUART MOORE) (1875-1941), a British mystic and influential author. She was born in Staffordshire, England, the daughter an attorney. She lived in London where she attended school. She was sent to a private school at Folkstone when she was sixteen years of age; graduated from King's College for Women in London; and in 1927 was made a fellow of her alma mater. She was reared in an Anglican church home but became interested in Roman Catholicism while visiting a Franciscan convent in 1907. She turned to the study of mysticism and became a follower of Baron Friedrich von Hugel. She married Hubert Stuart Moore in 1907 and continued her traveling, speaking, and writing. She wrote about her experiences and mysticism and translated writings of other mystics. Perhaps her most widely read book was *Worship* (1937), which included liturgy of the Orthodox churches. She wrote two volumes under the pseudonym John Cordelier: *The Spiral Way* and *The Path of the Eternal Wisdom.*

UNDERWOOD, LILLIAS HORTON (c. 1860-1927), medical missionary to Korea. She married Horace Grant Underwood in 1889. They were fellow missionaries in Seoul and were married there. She had a degree in medicine and considerable nursing experience in the Presbyterian Hospital in Chicago. She became the personal physician for the Korean queen and was able to be a Christian witness to her. During the war the queen was killed by the Japanese. Lillias organized womens meetings and had a ministry of Bible teaching in addition to her medical work. In 1916, after twenty-eight years in Korea, Dr. Underwood and her husband returned to America because of poor health.

URSULA (Fourth Century), although information about this princess is vague or indistinct, there is evidence that she was a British Christian who made a pilgrimage to Rome during the fourth century. Some believe perhaps as many as 10,000 people accompanied her. They were all massacred near Cologne, probably by uncivilized people of that area. Much later she was declared a saint.

URSULA OF MÜSTERBERG (c. 1495, d. after 1534), a nun who with two others left the convent of Mary Magdalene the Penitent in 1528 and went to Wittenberg to join Martin Luther and other Protestant converts. Her grandfather was King George Podiebrad of Bohemia and a cousin of Duke George and Heinrich, in whose home she lived after her parents died. She was placed in the convent when young but found life there disagreeable and difficult. George died in 1539 and Heinrich succeeded. He was definitely in favor of the teachings of Luther, and with the encouragement of his wife, Katherine, there was not only an infiltration of Luther's writings into the convent but a Lutheran chaplain as well. Some of Luther's books were said to have been sent there to be bound, but the nuns read them and a number of them were enlightened. Ursula and the other two nuns who went with her left the convent during the night of October 6, 1528, going first to a pastor at Leisnig and then to Wittenberg. Later, Ursula wrote a tract concerning her decision, using much Scripture to document her ideas. Luther wrote the preface to Ursula's tract. After that, she chose to live in seclusion, and her death date or place is not recorded.

V

VAN DEERLIN, MARGARET (1884-1978), a missionary-teacher in the Hawaiian Islands, appointed by the Episcopal church. She first went in 1931 and worked with her sister, also a missionary. She taught in an orphanage that bears her family name. She retired in 1947.

van de WERKEN, JOHANNA (1874-1949), a Dutch evangelist, hymnist, and commissioner in the Salvation Army. She served faithfully in her native country, the Netherlands, and in India, Indonesia, and Switzerland. Her linguistic abilities were unusual, and she wrote a number of songs widely used in services of the Salvation Army.

VAUGHAN, HARRIET PARKER (1867-1953), a missionary-physician to India, serving as the director of the American Hospital for Women and Children in Madura, South India. She founded the Dayapuram Leper Hospital and the Bird's Nest Orphanage, also in Madura. A native of Vermont, she attended Smith College and later the Women's Medical College of New York. She was sponsored by the American Board of Commissioners for Foreign Missions and in 1937 was decorated by the Indian government with the Kaiser-i-Hind medal for distinguished service to the people of India.

VERE MARY TRACEY (1581-1671), a noble Christian whose ancestors accompanied William the Conqueror in 1066. Only three days after Mary was born her mother died, and when she was eight, her father died. Details of her early childhood are vague. At the age of nineteen she married William Hobby, the son of a member of the Privy Council to Henry VIII. They had two children, both of whom died in infancy. After the death of Mr. Hobby, she married Sir Horatio Vere, Baron of Tilbury. They lived in Holland where they joined with the Presbyterians. She agreed with Calvinistic doctrine and was especially sympathetic toward the families of those persecuted for their faith. Mary and Sir Horatio attended the English church in The Hague, pastored by Dr. William Ames. They consistently exercised influence and support in obtaining devout and gifted ministers for the cause of Christ and Protestantism, such as the appointment of Dr. James Usher to the Archbishop of Armagh and Primacy of Ireland. In London their minister was Dr. John Davenport, a noted Puritan of St. Stephens. Sir Horatio died in 1635 and was interred in Westminster Abbey. She used much of her inheritance to help the poor and spread the gospel. She was described as having deep faith, a consistent prayer life, and was a student of the Scriptures.

VICTORIA, ALEXANDRINA (1819-1901), Christian queen of Great Britain and head of the Church of England for sixty-four years. She was born at Kensington Palace, London, the only child of Edward, Duke of Kent, and third in succession to the throne. Her father died before she was nine months old. Her education was by tutors, and she was a good student, devoutly religious, and serious as a youth. In 1837, when informed of the death of the king, she met with the Privy Council but requested two hours of solitude, during which time it is believed she prayed for wisdom and guidance. She then wrote a letter of sympathy to the widowed queen. Her coronation was in 1838 at Westminster Abbey. She immediately brought respect and dignity to the throne. Her long reign was filled with a succession of events that reflected her deep faith in the Bible and its application in daily living. She was married to Prince Albert of Saxe-Coburg-Gotha of Germany in 1840. Her great devotion to him was a remarkable example of personal love. His unexpected death in 1861 brought an extended period of personal mourning. She was widowed at age forty-two with nine children. Her long life and reign as queen brought influence for legislation that reflected Christian principles and her love for the Lord. She was not afraid to exercise her authority for good or to extend help to the needy, yet her personal witnessing was uniquely humble, often going unidentified until later. She was described as having transparent honesty and massive simplicity. She died in 1901 after a brief illness.

von BORA, KATHARINE. *See* **LUTHER**

von BUTTLAR, EVA. *See* **BUTTLAR**

von LASAULX, AMALIE. *See* **LASAULX**

von REUSS, BENIGNA. *See* **REUSS**

von MALLENCKRODT, PAULINE (1817-1881), founder of the Roman Catholic community Sisters of Christian Charity. She was born in Westphalia. The community began in 1849 in Germany, came to the United States in 1873, and its primary purpose relates to education.

WARD, MARY (1585-1642), born in Yorkshire, England, of noble parents. Details of her youth are obscure. She entered a convent of Poor Clares but was disappointed, so she founded the Institute of the Blessed Virgin Mary or Ladies of the Loretto in 1609 in Bavaria. It was a cloistered community for prayer and education and associated with the Roman Catholic church.

WARING, ANNA LAETITIA (1823-1910), born at Plas-y-Velin, Neath, Glamorganshire, Wales. Her family associated with the Society of Friends, but she became a member of the Church of England. A student of Hebrew, she was especially interested in Old Testament poetry. She wrote a number of well-known hymns including "Father, I Know That All My Life," and "In Heavenly Love Abiding." In 1850 she published *Hymns and Meditations*, and in 1858 *Additional Hymns*.

WARNER, ANNA BARTLETT (1821-1915), author and hymnist. She wrote several books of poems and hymns in addition to a number of novels. Her novels were written under the pseudonym Amy Lothrop. Many of her hymns were for children but have become popular with adults as well. She may be best remembered for her chorus "Jesus Loves Me, This I Know," written in 1858, and "A Mother's Evening Hymn." Her "The Song of the Tired Servant" was written in response to a letter she received from a pastor friend who expressed great physical weariness, yet pleasure in serving the Lord. She wrote two volumes of hymns: *Hymns of the Church Militant* (1848) and *Wayfaring Hymns, Original and Translated* (1869). Anna was the sister of Susan Warner (also an author), and used the pen name Elizabeth Wetherell. Anna and Susan made their home together, which was near West Point Military Academy. They were concerned for the spiritual needs of the West Point cadets and opened their home for Bible classes for them. In fact, their home was willed to West Point Academy and later made a national shrine.

WASTE, JOAN (c. 1500-1556), a blind woman of Derby martyred for her testimony and faith in Jesus Christ. Because of her blindness, she had memorized long portions of Scripture and was able to detect false teachings quite easily. She was not persuaded to deviate from Scripture truth in her testimony, so her refusal to communicate with those expressing antiscriptural views caused her to be apprehended for questioning. She did not alter her testimony and was sentenced to death. The day of her execution, August 1, 1556, she was led to the stake, knelt down, and fervently prayed, desiring spectators to pray with her. Her testimony for Christ was strong to the very end, when her body was engulfed in flames.

WATERS, ETHEL (1896-1977), a much-loved American gospel singer. She was converted as a youth and won fame as an actress and popular singer before dedicating her talents to the Lord. She won the hearts of many in singing for the Lord with the Billy Graham Evangelistic Team. Many recordings were made of her singing, and she was widely known for her profound Christian testimony.

WATT, AGNES (1846-1894), an influential Scottish missionary to New Hebrides. In 1868 she married William Watt in Glasgow. They took the gospel to the Island of Aniwa, where she had a special ministry among the women. The Aniwa culture had little respect for women, and the background of the people was barbarian. She was able to help them with domestic and scriptural matters. After Agnes and her husband returned home to Scotland, they translated the New Testament into Tannese, which was published by the National Bible Society of Scotland. They returned to Tanna better equipped to reach the people for the Lord.

WEBB, MURIEL S. (1913-1977), author, social worker, and official in administering refugee aid. A graduate of Connecticut College, she studied at Columbia University School of Social Work. A native of New York state, she served with the Episcopal church's executive council and later as director of a commission on interchurch aid, refugee, and world service of the World Council of Churches in Geneva, Switzerland. She wrote several articles on the role of the church in community and social welfare.

WEIL, SIMONE (1909-1943), European author of Jewish background. She was born in Paris, France. She studied philosophy and the Scriptures, and taught briefly. She became ill and while recovering in Portugal had a religious "experience" at the monastery in Solesmes, although she refused to accept all sacraments of the church. She and her family emigrated to New York. In 1942 she went to London and associated with the Free French Movement. Her writings, which were published posthumously, include: *Waiting for God* (1951); *Gravity and Grace* (1952); and *Oppression and Liberty* (1958).

WELSH, ELIZABETH KNOX (1568-1625), faithful Christian daughter of John Knox and his second wife, Margaret. She was about four years old when her father died, and later her mother remarried. She became acquainted with John Welsh when he preached at the Selkirk Parish at Fadownside. He was much like her father, faithful in preaching the Bible. When James VI came to the throne of England he tried to compel the Church of Scotland to conform to the ecclesiastical system of England. John Welsh resisted this action, and meetings were held regarding such. Welsh was arrested and taken to Edinburgh, then to the Castle of Blackness. In 1606 he was tried along with other ministers charged with holding a general assembly. Their family was eventually exiled on the Continent, but Mr. Welsh became quite ill from the conditions of the prison and never recovered his health. After fourteen years of exile they were permitted to return to England, though they much desired to return to Scotland. She went to the king for permission to go to Scotland, but the king became even more angry when he discovered that her father was John Knox, and denied her appeal. Soon after, John Welsh died. He had been one of the strong pillars of the church. He was buried in London; she went to Scotland, but survived her husband less than three years, leaving two sons and a daughter.

WESLEY, SUSANNA ANNESLEY (1669-1742), author, teacher, but perhaps best remembered as the devout mother of Charles and John Wesley. She had nineteen children altogether and is said to have set aside at least two hours daily for private devotions. Only nine of her children lived to be adults, all of whom she taught the basic subjects while disciplining them to study and read. Her father was Dr. Samuel Annesley, a well known Nonconformist minister with his doctorate from Oxford. He had even preached before the House of Commons. His parishes included St. Giles, Cripplegate, and London. She was the youngest of his twenty-five children. She married Samuel Wesley in 1689 and associated with the Church of England. They lived most of their married life at Epworth in Eastern England. She wrote three Christian textbooks for her children: *A Manual of Natural Theory, An Exposition of the Leading Truths of the Gospel,* and another directed to her daughter Emilia. Her son John, was the founder of Methodism and her son Charles was known for his many hymns. Susanna was a capable leader and family administrator when her husband was away.

WEST, ELIZABETH (1672-1735), author and wife of a Scottish clergyman. She was born in Edinburgh, but details of her youth are obscure. She wrote *Memoirs* or *Spiritual Exercises*, which influenced many.

WESTON, AGNES (1840-1918), teacher, author, musician, and missionary to the British Royal Navy personnel. Born in London, she was the daughter of an attorney, and her early years were spent in Bath. She studied organ and at the age of sixteen played at Gloucester Cathedral.

She visited hospitals and encouraged and witnessed to the poor and alcoholics as well as sailors. Her first work began in Devonport where she noted that there were many sailors roaming about with nothing to do, especially on Sundays. She organized a meeting and invited them to come and sing, share in Bible study, and enjoy Christian fellowship. These gatherings became so popular that with the help of a friend, Miss Sophie Wintz, Agnes opened the Royal Sailor's Rest, which included a book room. She wrote a monthly newsletter for sailors in the hospital, but others asked for it also. It was titled *A Monthly Letter Addressed to the Seamen, Marines, and Marine Artillery of the Royal Navy at Home and Abroad*, and the first year she distributed 500 copies each month. In 1872 the distribution grew to 1,500 copies a month and the circulation continued to multiply. Her work and meetings stressed temperance, and as donations came in another Sailor's Rest was established that included rooms for families of sailors to visit. She ministered to the social and physical needs of military wives and families but with an emphasis on evangelism. The Royal Sailor's Rests were the headquarters for the Royal Naval Temperance Society and the Royal Naval Christian Union, which included about twenty-five thousand members over the world. She wrote *My Life Among the Bluejackets*, a book about her work.

WHATLEY, MARY LOUISA (1824-1889), a British missionary to Egypt. She was born in Suffolk, the daughter of Archbishop and Mrs. Whatley of Dublin. It was apparently during the famine of 1846-1851 in Ireland when the Whatleys organized relief help that she became spiritually concerned for the potential outreach of the church. She devoted herself to the work of the church and in 1856 went to Cairo. She knew the Bible well, desired to teach it to the young women of the Cairo area, and hoped to establish a school for girls there. After investing much time and work, she did have a school for girls that later included boys. When the prince and princess of Wales visited Cairo in 1869, they were influential in getting a land grant for such a school outside the city. She was instrumental in opening a medical mission in 1879, after a qualified doctor arrived. She became well known among the people and went about teaching the gospel and distributing tracts.

WHITE, ALMA BRIDWELL (1862-1946), evangelist and founder of the Pillar of Fire Church. A native of Kentucky, she was educated at Millersburg Female College in Kentucky and at the University of Denver. She preached, held revival meetings, and organized camp meetings with much emphasis on holiness. She was criticized by her own denomination, the Methodists, because she worked independently of the church. In 1901 she withdrew from the Methodist church and established the Pentecostal Union, which is based on the old Wesleyanism. In 1917 the name was changed to Pillar of Fire, with headquarters established at Zerephath, New Jersey.

WHITE, ELLEN GOULD HARMON (1827-1915), author and cofounder of the Seventh Day Adventist church. She was born in Maine of Methodist parents. She was swayed by the teachings of William Miller, a Baptist minister much involved with the study of premillennialism, including datesetting for the return of Christ. His philosophies along with her own study and spiritual revelations formed the basis for founding the Seventh Day Adventist church in 1863. In 1846 she married James White and they established the headquarters for the church in Battle Creek, Michigan. She traveled and lectured in Europe and Australia after the death of her husband in 1881. She wrote many materials for the teaching of her faith. The church headquarters was moved to Washington, D.C., in 1903. Besides the teachings of Mrs. White in regard to the Scriptures, the work of the church is concerned with education, nutrition, and health, including the sponsoring of many medical centers. They have a sizable publishing business, and the denominational paper is *Review and Herald.*

WHITEFIELD, ELIZABETH BURNELL (c. 1705-c. 1757), devout wife of

George Whitefield. Little is recorded about this quiet, sincere Christian who married Whitefield in 1741. She was a widow of thirty-six years when they were married in Wales. Her maiden name was Burnell. They lived in London first as his preaching was centered there, but he did not allow marriage to interrupt his evangelistic meetings and was not home when their first child was born.

WHITMAN, NARCISSA PRENTISS (1808-1847), pioneer American missionary to the Indians of the Northwest Territory. She was the wife of Dr. Marcus Whitman, and a martyr. She was one of the first two white women to journey overland to the Oregon Territory. Born in Prattsburg, New York; her father was Judge Stephen Prentiss, a businessman; the family was Presbyterian. She was the third of nine children and attended the Female Seminary of Emma Willard in Troy, New York, and the Benjamin Franklin Academy at Prattsburg. In 1836 she married Marcus Whitman, a missionary physician, and immediately they proceeded to the Northwest. They had just one child, who was lost by a drowning accident. She provided foster care for several Cayuse Indian children at the mission. It was customary for this tribe to leave an ailing child in the woods to die. But when they found that Mrs. Whitman would care for their unwanted children, often a baby would be left at the mission house. In 1847, when they had eleven Indian children with them, there was an epidemic of measles. Dr. Whitman cared for them as best he could, but the Indians noted that several died, and they misunderstood, thinking the Whitmans were trying to kill them through this disease. Thus a controversy stirred that resulted in the famous Whitman massacre. Both Narcissa and her husband were martyred. Today near the site of the Waiilatpu Presbyterian mission where Narcissa Whitman spent the last eleven years of her life bringing the gospel to the Cayuse Indians, there stands Whitman College, sponsored by the Presbyterian Church.

WIEBE, ELIZABETH PAULS (1876-1957), a pioneer missionary who served with her husband as the first Mennonite missionaries to black people in the southern United States. She was born in South Russia and emigrated with her family from Chortitza Colony to midwestern America. Her father was a merchant. Elizabeth, or "Lizzie," as her family called her, became a Christian at an early age and was baptized in the Lehigh Mennonite Brethren Church in Lehigh, Kansas. She married Henry V. Wiebe in 1898. He was also from Russia, dedicated his life to mission work, and graduated from Bethel College in Kansas. After many obstacles were removed, they established a school and orphanage for blacks near the Tennessee-North Carolina border. Such pioneer work as this was not easy, largely because of racial tension. Nearly all of the adult blacks over the age of thirty-five had been born into slavery.

WIEBE, JUSTINA FRIESEN (1833-1916), author, brave immigrant, and devout wife of the first leader of the Krimmer Mennonite Brethren Church. She was born in South Russia, and her mother died when Justina was quite young. As a student she mastered Gothic script and wrote poetry. In 1857 she married Jacob A. Wiebe in Halbstadt, South Russia. After many unusual experiences they became a part of a group of thirty-five families who came to the United States by way of the Black Sea, Pedwollosk, through Austria, Krakan, and Oswiecim to England and then to the United States.

WILBRANDIS ROSENBLATT (1504-1564), influential in the Protestant Reformation of Germany. Born in Basel, her father was in the service of Emperor Maximillian. Before the age of twenty she married Ludwig Keller, known as Cellarius. He died in 1526, leaving her with a baby. Two years later she married a minister and professor at Basel named Oecolampadius, who died in 1531. The next year she married another reformer, Capito, who had just lost his wife. They had five children when again she was widowed. Her fourth marriage was to another leader of the Protestant Reformation, Martin Butzer, in 1542. Not only did she have children by each husband, but she was active in the cause of the Reformation. She communicated with the wife of Zwingli and others, encouraging them and assisting as appropriate. As a nurse she helped many Protestant refugees and was an active witness for Christ.

WILCOX, KATIE (1889-1974), a missionary educator and school founder. She attended Wesleyan University and Mt. Holyoke College, where she received her B.A. degree in 1911. She took graduate studies at Columbia and Cornell universities and was the first woman to receive Wesleyan's Distinguished Alumnus award. In 1961 she received an L.H.D. degree from Mt. Holyoke. She first went to India in 1915, served at the high school and Capron Hall Training School in Madurai and from 1938 to 1948 at the Orlinda Childs Pierce Memorial School. In 1948 she founded the Lady Doak College in Madurai, a Christian college for women of South India. She served until 1958 there as bursar and temporary administrator. The Indian Government recognized her work in 1947 by awarding her the Kaiser-i-Hind medal. Her missionary sponsorship was the Women's Board of Missions; American Board of Commissioners for Foreign Missions; and United Church Board for World Ministries.

WILKINSON, JEMIMA (1752-1819), founder of the cult Universal Friends. A native of Rhode Island, reared in a Quaker family. At the age of twenty-four she became quite ill, believing that she died and was returned to earth with a special mission. Her personality and preaching attracted large audiences especially in Massachusetts and Pennsylvania. In 1794 she formed a religious community called "Jerusalem Township." She believed in simple dress, pacifism, no slavery, and mystical interpretation of dreams. She did not discourage her followers from believing that she was a messiah. Like other such groups built around a personality, this cult sharply declined following her death.

WILLARD, FRANCES ELIZABETH CAROLINE (1839-1898), author, teacher, reformer, and founder of the world's Women's Christian Temperance Union. She was born at Churchville, New York, but when she was young her parents moved to Ohio and later to a rural area near Janesville, Wisconsin. She was taught at home then attended the Milwaukee Female College but finished and graduated with honors from the Northwestern Female College at Evanston, Illinois, in 1859. It was there that she made a profession of faith in Christ and later joined the Methodist church. She taught briefly and then traveled through Europe for several months. In 1869 she accepted a professorship at Northwestern Women's College at Evanston; then served there as the college president from 1871 to 1874. As she became more and more concerned with the temperance movement, she lectured and combined temperance and prohibition with the women's suffrage issue. Her popularity as a speaker grew. She became president of the Chicago Women's Christian Temperance Union and in 1879 served as president of the National WCTU. In 1883 she established a world WCTU and served as its president from 1891 until her death. She was founder and editor-in-chief of *The Union Signal* periodical; wrote four books: *Woman and Temperance*; *Nineteen Beautiful Years*; *A Great Mother*; and *Glimpses of Fifty Years* and many magazine articles. Her efforts did much to pave the way of victory for the Eighteenth and Nineteenth Amendments of the United States Constitution. She was the first woman to be honored with a statue in Statuary Hall in Washington, D.C.

WILLIAMS, HELEN MARIA (1762-1827), an author and hymnist born near London. Her father was an army officer. She wrote a variety of books, especially ones relating to history. Most of her life was spent in Paris, France; she was outspoken about her beliefs and was even imprisoned for expressing them. In 1786 she wrote the hymn "While Thee I Seek, Protecting Power."

WILLING, JENNIE FOWLER (1834-1916), author, editor, minister of Methodist persuasion, and leader in the Women's Christian Temperance Union. Born in Canada, she was married at nineteen;

had no children. She wrote a number of books and pamphlets on themes associated with Christian conduct and self-helps. She also became involved with the fight against alcohol and the work of the Women's Christian Temperance Union. She was the first editor of the WCTU paper *Our Union* and served as president of the Illinois chapter of the WCTU.

WILLOUGHBY, CATHERINE (1514-1580), an eminent Christian who helped many Protestants in perilous times. She was the daughter of William, Lord Willoughby of Ersley, by his wife, Mary of Salenes, of Spanish royalty. Orphaned quite young, she was placed in the custody of the Duke and Duchess of Suffolk (Brandon) in 1529, and they treated her as their own. The Duchess was formerly Mary Tudor, sister of Henry VIII. The Duchess of Suffolk died in 1534, and the Duke married Catherine, who thus became his fourth wife and took the title Duchess of Suffolk. She was fourteen and he was forty-nine, but apparently it was a happy marriage. They had two sons, Henry and Charles. Her spiritual life was influenced by the writings of Catherine Parr, although she was most influenced by Hugh Latimer. She was hospitable to John Fox, the martyrologist, and knew other prominent Christians of the day. Widowed in 1545, she married the Protestant Richard Bertie. Their home at Wessel housed Protestant refugees, and her compassion for them spread abroad so that even Tyndale, then in exile, and Viret dedicated some of their writing to her. Later she was forced to move to Palgrave in upper Germany for safety because of threats by Queen Mary. Many refugees followed her, and the Lord provided for their care and safety. After the death of the queen, they returned to England and enjoyed their final days in religious liberty. She and Bertie had two children, Susan and Peregrine, who grew up to serve the Lord. The boy, especially, as a revered Protestant leader.

WILLSON, MARY ELIZABETH BLISS (1842-c. 1895), American musician, hymnist, and only sister of the noted evangelist singer and hymn writer P. P. Bliss. She was born in Clearfield County, Pennsylvania, but soon moved to Tioga County. At the age of fifteen she went with her brother into Bradford County where he taught. They lived with a family named Young, and the daughter not only gave P. P. Bliss his first music lesson but became his wife. Both her brother and his wife were killed in a train accident in 1876. Mary Bliss taught a couple of years and in 1860 married Clark Willson of Towanda, Pennsylvania. The Willsons assisted Major Whittle in evangelistic work in the Chicago area. They served as gospel singers and were so successful that it became their life work. They worked with other evangelists and traveled in many places of the U.S. In 1882 they went to Great Britain with the Gospel Temperance mission work. She wrote several hymns; perhaps the best known are "Glad Tidings" and "My Mother's Hands." She wrote two volumes of gospel hymns: *Great Joys* and *Sacred Gems*. She also contributed both words and music to many Christian song collections over the years.

WILSON, ELEANOR (1891-1973), a pioneer educator, missionary, and author serving with the American Board of Commissioners for Foreign Missions and the United Church Board for World Ministries. She attended Simmons College and Biblical Seminary, went to Japan in 1925, and taught in several places; then was administrator for the Women's Evangelical School in Nishinomiya, Japan. Later she worked in Micronesia, Majuro, and Jaluit, the Caroline and Marshall Islands. She may be remembered by some for her spirit of adventure as skipper of MorningstarVII, for a book was written about this experience called *The Lady Was a Skipper*, by Maribelle Cormack. Although she served as a skipper first in an emergency situation, helped by the U.S. Navy, she used it as a means to distribute literature. She taught in several places through Micronesia, and at the same time she supervised the Christian school at Jabwor on the Jaluit Atoll. She wrote *Too Old? A Saga of the South Pacific* a story of life and work of the Baldwin sisters.

WINKWORTH, CATHERINE (1827-

1878), born in London, Miss Winkworth is especially remembered for her expertise in the translation of hymns from German. Her *Lyre Germanica*, published in 1855, had twenty-three editions, and a second series in 1858 that had twelve editions. In 1863 she published *The Chorale Book for England* and in 1869 translated *Christian Singers of Germany*. Some of the more familiar hymns of her translation are: "Praise to the Lord, the Almighty," "Lift Up Your Heads, Ye Mighty Gates," "From Heaven Above to Earth I Come," and "Now Thank We All Our God." Christian service for Catherine Winkworth was not limited to writing, for she did pioneer work in higher education for women and was one of the founders of Clifton High School for Girls.

WINTHROP, MARGARET TINDAL (1590-1647), pioneer Christian educator. She was the daughter of Sir John Tindal and the wife of John Winthrop, first governor of the Massachusetts Bay Colony. She had considerable influence on other pioneer women of the period. At the age of twenty-eight she married John Winthrop in her native England. He came to the new world first; she came in 1631. Their home was described as a family sanctuary, and she lived the Puritan concept that Christianity dominated her thinking and actions. They had three sons. Her influence on the growth of the church in the colony was notable.

WITTENMYER, ANNIE (1827-1900), outstanding American social worker and first president of the Women's Christian Temperance Union, founded in 1874. She was especially concerned with the care of soldiers during the Civil War and was recognized by President Lincoln for her efforts. In 1850 she founded an orphanage in Iowa, the Iowa Soldiers Orphans Home, and served as chaplain of the Women's Relief Corps, auxiliary to the Grand Army of the Republic. Although she was a Methodist, she crossed denomination lines to help those in need and in serving the Lord. She left some valuable writings, including a book on outstanding women of the Reformation period. Perhaps she is most remembered for her untiring efforts with the WCTU and promoting total abstinence from all alcoholic beverages.

WOOD, JOHNNIE BELL WHITAKER (1889-1981), an effective evangelist and teacher in the Church of God, in Cleveland, Tennessee; founder of the Ladies Ministries of that denomination. A native of Mississippi, she had a long and fruitful ministry and was loved by many.

WOOLEY, CELIA PARKER (1848-1918), remembered for her founding of one of the first settlement houses of Chicago, the Frederick Douglass Center. Started in 1904, this center was especially well-planned and effective. Her husband was a dentist in Chicago. She was one of the first women ordained in the United States, sponsored by the Unitarians in 1893. She pastored briefly before going into social work for which she is better known.

WOOLSTON, BEULAH (1828-1886), teacher and missionary among Chinese women. Born in Vincenttown, New Jersey, she graduated with honors from the Wesleyan Female College in Wilmington, Delaware. She taught there for a time while she engaged in missionary work and going as a teacher to Chinese missions. She and her sister worked together organizing and administrating a boarding school for girls under the Chinese Female Missionary Society of Baltimore. She served in this work for twenty-five years.

WRIEDEN, JANE ELIZABETH (1906-1970), a distinguished leader, author, and consultant in social services for women and children, serving with The Salvation Army. A native of New York state, she received her BA degree cum laude as well as a Master of Social Service degree from the University of Buffalo. She attained the rank of colonel in The Salvation Army. Influential in establishing and maintaining high standards of health and social welfare services in The Salvation Army in the United States, besides consultant work. She served as administrator of the Booth Memorial Hospital in Cleveland and as director of The Salvation Army Home and Hospital in

Jersey City, becoming a fellow of the American College of Hospital Administrators. She was active in several other professional organizations related to her work. In 1970 she was presented an award for her outstanding contribution to the field of health and welfare services by the Council for Health and Welfare Services of the United Church of Christ. She was much sought after as a speaker and represented the Salvation Army at many conferences, including the International Conferences of Social Work in Japan, Italy, Brazil, Greece, and Finland. At the Rome and Brazil Conferences she was secretary to the American delegation. She wrote many articles in her field of expertise and often was requested to conduct seminars.

WRIGHT, LYDIA MÜLLER (1882-1890), the only child of George and Mary Muller, British evangelist, and noted for work in establishing orphanages. Lydia and her husband took over the fruitful work begun by her parents.

WU, YI-FANG a significant Christian educator of China, she was reared in Ningpo in the province of Chekiang. Her father was an evangelist, and she attended the Sarah Batchelor Memorial School, then Ginling College. She received the degrees of B.A., M.A., and Ph.D., becoming president of Ginling College. As a distinguished medical missionary to her own people, she became known far beyond her native country.

Y

YAJIMA, KAJI (1834-1925), a Christian social worker among the women of Tokyo, Japan. She assisted in founding a branch of the Women's Christian Temperance Union in Tokyo and edited the WCTU publication. She later established a rescue home for girls and was influential in securing laws for the protection of Japanese women and children. The emperor of Japan recognized her for this work; she represented the Japan WCTU at an international conference in Boston; and she was recognized by President Franklin D. Roosevelt at the White House.

YAMAMURO, KIYE SATO (1874-1917), a pioneer evangelist and social worker who established the first Salvation Army Rescue Home for prostitutes in Japan. She was a native of Japan and the daughter of a prosperous silk manufacturer. She was first attracted to the Salvation Army by the personal devotion of the officers and their love for the Lord. Her Christian testimony and social work crossed denominational barriers; she was instrumental in establishing a sanatorium for tuberculosis victims and other social work. Her ministry extended from 1899 to 1917; she attained the rank of colonel in the Salvation Army.

YASUI, TETSU (early 1900s), eminent Japanese Christian educator who served in an administrative position at the Union Christian College for women. She graduated from a teachers college in Tokyo and was sent to England by the Japanese Department of Education. She spent three years at Cambridge University and was presented an honorary doctorate from Mt. Holyoke College.

YEO, ANNIE (1904-1983), a devout evangelist and missionary who ministered for thirty-three years among the Nupe people in Nigeria. Born in England, she moved with her family to Canada when she was seventeen years of age. She first served in Ontario with the Missionary church, known as the Mennonite Brethren in Christ. Her deep spirituality and rich prayer life influenced many young people in decisions pertaining to commitment and missionary service.

YODER, ALICE (c. 1877-c. 1939), one of the first Mennonite women to serve on a foreign mission field, although she went to India first in 1897 under the Christian and Missionary Alliance church. A native of Pennsylvania, she taught in an orphanage in Khamgaon during a difficult time of famine.

YODER, PHOEBE (1903-1981), teacher, translator, nurse, and outstanding pioneer missionary to Tanganyika (Tanzania) for thirty-four years. She was the daughter of C. C. and Susanna Kilmer Yoder and lived in McPherson County, Kansas. She attended Goshen College and Seminary; took nurses training at the LaJunta Mennonite School of Nursing, graduating in 1937 with RN certification. In Tanganyika she set up a dispensary, supervised the construction of ten school buildings, helped prepare and write school curriculum, and taught and assisted in translating the New Testament in both Jita and Swahili dialects.

YOU, Dr. ME KING a Chinese medical missionary. She practiced medicine under the Southern Methodist Mission and was the only Chinese woman who left China for study until the time of Dr. Hu King Eng. Believed to have been educated at a Methodist mission school, then sent to America for her medical training.

YOUNG NEAL COVINGTON (1891-1971), a native of South Carolina; taught and attended the Southern Seminary Buena Vista, Virginia, Winthrop College in South Carolina, and the Women's Missionary Union Training School, where she received the Bachelor of Missionary Training degree. She served as a missionary to Africa under the Southern Baptist

Convention; she also served as president of the Women's Missionary Union of Nigeria and Ghana for twenty-six years and the executive secretary of one of the other women's groups for thirteen years more. She encouraged many Nigerian women, and her Christian testimony was recognized even by government officials. A camp was named for her in Ede, Nigeria, where they called her "Iya ni Israeli," or "Mother in Israel," and in 1959 the Timi (king) of Ede conferred on her the honorary title "Iyalode Onigbagbo," meaning Queen of the Christians, for she had helped the king when enemies were attacking the throne.

Z

ZELL, KATHERINE (1497-1562), author, hymnist, active reformer, and devoted wife of German reformer, Matthew Zell. He was described as an "evangelical" preacher and was excommunicated of priesthood because of his marriage to Katherine. They lived in Strasbourg, Germany, where their home became a refuge for reformers. She wrote a tract for women of Kensinger and in 1534 had published a collection of hymns. Her life was a comfort and help to many. She risked her life to visit and give aid to the needy in prison. When her husband died in 1548, she delivered the funeral message and took active part in the cause of the Reformation.

ZOE (c. 255-286), a Christian martyr of Rome. Her husband was the jailer who had charge of the Christians facing death because of their faith. Details of her early life and even her full name are lacking, but it is recorded that she became a Christian after observing and hearing discussions by Christians facing martyrdom. She had a physical disability that would not permit her to express herself except in gestures. The Christians instructed her in the faith and when she responded in belief, they told her to pray for freedom from her disability. She did so and was healed and able to speak. Her husband witnessed this miracle and accepted the Lord as his Savior. This situation enraged the enemy, and she was greatly tortured and then killed for her faith.

ZWINGLI, ANNA REINHARD (c. 1487-1538), compassionate mother and devoted wife of Ulrich Zwingli, the Swiss Reformer. She was the daughter of Oswald Reinhard and Elizabeth Wynzuern. She married and was widowed with three children. She attended Zwingli's church in Zurich and he first became fond of her children. They were encouraged by his preaching, and although Zwingli was at one time a priest, he had been preaching against clerical celibacy since 1519. It was in 1522 that he and Anna Reinhard were married privately, but openly celebrated later. She and Zwingli had four children, although he never ceased to be interested in her children by the former marriage. In fact, he dedicated to her boy the publication *Little Manual of Christian Education for Youth,* which became an educational treasure of its time. Zwingli died in the Catholic-Protestant battle at Kappel in 1531 as did Anna's son, Gerrold, and other relatives. Again, Anna was left a widow with several children to be cared for and taught. It was Heinrich Bullinger, Zwingli's successor, who took in Anna and her family. She remained in the Bullinger home until her death and along with Anna Bullinger cared for Protestant refugees and their children during this dark period.

Bibliography

Abbott, W. J. *Notable Women in Church History*. Philadelphia: John C. Winston, 1913.

Albus, Harry J. *A Treasury of Dwight L. Moody*. Grand Rapids: Eerdmans, 1949.

Anderson, J. *Memorable Women of the Puritan Times*. London: Blackie & Son, n.d.

Bacon, Ernest. *Spurgeon, Heir of the Puritans*. Grand Rapids: Eerdmans, 1968.

Bainton, Roland H. *Women of the Reformation in France and England*. Minneapolis: Augsburg, 1973.

———. *Women of the Reformation in Germany and Italy*. Minneapolis: Augsburg, 1971.

Barker, William P. *Who's Who in Church History*. Old Tappan, N.J.: Revell, 1969.

Bender, Harold S., and Smith, C. Henry., eds. *The Mennonite Encyclopedia*. 4 vols. Scottdale, Pa.: Mennonite Publishing House, 1955-1959.

Bingham, Helen E., *An Irish Saint: Life Story of Ann Preston*. Noblesville, Ind.: Newby, 1972.

Bowden, Henry W. *Dictionary of American Religious Biography*. Westport, Conn.: Greenwood, 1977.

Boyer, P. *Women in American Religion*. U. of Pennsylvania, 1978.

Burder, S. *Memoirs of Eminently Pious Women*. Philadelphia: Woodward, 1836.

Burton, Margaret E. *Notable Women of Modern China*. New York: Revell, 1912.

Carey, Rosa Nouchette. *Twelve Notable Good Women of the XIXth Century*. New York: Dutton, 1901.

Cassidy, Bertha. *China Adventure*. Brookline, Mass.: American Advent Mission Society, 1962.

Cecil, Richard. *The Life of John Newton*. Grand Rapids: Baker, 1978.

Charles, Ray. *Mrs. C. H. Spurgeon*. Pasadena, Texas: 1903. Reprint, 1973.

Charles, Mrs. Rundle. *Martyrs and Saints of the First Twelve Centuries*. London: Society for Promotion of Christian Knowledge, 1898.

Creegan, C. C. and Goodnow, Josephine. *Great Missionaries of the Church*. New York: Books for Libraries, 1895, Reprinted in 1972.

Cross, F. L., ed. *The Oxford Dictionary of the Christian Church*. New York, Toronto: Oxford U., 1957.

d'Aubigne, J. H. Merle. *The Reformation in England*. 2 vols. London: Banner of Truth Trust, 1963.

Dawson, E. D. *Heroines of Missionary Adventure*. Philadelphia: J. B. Lippincott, 1909.

Day, Richard E. *Bush Aglow*. Grand Rapids: Baker, 1936.

Deen, Edith. *Great Women of the Christian Faith*. New York: Harper, 1959.

Dehey, E. T. *Religious Orders of Women in the U.S.*. Hammond, Ind.: W. B. Conkey, 1930.

Dickson, Lillian. *These My People*. Grand Rapids: Zondervan, 1958.

Douglas, J. D. *The New International Dictionary of the Christian Church*. Grand Rapids: Zondervan, 1974.

Drewery, Mary. *William Carey, A Biography*. Grand Rapids: Zondervan, 1979.
Farrell, Monica. *From Rome to Christ*. Australia: Protestant Publications, 1947.
Gies, Frances. *Women of the Middles Ages*. New York: Barnes & Noble, 1978.
Guyon, Madame. *Madame Guyon*. Chicago: Moody, n.d.
Hardesty, Nancy. *Great Women of Faith*. Grand Rapids: Baker, 1980.
Howell, Beth Prim. *Lady on a Donkey*. New York: E. P. Dutton, 1960.
Hubbard, Elbert. *Little Journeys to the Homes of the Great: Famous Women*. New York: Roycrafters, 1928.
Hubbard, Ethel Daniels. *The Moffats*. New York: Friendship, 1917.
Jones, F. A. *Famous Hymns and Their Authors*. Detroit: Singing Tree, 1970.
Julian, John A. *A Dictionary of Hymnology*. New York: Scribner, 1892.
Karr, Jean. *Grace Livingston Hill: Her Story and Her Writings*. New York: Grosset and Dunlap, 1948.
Kavanagh, Julia. *Women of Christianity*. London: Smith, Elder & Co., 1852.
Latourette, Kenneth Scott. *A History of Christianity*. New York: Harper, 1953.
Lawrence, Una Roberts. *Lottie Moon*. Nashville: Sunday School Board of the Southern Baptist Convention, 1927.
Lillenas, Haldor. *Modern Gospel Song Stories*. Kansas City, Mo.: Lillenas, 1952.
McLeister, Clara. *Men and Women of Deep Piety*. Syracuse, N.Y.: Wesleyan Methodist, 1920.
Matthews, Winifred. *Dauntless Women*. New York: Friendship, 1947.
Mattson, Sylvia, *Missionary Footpaths*. Salem, Oregon: Mission Mill Museum Association, 1978.
M'Clintock, Rev. John, and Strong, James. *Cyclopaedia of Biblical, Theological, and Ecclesiastical Literature*. 10 vols. New York: Harper, 1881. Supplemental vols.: 1884, 1887.
Moffat, John S. *The Lives of Robert and Mary Moffat*. New York: A. C. Armstrong & Son, 1885.
Moody, William R. *The Life of Dwight L. Moody*. New York: Revell, 1900.
Moyer, E. S. *Wycliffe Biographical Dictionary of the Church*. Chicago: Moody, 1982.
________. *Great Leaders of the Christian Church*. Chicago: Moody, 1951.
________. *Notable American Women*. Cambridge: Belknap Press of Harvard U., 1971.
Price, Carl F. *One Hundred and One Hymn Stories*. New York: Abingdon, 1923.
Randall, Ruth Painter. *Mary Lincoln, Biography of a Marriage*. Boston: Little Brown, 1953.
Reynolds, William. J. *Hymns of Our Faith*. Nashville: Broadman, 1964.
Rich, Elaine Sommers. *Mennonite Women: A Story of God's Faithfulness, 1983-1983*. Scottdale, Pa.: Herald Press, 1983.
Rogal, Samuel J. *Sisters of Sacred Song*. New York: Garland, 1981.
Ryden, E. E. *The Story of Christian Hymnody*. Rock Island, Ill.: Augustana, 1959.
Sanville, George W. *Forty Gospel Hymn Stories*. Winona Lake, Ind.: Rodeheaver Hall Mack, 1945.
Schaff, Philip. *History of the Christian Church*. 3d ed., 8 vols. Grand Rapids: Eerdmans, 1974.
Seventh Day Adventist Encyclopedia. Vol. 10. Washington, D.C.: Review and Herald, 1976.
Shelley, Bruce. *Church History in Plain Language*. Waco, Texas: Word Books, 1982.
Singmaster, Elsie. *A Cloud of Witnesses*. Cambridge, Mass.: Central Committee of the United Study of Foreign Missions, 1930.
Smith, Eva Munson. *Women in Sacred Song*. Boston: Lothrop, 1885.
Speer, R. E. *Servants of the King*. New York: Board of Foreign Missions of the Presbyterian Church of U.S.A., 1970.
Steinbock, Evelyne. *"Miss Terri!"* Lincoln, Neb.: Back to the Bible Broadcast, 1970.
Sumrall, Lester F. *Lillian Trasher, The Nile Mother*. Springfield: Gospel, 1951.
Taylor, Mr. and Mrs. Howard. *The Triumph of John and Betty Stam*. Chicago: Moody, 1935.
Thomas, Henry and Dana. *Living Biographies of Famous Women*. New York: Garden City, 1942.

Thompson, Phyllis. *Each to Her Post*. London: Hodder and Stoughton with the Overseas Missionary Fellowship, 1982.
Thomson, Ronald W. *Who's Who of Hymn Writers*. London: Epworth, 1967.
Wells, Amos R. *A Treasure of Hymns*. Boston: W. A. Wilde, 1945.
Wiebe, Katie Funk., ed. *Women Among the Brethren*. Hillsboro, Kan.: Board of Christian Literature of the General Conference of Mennonite Brethren Churches, 1979.
Wilson, Dorothy Clarke. *Granny Brand*. Chappaqua, N.Y.: Christian Herald, 1976.
————. *Lincoln's Mothers*. Garden City, New York: Doubleday, 1981.
Wilson, Kenneth L. *Angel at Her Shoulder*. New York: Harper, 1964.
Wittenmyer, Annie. *Women of the Reformation*. New York: Phillips and Hunt, 1885.
Woodham-Smith, Cecil. *Florence Nightingale*. New York: McGraw-Hill, 1951.
————. *Queen Victoria. New York: Dell, 1972.*

Several valuable sets of reference books include the *Encyclopaedia Brittannica, International Who's Who, Who's Who in America,* and various encyclopedias of denominations.

Moody Press, a ministry of Moody Bible Institute, is designed for education, evangelization, and edification. If we may assist you in knowing more about Christ and the Christian life, please write us without obligation: Moody Press, c/o MLM, Chicago, Illinois 60610.

BOSTON PUBLIC LIBRARY
3 9999 04677 164 6